KU-167-820

RADICAL HAPPINESS

LIBRARIES NI
WITHDRAWN FROM STOCK

Moments of Collective Joy

RADICAL HAPPINESS

LYNNE SEGAL

VERSO
London • New York

For Agnes, Andreas, Éamonn and Zim

First published by Verso 2017
© Lynne Segal 2017

All rights reserved

The moral rights of the author have been asserted

1 3 5 7 9 10 8 6 4 2

Verso
UK: 6 Meard Street, London W1F 0EG
US: 20 Jay Street, Suite 1010, Brooklyn, NY 11201

versobooks.com

Verso is the imprint of New Left Books

ISBN-13: 978-1-78663-154-1
ISBN-13: 978-1-78663-744-4 (EXPORT)
ISBN-13: 978-1-78663-157-2 (US EBK)
ISBN-13: 978-1-78663-156-5 (UK EBK)

British Library Cataloguing in Publication Data
A catalogue record for this book is available from the British Library

Library of Congress Cataloging-in-Publication Data
A catalog record for this book is available from the Library of Congress

Typeset in in Fournier by MJ & N Gavan, Truro, Cornwall
Printed in the UK by CPI Mackays

Contents

He who binds to himself a joy
Does the winged life destroy;
He who kisses the joy as it flies
Lives in eternity's sunrise.

William Blake, 'Eternity'

Preface

Not at the eleventh hour, but with this book in production, I had to recall its galleys to meddle with my preface. All of a sudden, I had just experienced a night of collective joy with my friends, watching the election results from 8 June 2017. We listened with mounting glee as the Labour Party massively increased its vote in so many areas across Britain, winning seats that had been unwinnable for decades, even centuries, the largest swing since 1945. Despite all the effort we had put into the campaign, it was the surprise of this outcome that was so thrilling. Almost every mainstream newspaper had written off the Labour Party as 'unelectable' under the leadership of Jeremy Corbyn, who was vilified relentlessly in its most popular outlets, indeed who had been dismissed by friends and enemies alike as an impossible leader. In the end, the party did not win an outright majority, but jubilation lingered, knowing we had witnessed a momentous swing against the seemingly unstoppable policies of austerity and privitization that had been deepening inequality and devastating so many over the last thirty years and more. Instead of the predicted death-knell of social democracy, there was suddenly renewed energy and hope that something different might emerge in the future. The alignment of this moment of hope with my objectives in writing *Radical Happiness* seemed almost uncanny.

Nevertheless, writing a book on happiness is surely one of the most foolish hostages to fortune I have ever given. Who am I to lay claim to any expertise on the matter? Like many of us, I am often preoccupied by the miseries of the world, including my own familiarity with loneliness, regret and thwarted desire. Certainly, 'happy' is not the box I would readily tick if asked to scale my present feelings, despite having been personally fortunate in so many ways. But then, that is not my reason for writing this book.

Preserving what personal pleasures and comforts I have may guide much of my waking time, but like all the people I know, I am in countless ways immersed in public life. Public awareness easily blurs into private emotions, leaving us raging against the ubiquity of injustice all the more bitterly when we are feeling desolate. The older we become, the more obvious it should be that there is a public as well as a private aspect to our feelings. Above all, as I explore throughout this book, feelings of happiness are entwined with our ties to the world, mostly to other people, but also to all that we are able to do or are restricted from doing. This is just one of the reasons why feminists have said that the personal is political, although we used to be clear that the political can never be reduced to the personal.

As a feminist, I have always taken the pleasures and joy of others seriously, as well as the misery and fear that are increasingly evident, both close to home and across the globe. Thus, the sexual politics I have written about for over forty years begins and ends with reflections on personal agency and pleasure, while confronting the many, sometimes accumulating, impediments that stand in its way.[1] These barriers can at times be stark. Knowing his country's fetishization of happiness, Tennessee Williams was, I am sure, partly teasing the reporter who asked him to define happiness when he responded, 'Insensitivity, I guess.'[2] Nevertheless, I do not understand people who feel able to separate their own wellbeing entirely from that of others, or from public life more generally. Acknowledging the sadness of others, doing work we find interesting, sharing friendship and love through good times and bad while facing the tribulations life hurls at us, with help when we need it, seems to me the essence of pursuing any good life. As the world becomes an ever lonelier place, it is sustaining relationships, in whatever form they take, which must become ever more important. An act of defiance, even.

Yet this is exactly what is missing from the debates on the politics of happiness. Ridicule more than rage was no doubt most appropriate when George H. W. Bush made Bobby McFerrin's one-hit wonder, 'Don't Worry, Be Happy', the official campaign song of his (sadly successful) presidential bid in 1988, and not only because he did so without McFerrin's endorsement or permission. This seemed to herald a wind of change globally. Ten years later, Tony Blair's New Labour regime promoted the use of measures of wellbeing and happiness to steer government policy. Successive governments have continued this policy. In 2010, David Cameron launched his own, still ongoing, wellbeing project, dedicating £2 million a year to data collection, with one of the key questions in its research being: 'How happy did you feel yesterday?'[3] For what it's worth, in the rankings of nations around the globe for national happiness the UK usually hovers somewhere around the halfway mark, which is not very impressive.[4]

What sense should we make of this official happiness agenda? How can we compare other people's notions of happiness, which will doubtless range from the weighty to the trivial? As the celebrated literary critic Terry Eagleton notes, 'We can experience intense pleasure without being in the least happy,' or 'Be happy for dubious reasons,'[5] or perhaps, 'Relish morally disreputable pleasures, like rejoicing in your enemy's discomfort.'[6] The happiness agenda has little time for our being rather unsure about quite what we are feeling when we are getting on with our daily tasks. It is a project that insists on our accepting or rejecting simple descriptions, which are unlikely to capture any uncertainties about our thoughts, feelings and actions were we to put them to deeper probing.

Interestingly, the more intense our emotions, the more complex they may seem to us. In all the chapters to come, there will be more than enough to illustrate that what gives us greatest happiness one moment, such as the laughter of those we care about, brings greatest pain the next, when we feel their hurt – and all the more so when we have caused it. In *Radical Happiness*, therefore, I examine why this official interest in happiness is such a dubious development. The eager promotion and quantification of our contentment goes along with the disavowal of the actual presence of its antithesis: the precipitously rising rates of anxiety and depression all around us, and the accompanying pathologizing of personal misery.

It is therefore the multifarious meanings of the notion of 'happiness' itself that I want to explore in my opening chapter, with all its challenges and ambiguities. Happiness is usually seen today as a distinct – and measurable – state of mind. However, this was not always so. For a long time it was understood as the outcome of certain types of worthwhile actions, pursued for their own sake. It is clear that this definition encompasses a shared and public life.

Since our own survival and identity depend upon the existence of others and the communication between us, neither our emotions nor our deeds are ever purely private affairs. What we say and do emerges from how we try to make sense of and give significance to the nebulous muddle of our experience and exertions. Sometimes, though, meaning may fail to cohere at all, as when the degree of trauma crushes any manageable response to it. Moreover, happiness itself is something we usually report in retrospect, not as and when we feel it – even if we are singing along to the perverse ironies of Pharrell Williams's global hit, 'Happy': 'Clap along if you feel like happiness is the truth'. For anything we call happiness to endure and be cherished, it needs to be recognized and shared with others, always hovering somewhere between the strictly personal and the potentially public. As well as sharing these individual pleasures, we also need to claim the spaces and places out there in the world where it becomes easier to escape our own personal dilemmas, enjoying collective moments of pleasure.

It is clear that few emotions – joy or sorrow, love or hate, acceptance or rage – arrive in any pure form, untouched by hints of their opposite. That which makes us happy also makes us vulnerable; all the more so when it is tied up, as it so often is, with confirmations of identity. Hence in my next chapter I look at that shadow-land that haunts us all, one which we are encouraged to repudiate, including acute episodes of depression. Yet, as we'll see, those who have survived the depths of acute depression often agree that despite all the anguish, their suffering not only expanded their horizons, rendering them more sensitive to the pain of others, but also left them better able to cherish joyful moments when and as they occur.

It is worth noting that while there is much official talk about happiness today, it rarely includes any rhetoric of joy, least of all mention of collective joy. Yet such contagious delight is not so hard to observe, though it is nowadays usually confined to very particular times and places, often with their own competitive formulas – as in the noisy delight many feel in pubs or fans' reaction on football terraces when their team scores. Barbara Ehrenreich's book on the topic attributes the acknowledged widespread depression to the suppression of most earlier forms of spontaneous public carnivals and other festivals where people could be, literally, dancing in the streets.[6]

I therefore move on to delve deeper into manifestations of 'joy' across the centuries. From its religious origins, through to the Romantics' love of nature, in moments of shared political passion or in what remains today of public festivals, joy is most often associated with experiences that take us altogether outside ourselves. They are either intense feelings of pleasure that we share with others, or that others, at least potentially, might share. I think this also tells us something about personal happiness. As in drug-induced euphoria, what we recall later as pleasurable often occurred when we were fully absorbed in our experiences of the moment, whatever the context, whether reading a book, gardening or arguing passionately with friends. In these moments, we do not worry about whether we are happy or not, any more than a child does when fully engrossed in life at large.

More often, however, we feel ourselves at the mercy of situations we neither control nor value. The anthropologist David Graeber, for instance, sparked international controversy with his dramatic account of the 'bullshit jobs' thrown up by the changing nature of paid work. He noted that both productive and service workers have been increasingly squeezed out of jobs or are finding their conditions of work and pay deteriorate, as there has been a simultaneous huge expansion of better-paid but unnecessary jobs seen by their occupants themselves as pointless and stupid.[7] (An ensuing YouGov Survey did indeed find that 35 per cent of British workers believed their jobs were pointless.[8])

The dilemmas of happiness remain central in subsequent chapters, in which I explore the risks of love. In our time, happiness and love – especially romantic love – are seen as inextricably entwined, despite all we know of its inescapable uncertainties and ambivalence. As I suggested in my last book, *Out of Time*, single people routinely face pity or contempt from those around them, on the assumption that to live uncoupled is to be lonely and miserable. Others, however, have pointed out the perils and dangers of searching for happiness exclusively within the domestic bond, knowing how prone such relationships are to disappointment and failure, especially in what has been termed our 'liquid modernity'.[9]

In this book, therefore, I will be roaming well beyond any governments' or employers' interest in happiness, or the lack of it, that hides so much of the ideological underpinning of the current managerial agenda. Nevertheless, while I suggest how much lies buried in mainstream measurements of and debates surrounding happiness, we need to guard against such suspicions hurling us into troughs of cynical pessimism. For without our own sources of optimism, we inevitably give up on the search for sharing possibilities for the enjoyment of life, however fleeting these possibilities might prove to be.

So, in later chapters, I return cautiously to notions of 'public happiness', a term used by the German-born, Jewish-American political theorist Hannah Arendt. By this, Arendt meant the opportunities created within any society for people to move outside their personal concerns, whether happy or miserable, into conscious participation in public life and politics. In her view, it was here that people, whoever they were and wherever they lived, should be able to engage collectively in the affairs of the day, each person being respected as a potential agent in the world at large. Indeed, she argued, such political engagement was necessary to sustain happy and healthy societies and vice versa. Sadly, Arendt's reasoning may strike us as almost absurdly utopian today, when the opportunities for democratic participation in affairs of state are so very reduced.

As we see in my final chapter, nowadays most nation states themselves, whether willingly or not, have ceded much of their sovereignty to global corporate interests, selling off state-run assets and resources to an ever-shrinking number of commercial oligopolies. Thus, throughout this book and especially in its later sections, I will explore what impact this pervasive expansion of commercial values and interests has had on both personal and public life.

At the same time, however, I note that spaces of collective resistance and renewal never completely disappear. Indeed, rather as Arendt suggested, those participating in resistance to or a process of collective deliberations on the harms of the present, sometimes trying to build alternatives, often do find within these strategies sources of fulfilment, resilience, even moments of shared joy, alongside the inevitable frustrations and conflicts that emerge in political life and struggle.

It was the sudden appearance of just such political collectivity that provided the mood and momentum of my younger life, when the women's army was marching in the passionate beginnings of the women's liberation movement at the close of the 1960s. It is the lasting significance of those years that has helped many an ageing feminist keep a certain political optimism alive, whatever gloom we may feel about the present. Sharing those stories still hurls us back to the hopes of that time when, as others recall, we knew 'the miraculous revolutionary power of joy'.[10]

Hence, I also use these pages to consider why utopian thinking, in whatever shape or form, has been systematically discredited over recent decades. Dystopias, not utopias, capture the popular imagination nowadays, whether in some of our most applauded literary fiction or in box-office hits. Fear and paranoia are writ large, for instance, in the most successful work of leading literary figures, including Kazuo Ishiguro, Margaret Atwood, Don DeLillo or Dave Eggers, as well as in the huge cinematic appeal of *The Hunger Games*, *Divergent* or *The Maze Runner*. I look at the immense appeal of this dystopic narrative, while suggesting that a more utopian spirit may actually be necessary for us even to envisage real social change, that is, may be essential for us to resist mere accommodation to the known harms of the present. It is what many radical thinkers have argued throughout history, though often meeting derision.[11]

This function of utopianism is just one of many reasons why any serious promotion of happiness needs to embrace not just the personal, but also efforts to change a larger world that so firmly impedes possibilities for greater joy in the lives of so many. Or, at the very least, the pursuit of happiness must refuse to abandon the desire to see such change.

1

What's Wrong with Happiness?

'Why be happy when you could be normal?' the British writer Jeanette Winterson recalls her mother saying in response to her falling in love with a woman. Winterson had just tried to explain her feelings to her mother: 'When I am with her I am happy. Just happy.'[1]

It is startling to read this. The exchange was not so long ago, a mere twenty-five years, yet it sounds especially odd today. For over the last two decades, it is 'happiness' itself that been insistently promoted as the normality to which we should all aspire. Nowadays it is not 'normal' to neglect the pursuit of happiness. We are told that we should personally work on ensuring our own contentment in every aspect of life. This outlook has resulted in certain legal reforms that we should all be able celebrate. These include the acceptance of gay and lesbian civil partnerships around much of the Western world – despite significant resistance from many quarters, and much left to be done on trans and queer rights. What's not to like, many might ask.

The problem with happiness, however, is that while we are all for it, in general (or almost all of us), it is not so easy to pin down the nature of the thing itself. It is even harder to be sure of quite how to go about obtaining it. Indeed, it is plausible to suggest that it is the constant search for happiness that itself generates frustration, unease and a sense of failure. This is hardly surprising when emotions have a volatile and complicated life, with laughter and tears, pleasure and displeasure often entangled, or in other ways unstable, and constituted in part by the ambience around us. We know that feelings can be hard to describe, at times seeming almost impenetrable, with words either failing us or oversimplifying the complexity of, if not actually distorting, our feelings. We need poets, Auden wrote in 1940, to capture the complications of the human heart: 'Poetry might be defined as the clear expression of mixed feelings'.[2]

Today we have a new 'science of happiness', which many hope might clarify some of these complexities. But this has yet to happen. What has been apparent so far is that those who champion this science have proved the *least* likely to encourage any deeper reflection on mixed feelings. The new agenda encouraging us to choose happiness, and the plethora of books designed to tell us exactly how to do this, have little time for any nuance of feelings. For example, one of the most esteemed British psychologists offering 'new routes to happiness' is the psychologist Paul Dolan, from the prestigious London School of Economics (LSE). In his book *Happiness by Design*, he devotes a few short sentences to the definition of happiness:

> Having worked at the interface of economics, psychology, philosophy, and policy for two decades, I think I am well placed to make a strong case for the following definition: *happiness is experiences of pleasure and purpose over time* ... It is also measurable, which is vital if we are to advance our understanding of happiness.

Complexity of any sort has little or no place in the new 'science of happiness', except as something to be eliminated. Thus Dolan continues:

> Many of the assumptions we make about happiness and about ourselves have a lot to do with the fact that we generally pay more attention to what we think *should* make us happy rather than focusing on what actually does.[3]

'Do what makes you happy' is the mood music of the moment. No other ethical considerations seem to apply, unless you are labelled a paedophile, an immigrant or a terrorist. Some instance of this hollow happiness is offered up to us on every other billboard: the latest arresting one I noticed portrayed a young black woman on a bicycle, with Barclay's Bank generously informing her, and the world, 'We're here to make you happy being You'. Yes, of course they are, so just make sure you keep smiling when next you're overdrawn or your credit card is cancelled.

There is no surprise, of course, in noting the questionable promises issuing from the commercial world. The arousal of our desires and manipulation of our behaviour is the raison d'être of advertising, which I will return to in chapter three. It is rather the attention to our 'happiness' coming from governments themselves at present that is less expected. This is all the more peculiar in these days of austerity and global fears of rising rates of depression and mental illness, not to mention of war, ethnic conflict and environmental catastrophe.

It is very much in tune with the zeitgeist of an era labelled as one of 'turbo-charged' capitalism that most of the influential happiness researchers are behavioural economists.[4] It is even more peculiar that one of the oft-repeated claims of these economists is that, above a certain minimal level, economics has nothing to do with happiness. This idea has been labelled the 'Easterlin Paradox' and is associated with the American economist Richard Easterlin, who surveyed the factors contributing to happiness in 1974.[5] His research showed that in the long term extra money beyond a certain threshold does not *necessarily* guarantee increased happiness.

This claim has been routinely repeated by happiness experts, including another US economist, Andrew Oswald, working at the University of Warwick, as well as by the premier thinker in the field, Richard Layard. Layard, who was promoted to the House of Lords in 2000, has been at the centre of successive British government initiatives on wellbeing from their inception, and co-edited the World Happiness Report in 2012.[6]

There have been challenges to the theory, however. For instance, in the USA, two economists Betsey Stevenson and Justin Wolfers recently produced rival statistics showing that money does matter. Indeed, they found no evidence for the claim that once 'basic needs' have been met, higher income is no longer associated with higher assessments of subjective wellbeing, whether making comparisons between or within different countries. Instead, Stevenson and Wolfers argue that the relationship between incomes and happiness does not diminish as incomes rise: 'If there is a satiation point', they note, 'we have yet to reach it.'[7]

What can we make of the squabbles between these economic bean counters? They certainly suggest why it is all the more necessary for those of us concerned with personal and social wellbeing, and the ties between them, to explore more fully what exactly is being discussed, or perhaps ignored, when our pleasures, sorrows and survival are being measured and used to develop policies concerning our social health. They challenge us to understand the inconsistencies in public conversations and computations around notions of happiness, if only to move beyond them.

Here, the first thing I notice is that the contemporary happiness agenda might be better described as its opposite: *a misery agenda*. The recent interest in happiness shown by both governments and employers has been triggered not by outbursts of benevolence towards us, quite the contrary. Rather, the disingenuous 'happiness agenda' is concerned above all with softening the costs of ever-rising social wretchedness. This is obvious, for instance, from examining those whom the British government turned to for advice.

Conspicuous Reversals

Richard Layard, the original 'Happiness Tsar', appointed by Tony Blair in the 1990s, was a labour economist, whose early work was concerned with reducing unemployment and inequality because of its effects on social misery, depression and mental illness. After that he headed up government-sponsored research on depression, which resulted in *The Depression Report*, published in 2006. The chief finding here was that: 'Crippling depression and chronic anxiety are the biggest causes of misery in Britain today. They are the great submerged problem, which shame keeps out of sight'. Citing psychiatric reports, the study suggested that one in six of us is likely 'to suffer from depression or chronic anxiety, which affects one in three of all families'.[8]

Overall, the report concluded by calling for massive state funding for cognitive behavioural therapy (CBT), not just to alleviate the devastating levels of social misery but also, in the language we might anticipate nowadays, in order to improve business efficiency, estimating that the 'loss of output due to depression and chronic anxiety is some twelve billion a year' – 1 per cent of our total national income.[9]

Interestingly, but again very much in line with ruling ideas of the moment that stress only the significance of individual aspirations, Layard's report chooses to ignore the effects of structural inequality on the emotional distress it measures. Thus *The Depression Report* lacks any data on the correlation between mental illness and levels of unemployment, poverty, debt and social inequality – even though Layard himself was once well aware of the effects of these issues.[10] Instead, despite and no doubt because of these times of soaring inequality, attention to the effects of social disadvantage was consistently under-played, buried by correlational data highlighting an alternative assertion: that there is no direct correlation between wealth and happiness. We now know that this is a highly contested claim.

However, even were we to accept the claim, it would be neither surprising nor especially interesting to be told that money, alone, does not bring happiness. It may perhaps appear a little unexpected to see in Paul Dolan's book a table of measurements suggesting that hairdressers, beauticians and florists are recorded as providing the highest percentage scores on happiness (between 70 per cent and 87 per cent), while bankers stood out as scoring the lowest, reaching a mere 44 per cent.[11] But this does not change people's behaviour about wanting more money.

I also notice that this disconnection between significant affluence and happiness has never been used to encourage governments to abolish bonuses for those apparently unhappy bankers, or to tax them at 70 per cent, insisting that their wealth brings them no added joy. Instead, this disputed finding is deployed selectively to support the delusion that anyone, however poor, overworked, indebted and unappreciated, can decide to 'choose happiness' despite their situation. Meanwhile it also resonates with those voices that blame the supposedly 'work-shy' for their own low wages, or their inability to find fulfilling employment.

Furthermore, this sort of correlational data on happiness is rarely sufficiently transparent or consistent to offer any simple conclusions. There is more than enough evidence pointing to the politics behind the selective interpretation of measurements. For example, while Layard and his team ignore the effects of economic matters on our health and wellbeing in the research he led at one college of the University of London, the LSE, a different team led by the British epidemiologist Michael Marmot emphasizes their grim impact at another, the UCL (University College London), little more than a twenty-minute walk across the city. In contrast to Layard, Marmot has convincingly researched the quite devastating effects of poverty and inequality on social misery generally, and individual psychic health in particular. He found that 'children and adults from the lowest 20 per cent of households are three times more likely to have common mental health problems than the top 20 per cent, and [were] an extraordinary nine times as likely to have psychotic disorders'.[12]

Marmot's research is in line with that of many others, including Richard Wilkinson and Kate Pickett, authors of the acclaimed book *The Spirit Level*, which stresses the toxic consequences of social inequality on overall levels of mental illness and physical health, in Britain and elsewhere around the globe.[13] In 2015, Marmot warned that more than 200,000 people in the UK are dying prematurely because of existing social inequalities. We live in a rich country in which the poor, on average, die seven years sooner than the wealthy and are likely to become disabled almost two decades earlier. Indeed, even the middle classes have life expectancies eight years lower than the very richest. Death and disability provide far more robust statistics than measures of happiness, which tells us something about that supposed lack of correlation between income and measures of wellbeing.[14]

I have a personal connection with all of this, having lived for almost half a century in what is viewed as the affluent, distinctly desirable London borough of Islington. Unless you are allergic to cities, who wouldn't want to live here? However, rocketing rent and house prices mean that hardly anyone nowadays could actually choose to do so. Arrestingly, apart from my presence (of little interest to the world at large), Islington has one or two other little-known but unique features: the borough has the highest level of depression and psychosis in the whole of England, and men who live here have the lowest life expectancy in London.

These figures become a little less surprising when we realize that Islington is one of the most socially unequal areas in the land, with the average homeowner earning over five times more than someone in social housing – a mean that compresses far more obscene levels of inequality.[15] Thus Kristina Glenn, the director of the Cripplegate Foundation, which has been fighting poverty in Islington for over 500 years, sums up the statistics on Islington as follows:

The fourth-highest child poverty in the country. The four-
teenth most deprived borough. A third of children living in
overcrowded conditions. Forty per cent of older people living
in poverty. The lowest life expectancy in London. The highest
number of serious mental health issues in the country. The
highest levels of depression in England ... the highest level of
male suicides in Britain.[16]

That might seem a lot of bleak data for the borough's more affluent residents to counterbalance, especially when, as Wilkinson
and Pickett found, visible inequality makes life worse for everyone, especially in terms of levels of violence, status anxiety and
fear of failure. This might explain why Islington suffers from
some of the highest levels of criminality, drugs and violence
across the country; as well as showing the second highest levels
of crime across all London boroughs.[17]

Once we place endemic depression in a broader political
context, there is always so much more to say. It is all at odds
with those strictly personal solutions recommended by what
William Davies and others call the happiness industry, but very
much in line with the inevitable cycles of debt that trap so many
today in economic misery.[18]

Some fifty years ago, Marxist economists such as Paul Baron
and Paul Sweezy foresaw the rise of unregulated financial capitalism over productive investment as a way of ensuring fast
profits, while threatening mounting inequality both nationally
and globally.[19] However, it took a few more decades still to install
the current world order, broadly – if loosely – characterized as
'neo-liberalism'. This new world order has included the rapid
movement of the private sector, dominated by finance capital,
into increasing control over the public sector in economic matters.

From the close of the 1970s, the triumphal march of the right, steered by Margaret Thatcher in the UK and Ronald Reagan in the US, followed in the wake of the global oil crisis and the subsequent stock market collapse of the mid 1970s. Once in government, Thatcher changed the political agenda, initiating a programme of confronting and defeating the trade unions, underinvesting in industry, selling off public housing and beginning the process of privatizing public services, while perilously encouraging the complete deregulation of finance capital.

Since then, there has been an overriding emphasis on markets and profits, yet as the British political scientist Colin Crouch illustrates, in actuality the steady global penetration of monopolistic multinational corporations and the financialization of capitalist accumulation has meant the closing down of both markets and profits other than for the super-rich.[20] Thus today the oligarchy of financial institutions looms like an ogre over markets and governments alike. The profits of the biggest corporations rest upon the selling and reselling of credit and debt, incurred at personal levels by the many trying to maintain their living standards, even as wages have stagnated or fallen since 2007, while house prices have continued to soar due to low interest rates on borrowing.[21]

This is the context in which so many people, and households, are on the verge of tumbling into unmanageable indebtedness, whether from job losses, divorce, relatives in need of care, or any number of unpredictable mishaps, rendered all the more precarious by the removal of welfare safety nets. Alongside Marmot, other researchers have also been busy collecting data on the physical and mental harm experienced by people struggling with mountains of debt. Misery becomes concentrated in all the poorest areas of the country, where local economies are weakest and the effects of continual government cutbacks to municipal authorities are greatest, largely preventing local councils from improving the lives of those in most need.[22]

Accompanying the impact of economic anxieties, although often overlapping with them, there are a host of mental health issues stemming from the effect of sexism, racism and other clear patterns of social neglect, bullying and exclusion. For instance, Laura Bates, who founded the Everyday Sexism Project in 2012, highlights the growing miseries of teenage girls. A recent British survey of 1,500 girls and young women reported that almost half of those aged between 17 and 21 had psychological problems, with self-harming topping the list, closely followed by depression and eating disorders.[23]

Already suspicious of the official happiness agenda, the Political Economy Research Centre at Goldsmiths College, also part of the University of London and headed by sociologist Will Davies, has recently been monitoring the websites used by people in serious debt. This gave them access to the intense anguish caused by spiralling debt.[24] As their research indicates, it can be hard to assess the exact causes of the widely reported rise in mental health problems such as depression, since once stress and anxiety are aroused people find themselves trapped in a degenerating cycle. Nevertheless, they provide more than enough material to highlight the social underpinning of much of the emotional turmoil they witnessed online, leading them to argue: 'The emotional injuries of debt need to be understood as both widespread and ... socially embedded ... people in particular socioeconomic categories such as those with low income, women and young people are overrepresented among the population with mental health issues and with high levels of personal debt'.[25]

Moreover, they notice that the more individuals blame themselves for accruing debt in the first place, as indeed they are encouraged to do, the greater the levels of anxiety and panic, triggering largely futile attempts to escape a sense of shame and failure. Thus, we learn that overall 'about 50 per cent of people with debt in the UK have a mental disorder, compared to 14 per cent amongst people with no debt'.[26] These researchers conclude that in economies now built and sustained by debt, widespread 'financial melancholia' is endemic, as 'the past devours the future', the chilling words they borrow from the French economist Thomas Piketty, in his landmark book *Capital in the Twenty-First Century*. The debt accrued in the past devours the future's ability to be free of distress, and any sort of social life can begin to fade for those trapped in financial melancholia.

Here's a flavour of the narratives these Goldsmith researchers collect, in this case from postings to the online forum Consumer Action Group (CAG), which was set up in 2006 and now has around 250,000 members:

'I am afraid of the post arriving (my husband is on antidepressant[s] and can't cope with even a gas bill) ... I hate to answer the phone in case it's a debtor chasing money'.

'Blinds were pulled, doors doubled locked, we didn't go out ...'

'Nothing the doctor can do except diagnose me with moderate depression, anxiety, stress, etc. and give me sick notes. Seeing a counsellor and various other medics, but fundamentally the money side isn't their problem, is it?'[27]

Finally, Davies and his co-workers conclude that urging only personal solutions for those trapped in debt crisis can actually deepen the trauma and harmful behaviour it can potentially trigger. More successful strategies to combat personal calamity involve seeking help and sympathy from others, as well as collective attempts to understand and share one's problems. Financial institutions and debt collectors have even tried, unsuccessfully, to lobby against and close down online consumer forums allowing people to share advice about dealing with debt problems and taking on financial institutions, suggesting to me the possible effectiveness of this alternative strategy.[28]

Davies himself has much more to say about this in his widely researched book, *The Happiness Industry*. He illustrates, for instance, how an employer's seemingly benevolent attention to the apparent cheeriness of their workers can easily become a way of further manipulating and controlling them – by perhaps literally monitoring smiles. Meanwhile, the necessity for a cheerful demeanour is imposed alongside a stubborn refusal to admit that it is long hours, workplace competitiveness, low wages and more that really underpin workplace misery.[29]

Recently, there has been some public exposure of these coercive 'happiness' regimes in a few of the major oligopolies, with Amazon providing just one of the better-known examples. From their various outlets around the world, Amazon employees have repeatedly described working conditions as a 'soul-crushing experience'. The recollections of one worker on his brief time at an Amazon warehouse is typical of many available: 'I can confirm that no one is ever happy or smiling, except the security guards who are on the front lines as the face of the company, so they get paid to be happy'.[30]

Using reports from Amazon warehouses, the organizational researchers Carl Cederström and André Spicer offer their own damning appraisal of the burdens of corporations' commitment to the 'happiness ethos', miserable though their workers may be: 'Although they are in a precarious situation, they are required to hide these feelings and project a confident, upbeat, employable self.'[31] Today there is a booming field of management research on positivity at work, all designed to keep employees working longer, with corporations such as Google even installing play equipment in their workplaces. Yet Spicer argues that what he calls 'the cult of compulsory happiness' can actually render workplaces more miserable, since the implicit ban on negative sentiment often proves 'emotionally stunting for employees', especially in difficult situations, by preventing them from expressing the full range of their emotions.[32]

Meanwhile, any collective strategies of resistance and mutual aid for combating personal stress and misery are quite distinct from (though not necessarily wholly incompatible with) the recommendations of those such as Richard Layard, who use their authority to promote wellbeing via calls for funding for what they see as the most cost-effective form of individual therapy: CBT. However, the ironic bottom line is clearly that the happiness economists do actually fear that we now live in an era of mounting disquiet and foreboding.

Many of us share their premonitions. 'Beware the happiness gurus' seems useful advice, when they offer only personal solutions in line with the ruling elites' supposed commitment to promoting general wellbeing. This facilitates rather than disrupts a climate in which most of us will be working longer hours, in more precarious jobs, in harsher times overall. It requires effort to remain entirely blind to the misery of others, near and far, however much the political reiteration of reactionary 'common sense' tries to privatize misery and distract us from the suffering of others.

My fear, then, is that people have overall actually become more miserable in recent decades, but the pressure is on for us to disavow this knowledge. 'Cruel optimism' is the term the astute American literary scholar Lauren Berlant coined to encompass the particular anguish of being encouraged to aspire to what in practice you have not the remotest chance of achieving, thus ending up blaming only yourself and feeling guilty for your failure. As she illustrates so poignantly, people are wounded by their attachment to objects associated with fantasies of the 'good life', a 'good life' which social conditions have rendered entirely unobtainable. It holds them back from imagining alternative ways of living in the present: 'In a relation of cruel optimism our activity is revealed as a vehicle for attaining a kind of passivity.'[33]

Similarly, in her powerful essay 'Find Your Beach', the perceptive Zadie Smith ponders her life in Manhattan, with the public command beaming out from every other billboard to assert not collective pleasure, but your very own personal bliss: 'The pursuit of happiness has always seemed to me a somewhat heavy American burden, but in Manhattan it is conceived as a peculiar form of duty ... Our happiness, our miseries, our anxieties, our beaches, or our blasted heaths – they are all within our own power to create or destroy.'[34]

Philosophical Puzzles

Aware of all its ritual incantation and false promises, many critics now disdain the topic of happiness altogether. Such repudiation would not surprise many of those who have puzzled over the history and uses of the notion of happiness. As we have seen, the work of contemporary government advisers on personal wellbeing has its own shadow, the study of happiness is forever haunted by its antithesis. It is easier to invoke and recall moments of misery and pain, it would seem, than the absence of suffering.

We could go right back to the birth of Western philosophy, to the ancient Greeks, for whom happiness was, for the most part, reserved for the immortal gods. Classic Greek tragedies are replete with tales of human misery: 'O unhappy race / Of mortal man! doomed to an endless round / Of sorrows, and immeasurable woe!' as Sophocles had his chorus chant, in the fifth century BCE.[35]

Importantly, however, in Greek philosophy and most notably in Aristotle, happiness (or *eudaimonia*) is not so much an emotion, a psychic state or inner disposition, but rather a way of acting in the world, a form of human flourishing, through the use of all one's faculties in pursuit of a good life: 'Happiness is good activity, not amusement.' Happiness, Aristotle argues, can only stem from those activities that we desire to do for their own sake, which are therefore both noble and good. Moreover, fortunately for the scholar, since happiness is an activity in accordance with virtue, the highest form of happiness is the contemplative life, hence, 'The philosopher will more than any other be happy'.[36] The specialist in ancient Greek and Roman philosophy Martha Nussbaum points out that in the *Nicomachean Ethics*, Aristotle offers two slightly different conceptions of happiness. In the first, he identifies pleasure with unimpeded activity; in the second, better-known account, quoted above, he links it to a type of healthy, virtuous activity, 'like the bloom on the cheek of youth'.[37]

In neither, however, would happiness be seen as any sort of

permanent or measurable thing. Only the noble or 'godlike' few are even thought capable of this type of truly virtuous action through a life of reflection and the contemplation of truth, as Darrin McMahon confirms in his rich overview of historical reflections on happiness: 'For much of Western history, happiness served as a marker of human perfection, an imagined ideal of a creature complete, without further wants, desires, or needs'.[38] It was only approaching modern times, in the late seventeenth century, McMahon suggests, that the more familiar hedonistic notion of happiness comes to the fore, with the British philosopher John Locke writing in his *Essay Concerning Human Understanding* in 1689: 'Happiness then in its full extent is the utmost Pleasure we are capable of, and *Misery* the utmost pain'.[39]

Furthermore, it was only with the Industrial Revolution and improvements in health, longevity and overall living standards beginning in the late eighteenth and nineteenth centuries that the harshness of daily life gradually lessened for more of the population. It was in this period, in the late eighteenth century, that Jeremy Bentham developed his famous principles of utilitarianism, broadcasting his dream that governments should aim to promote 'the greatest happiness of the greatest number'.[40] Moreover, it is he who first suggested that this happiness is straightforward and quantifiable, not a volatile emotion that so frequently arrives shadowed by its antithesis.

Yet, though Benthamite utilitarianism has remained the dominant conception of happiness in the Anglophone world, it hardly existed unchallenged by shrewder observers. Nobody expressed this more passionately than the notoriously mystical William Blake, in almost everything he wrote:

Joy & Woe are woven fine
A Clothing for the soul divine.
Under every grief & pine
Runs a joy with silken twine.[41]

Indeed Blake, like other poets before and since, expressed the potentially destructive side of any happiness agenda, focused upon avoiding pain:

He who binds to himself a joy
Does the winged life destroy;
But he who kisses the joy as it flies
Lives in eternity's sunrise.[42]

Blake's poetic mysticism brings me to another enduring philosophical tradition, which is associated in particular with the short life of that heretical, lens-grinding Dutch Jew Baruch Spinoza. Writing in the century before Blake, he was busy cataloguing human passions, seeing joy and sadness as the two basic passions (which today we would call emotions). 'Joy' he saw as that which exercised the greatest capacity for action, and 'sadness' as resulting whenever one's capacities for action are blocked or rendered passive. Joy is 'that passion by which the mind passes to a greater perfection', while sadness is 'that passion by which it passes to a lesser perfection'.[43] However, with its Aristotelian echoes, Spinoza's thought cannot be aligned with the contemporary ethic of individual self-empowerment because he did not see people as separate, autonomous creatures with their own inherent natures, but always as interconnected.

Spinoza's notion of joy as movement has influenced many later philosophers, in particular Gilles Deleuze, who uses

Spinoza to define joy as 'everything that consists in satisfying a capacity'. Conversely, 'sadness' is 'when I am separated from a capacity of which I believed myself, rightly or wrongly, capable ... all sadness is the effect of a power over me'. Joy is using one 'maximum capacity for life and for resistance to any power that interferes with such capacity.'[44]

In modern times, it is German philosophers in particular who highlighted the trouble with happiness. Writing in the early nineteenth century, Hegel noted that 'history is not the soil in which happiness grows. Periods of happiness in it are the blank pages of history'.[45] At much the same time, Arthur Schopenhauer argued that happiness would always be defeated by painful craving, and recommended renouncing any search for pleasure: 'Everything in life proclaims that earthly happiness is destined to be frustrated or recognized as an illusion. The grounds for this lie deep in the very nature of things.' Earthly happiness will not only be frustrated, but in his many axioms on life Schopenhauer would add: 'We find pleasure much less pleasurable, pain much more painful than we had anticipated.'[46]

Both philosophers drew upon the canon of their eminent predecessor, Immanuel Kant, who thought that while we all seek happiness, it is so indeterminate that no one can say 'definitely and consistently what it is that he really wishes and wills'.[47]

By the close of the nineteenth century, Friedrich Nietzsche made the same thought axiomatic, with a swipe at the earlier British utilitarianism that continues in Anglophone thought to this day: 'Man does not strive for pleasure; only the Englishman does'.[48] This was at much the same time that Sigmund Freud, who had read Nietzsche, was laying down the groundwork for psychoanalysis. However, if there is one thing people know about Freud's writing, apart from but relating to his foundational account of the fierce attachments of early infancy, it is that he believed that our most basic human energy, the source of all desire, the libido, is pleasure seeking from the very beginning. Moreover, as he wrote in his classic *Three Essays on Sexuality* (1905), our first encounters with the world are constant sources of desire – and, at the very same time, of frustration: 'A child's intercourse with anyone responsible for his care affords him an unending source of sexual excitation and satisfaction from his erogenous zones'.[49]

The problem, however, is that, girl or boy, our wishes are inevitably frustrated at every turn by the removal of satisfaction, the absence of that 'object' responsible for our satisfaction, whom we soon come to recognize as a person and usually, in those crucial early years, our mother.

Thus, Freud's position is certainly quite as gloomy as all the other German philosophers mentioned, since our desires can never be fully satisfied, but will always encounter obstacles. In *Civilization and its Discontents*, the book he wrote towards the end of his life, Freud concluded: 'The programme of becoming happy, which the pleasure principle imposes on us, cannot be fulfilled'. Nevertheless, he believed, we rarely give up the struggle to pursue what little happiness we might find. This led him to caution us not 'to look for the whole of our satisfaction from any single aspiration'.[50] We are destined to seek happiness even though we can never escape the tragic in life.

Consistent throughout his writing on this point, Freud ends where he had begun: by noting the inevitable sorrow of human existence. In the finale of his very first book, *Studies in Hysteria*, Freud believed the only promise he could give a patient was that he might succeed in turning their 'hysterical misery into common unhappiness', thereby making it easier for them to defend themselves 'against that unhappiness'.[51]

Today, we are less likely to be diagnosed as suffering from hysteria. However, many have argued that the widespread depression we hear so much about is the cultural equivalent of hysteria. Depression has become an expanding blanket enfolding all manner of individual miseries and fears. Attempting to update Freud's views, the Lacanian psychoanalyst Darian Leader notes that the way we talk about depression nowadays has little merit. The widespread hubbub about 'depression' merely mirrors its supposed opposite, the vacuous noise surrounding 'happiness': both categories are empty of any real meaning. Despite their differences on other matters, most clinicians agree with Leader's arguments in his book *The New Black*, in which he suggests that the belief in quick fixes for depression, whether through psychotropic drugs or CBT, are themselves merely a 'mirror of the malady' itself. The daily pill or the individual cognitive goal of replacing negative thoughts with positive ones primarily reflects back the 'bleak image of us all as separated units ... each ... taken to be an isolated agent cut off from others and driven by competition for goods and services in the marketplace rather than by community and shared effort'.[52]

It is not reinforcing such individualizing outlooks but rather thinking about our shared humanity that those who criticize quick fixes, including myself, want to stress. This suggests that in dealing with contemporary unhappiness we need to begin by seeking out the varied and nuanced human stories behind it: stories that involve loss, lack, abandonment, separation and mourning, all exacerbated by the stress, pessimism and feelings of isolation so many now feel. It is only holding on to the complexity of emotions and the inevitability of pain and loss that accompanies our desires and their satisfaction that can provide a fuller picture of either happiness or sorrow. Happiness and sorrow are never fully separable.

No one saw human life in bleaker terms than the post-war German philosopher and social theorist Theodor Adorno, who was also influenced by Freud and psychoanalysis, and nothing enraged him more than promises of 'happiness' in a world dominated by the grinding logics of production and consumption:

> It is part of the mechanism of domination to forbid recognition of the suffering it produces, and there is a straight line of development between the gospel of happiness and the construction of camps of extermination ... that each of our own countrymen can convince himself that he cannot hear the screams of pain. That is the model of an unhampered capacity for happiness.[53]

Yet, even those who are all too aware of the pains of life have sometimes managed to capture something of the fleeting nuance of happiness. If often less noisy than depictions of sorrow, happiness is not always silent; it is not only Hegel's 'blank pages of History without record'. It is just that it is neither stable, nor free from memories of pain. The descriptions of happiness we find most compelling are usually passing memories of discrete moments, which we later recollect as precious. This thought is well expressed in a poem published the very day I was writing this page, by the young English poet Jack Underwood, entitled 'Happiness'. It captures elegantly some of those fleeting moments, little and large, diverse and mundane, such as in his final memory of happy moments:

privately with you, when we're watching television and everyone else can be depressed as rotten logs for all we care, because variously and by degrees as it is, we know happiness because it is not always usual, and does not wait to leave.[54]

Passion and Politics

It is partly the culturally orchestrated ideology of individual happiness, however, accompanying the ubiquitous commercial incitements to pleasure, which makes it harder to know how to write about joy in our times. I will return to this topic again in my chapter 'Where Is Joy?', but for now I will merely say that the triggers for joy are almost always something others might share, at least potentially, even if we experience them alone. Opening his cultural history of the notion of joy, Adam Potkay begins: 'Joy is the mind's delight in a good thing that comes to pass or seems sure to happen soon.' However, he hastens to add that emotions are not just aspects of our individual psychology or physiology, but 'shaped as well by histories: the case history of each individual and the cultural history of each emotion term'.

Potkay confirms what I have already suggested, which is that in contemporary cultural life there is scant reflection on joy. In contrast, looking backward we can see that the most enduring accounts of joy we have all point to some more transcendent pleasure that we want to share. Thus in his famous 'Ode to Joy' in 1786, the brilliant eighteenth-century German poet and philosopher Friedrich Schiller wrote about his concept of joy, which Beethoven would later set to music in his Ninth Symphony (later to become the international anthem of the European Union):

> Thy enchantments bind together,
> what did custom's sword divide,
> Beggars are a prince's brother,
> where thy gentle wings abide.[55]

Drawing on Schiller, as well as England's own more melancholy Romantic poet Samuel Taylor Coleridge, and many others who tried to describe the lineaments of joy in former times, Potkay comments: 'Joy breaks down the boundaries that separate self from other, humanity and nature. It bestows a glorious we-mode upon earth, making it seem like heaven'.[56]

Thus, while nowadays we are encouraged to see happiness as something embedded within us, the type of euphoric happiness we call 'joy' takes us beyond or outside ourselves. Writing in her diary as she fled Paris in 1939 to resume residence in New York, Anaïs Nin reflected: 'Over and over again I sail towards joy, which is never in the room with me, but always near me, across the way, like those rooms full of gayety one sees from the street, or the gayety in the street one sees from a window. Will I ever reach joy?'

Can one ever reach joy? For once I think this usually self-obsessed diarist does indeed capture something about its substance. She continues: 'I want the joy of simple colours, street organs, ribbons, flags, not a joy that takes my breath away and throws me into space alone where no one else can breathe with me, not the joy that comes from a lonely drunkenness '.[57] Lonely drunkenness, surely, is the very antithesis of joy, hardly the ushering in of a better future. Moreover, Nin did come to experience the most extraordinary moment of shared joy, as she wrote in her diary on the day of the liberation of Paris, 19 August 1944:

Liberation of France!
JOY. JOY. JOY. JOY. JOY. JOY. JOY. JOY. JOY.
Such joy, such happiness at the hope of war ending. Happiness
in unison with the world. Delirious happiness ...
A joy you share with the whole world is almost too great for
one human being.[58]

One does not have to have experienced an event quite as momentous as the end of the Second World War to agree that the ordinary nature of joy is enhanced when we are able to rejoice with others. And it is even greater, although Nin does not mention this, in situations we feel we have worked to help create. The desire to move outside and beyond oneself, the search for some sort of shared laughter or joy, one with another, that 'we-mode', is certainly one way of overcoming the gloom that can threaten to engulf us.

This is why, from the shakiest of foundations, although with plentiful memories of the joys I have shared with others, I want to reclaim more of those moments and those spaces in public life where collective energy binds us together in ways that transcend our personal worries. Furthermore, things we have helped create in the past can provide blueprints for their possible recurrence – never exactly as they arose before, but rather in new forms shaped by the dynamics of the present.

To provide a sense of this, in my own lifetime, the joy with which women's liberation burst onto the political scene at the close of the 1960s will remain unique, even though some feminists have struggled to remain true to their early utopian hopes. In the USA, this would include tens of thousands of women, such as that ground-breaking feminist fighter, the late Ellen Willis, who helped found New York Radical Women in 1967, then Redstockings in 1969, and whose refrains until the day she died at only sixty-four remained much the same: 'Radical politics is about being happy, not about being good'; 'Feminism is a vision of active freedom, of fulfilled desire, or it is nothing.'[59] In the same era, black American feminist Audre Lorde wrote in *Sister Outsider*: 'The sharing of joy, whether physical, emotional, psychic, or intellectual, forms a bridge between the sharers which can be the basis for understanding much of what is not shared between them, and lessens the threat of their difference.'[60]

In the UK, feminists of every stripe often shared similar sentiments. The iconoclastic writer Angela Carter was determined to find a language for expressing women's pleasure while stressing in all her prose and fiction the many possibilities for transformation through rebellion and women's desire for shared joy and connection with each other – however fragile and temporary. She summed up such doggedly ironic optimism in the very last line of her carnivalesque novel *Wise Children*, written after she was diagnosed with the terminal cancer she died from at only fifty-one. Tracking the vivid but precarious lives of Dora and Nora Chance, two ageing ex-chorus girls still defiantly facing the many bumps and shocks of their lives in a fiercely male-dominated world, she signed off this, her last novel, with them both proclaiming in its concluding line: 'What a joy it is to dance and sing!'[61]

During its early years, all around the world many women spoke of becoming involved in second-wave feminism as rather like 'falling in love', and sharing the type of radical joy so often expressed in freedom struggles. It is when more inclusive spaces open up for particular groups of hitherto marginalized or subordinated people to find themselves anew, in affirmative identifications with one another. Ursula Owen, one of the founders of Virago Press in 1974, captures the exhilaration of many women's desire to be part of that sudden feminist cultural renaissance: 'You couldn't have asked for more joyousness or pleasure from people about the existence of Virago ... people came up to me all the time, even on holidays, seeing me reading a Virago book ... it was extraordinary really, young women just felt their lives had been changed.'[62]

This was the utopian feminist moment I shared. As I have written about elsewhere in my political memoir *Making Trouble*, it would pass, as such moments do, facing inevitable setbacks, failings and conflict, from within and without.[63] Moreover, I am aware that a passion for politics is just one form of collective bonding, though as we'll see again it is regularly an enduringly significant and transformative one.

Personally, despite the greater caution and lowered certainties I now often bring to political engagement, I still see diverse forms of solidarity drawing people together in movements of collective hope, when they try to offer some resistance to the disorders of the present. Once we acknowledge the injustice and suffering all around us, affirming at least some possibility for resistance and change is always possible. Further, with the forging of any new radical communities, that same sense of meaning and shared energy I described above in the early days of women's liberation can easily recur. Indeed, I first came across the term 'radical happiness' when it was used by that enduring feminist mentor the American poet Adrienne Rich to describe the joy she sometimes saw flowing all around her when people shared a sense of 'true participation in society', usually in celebration of what they had achieved, or might soon realize. She had experienced such radical happiness at a mass poetry festival after the arrest of Pinochet in Chile in 2001, as well as in noting the shared energy at one of the early 'anti-globalization' protests in Seattle the same year.[64] Rich was herself drawing upon Hannah Arendt's notion of 'public happiness', which I mentioned in the preface.

Arendt had written about 'public happiness' in her book *On Revolution*, published in 1963, following an earlier essay entitled 'Revolution and Public Happiness' in 1960.[65] What Arendt hoped to revive and foster was the sort of radical spirit that energizes people in revolutionary moments, bringing the mass of people into active engagement with politics to create better societies and produce a fairer, more egalitarian world where everyone can have what Arendt saw as the pleasure of participating in public debate over critical issues.

Arendt rejected the idea of leaving politics to elected representatives in government, believing people's active participation was necessary to check the possible weaknesses of representative democracy, in its potential to distance itself from the people, or at least, given competing social interests, from certain segments of them. Thus, true happiness, Arendt argued, could not be simply a private matter, but comes as much from the sense of purpose and significance gained through lively participation in public affairs. Just as much, the active engagement of the majority in politics is necessary for creating public happiness. Arendt used the earlier republican ideals of Thomas Jefferson to argue that 'no one could be called happy or free without participating, and having a share, in public power'.[66] It is thus some notion of genuine participatory democracy that is both the enabler and the product of public happiness, in Arendt's writing. However, we can hardly desire any return to the ancient Greek *polis* on which Arendt founded her visions of radical democracy. This is because it was a place where the possibility and freedom of its male citizens to spend so much of their time discussing politics in designated spaces of their cities, as in the agora of Athens, itself rested upon the labour of slaves and the subordination of women, both denied rights of citizenship.

Nevertheless, I hardly need convincing that creating more social spaces for facilitating people's greater sense of involvement and agency in public affairs could help promote healthier, happier, less atomized communities. Yet for many reasons I see only sporadic, if recurrent, possibilities for successful collective engagements in today's political world, however engaged a minority is in trying to help create and sustain such moments. I have already mentioned that the seemingly unstoppable commercial dominance of a small number of global corporations and financial oligarchies has for decades now been undermining the ability of nation states to shape their own domestic policies, let alone of people's power to control government policy.[67] Moreover, some political theorists today, such as Wendy Brown, suggest that the ubiquitous promotion and near blanket acceptance of a neo-liberal logic of market principles and competitiveness have meant the further 'extending of economic values, practices, and metrics to every dimension of human life', thereby rendering us individually 'roving bits of human capital', where any collective affirmative politics becomes almost unthinkable.[68]

I certainly recognize the world Brown is describing, but not the unremitting degree of cultural and political pessimism in her analysis. No doubt the sparse optimism over transforming these mean and increasingly unequal times feeds into the melancholy of those who have been busy exploring the nuances of feelings, emotions and 'affect' in scholarship in recent years, which has been concerned almost exclusively with tracking negative feelings.

As I discuss in my next chapter, there has been much significant and lyrical reflection on shame, guilt, loss, trauma, loneliness, self-hate, depression and melancholy, especially noticeable among cutting-edge feminist and queer scholars in cultural studies.[69] More generally, it seems to me that positive affect, our moments of joy and happiness, are seen as more trivial, less stirring, interesting or memorable than the tragic, and closer to what is seen as dull and coercive normality: 'All happy families are alike'. Yet I see no compelling reason to accept this, however fascinating Tolstoy's unique domestic miseries.

We need to resist the happiness imperative beamed down on us from every other billboard or packaged in a thousand self-help manuals. The black American scholar Cornel West, for instance, distinguishes the usual talk of happiness from what he, like so many before him, sees as the joyful possibilities of collective resistance. Pleasure, under commodified conditions, tends to be individual and inward, but joy, he suggests, can cut across that: 'Joy tries to get at those non-market values – love, care, kindness, service, solidarity, the struggle for justice – values that provide the possibility of bringing people together'.[70] Bringing people together, as we'll see in later chapters, can only endure when there is also space for the recognition of a plurality of differences, which – in consciously combating the hierarchies of privilege and power consolidated around difference – creates spaces of excitement, respect and hope.

2

Sing No Sad Songs for Me

Happiness does not wait to leave, as poets note. So, it is the paradoxes surrounding today's notion of 'depression' that force us to acknowledge that a book about happiness must also be one that addresses sorrow and loss. 'Depression is ordinary', the North American professor of English and Gender Studies Ann Cvetkovich says in her genealogical survey and personal memoir of its crippling symptoms, *Depression: A Public Feeling*. It certainly would seem so, given the extraordinary numbers of people around the globe currently diagnosed with this malady.

However, Cvetkovich's multilayered reflections on the history of melancholy feelings are completely at odds with publicly endorsed trends encouraging us, if we can't conceal sorrow, hastily to alleviate it, most often with drugs or diverse forms of cognitive behavioural therapy (CBT). This is because Cvetkovich believes, along with a significant minority of others, that dwelling with feelings of depression, or melancholic experiences of loss, trauma or abandonment, is not necessarily at odds with finding ways of surmounting them, and perhaps even helping others to do the same.[1]

In her typically acerbic, witty way, the writer Barbara Ehrenreich says something similar, though more directly political, when she explores the tyranny of positive thinking in her bestselling book *Smile or Die: How Positive Thinking Fooled America and the World*. Here she expresses her rejection of the magical thinking that is ubiquitously urged upon people, especially in the USA, as a way of disavowing grim realities and mortal threat. She castigates in particular the motivational coaches of positive thinking, arguing that they actually encourage both widespread self-blame and political passivity and ignorance. Barely submerged in this agenda, she argues, is something else: 'Always, in a hissed undertone, there is the darker message that if you don't have all you want, if you feel sick, discouraged, or defeated, you have only yourself to blame. Positive theology ratifies a world without beauty, transcendence, or mercy.'[2]

Ehrenreich's argument addresses what happens to those with little or no chance of altering the conditions that threaten and impoverish them, crushing their hopes. People encouraged to waste time and money on false promises of 'improving' themselves thereby sideline any anger against the many exploitative and damaging contexts that may indeed be harming them. As we saw in the last chapter, these begin with the massive expansion of insecure, low-waged jobs, which can be lost on the whim of employers, accompanying the general removal of welfare benefits and public provisions. These 'personal' calamities occur in the context of increasingly carcinogenic environments, the continuing fiscal recklessness of financial capital and what have proved foolhardy military ventures. In the pursuit of greater overall happiness, Ehrenreich will not overlook these huge impediments keeping us miserable:

In my own vision of utopia there is not only more comfort, and security for everyone – better jobs, health care, and so forth – there are also more parties, festivities, and opportunities for dancing in the streets ... But we cannot levitate ourselves into that blessed condition by wishing it. We need to brace ourselves for a struggle against terrifying obstacles, both of our own making and imposed by the natural world. And the first step is to recover from the mass delusion that is positive thinking.[3]

The deep fault line in the delusion that positive thinking can cure depression should be obvious as soon as we notice that the nation most committed to imparting its benefits consumes two-thirds of the global market in anti-depressants. Anti-depressants are indeed one of the most commonly prescribed drugs in the USA, swallowed by a staggering 31 million Americans, including one in four women in their forties and fifties.[4] With figures such as these, however, we face another knotty issue. If the trouble with the different ways we think about happiness today is masking escalating depression, we surely need to wonder why misery seems to have engulfed the human condition, especially in the very countries apparently most committed to eliminating it.

The Many Shades of Melancholy

Has depression always been with us? Many would suggest that it has. In the ancient world the Greek physician Hippocrates wrote that melancholia resulted from too much black bile in the spleen. However, both our understandings of melancholic conditions, and above all the prevalence of specific forms of misery, have changed remarkably since then.

It was Aristotle, or someone writing in his name, who suggested that it was in the nature of the most distinguished, creative, even witty men to suffer from melancholy: 'Why is it that all those who have become eminent in philosophy or politics or poetry or the arts are clearly melancholics?'[5] Ever since, others have also claimed links between melancholy and creativity or merit. Still, many simply wrote of its inevitability as a part of life, as did Shakespeare in his comedies and tragedies alike, most of them written around the 1590s: 'I hold the world but as the world ... A stage where every man must play a part, and mine a sad one'.[6]

A few decades later, the Renaissance scholar Robert Burton's *The Anatomy of Melancholy* (1621) quickly became the most famous English historical text on the topic of melancholy. It has retained admirers right up to the present, from Samuel Johnson through John Keats and Samuel Beckett, to Philip Pullman and Nick Cave. Burton wrote his tome, he said, to keep himself busy in order to avoid melancholy himself. It seems to have worked, at least up to the time of his death at sixty-three, since he never stopped writing till the day he died. By this time, he had completed three volumes and around 1,400 pages, leaving on his deathbed notes for further revisions.

When Burton began, he was writing about what he saw as an epidemic of melancholy, a condition so prevalent that few could be said not to suffer from it at all. His goal was to encompass every dimension of misery in his work, from the most common to the most esoteric. Burton's 'melancholy' was therefore a broader concept than the condition we think of today as depression. He believed it could be understood and treated medically, but Burton also described the diverse patterns of melancholy as forms of moral and spiritual disease tied in with the background misery of his times. His was a period of both political and religious strife that had continued across Europe after the Protestant Reformation, reaching England in the early seventeenth century.

Burton was far from the only member of the early modern learned community writing about the passions who saw melancholy as shaped by the anxieties and conflicts of the day, along with the licentiousness the passions were also seen as generating.[7] As the historian of emotions Thomas Dixon argues, widespread interest in melancholy and the approval of tears were present in British history right up to the middle decades of the twentieth century. Indeed, in 1733 the pioneering British physician Dr George Cheyne would write about 'melancholia' as *The English Malady*.[8]

However, the earlier notions of melancholia as a type of imbalance of the humours, or dark spirits circulating in the body, shifted with the strong turn to science during the British Enlightenment in the second part of the eighteenth century. In particular, the physician and medical scholar William Cullen, a key figure in the Scottish Enlightenment and friend of the philosopher David Hume (as well as his physician), sought to explain all diseases as linked to the physiology of the nervous system, especially the brain. For Cullen, melancholia was 'partial insanity' and, although he did not depart altogether from the old notion of 'noxious' humours, he did pave the way for the gradual reinterpretation of melancholy as 'depression', later seen as a neurological or 'affective' disorder.[9]

Thus by the early nineteenth century, a strictly medical model of mental illness was emerging. As the century progressed, sadness, in whatever form, was no longer attached to the idea of melancholy as a disorder of the intellect, but rather melancholia and depression were seen as a mood or 'affective' disorder, according to the philosopher of science Clark Lawler.[10]

By the end of the century, the stage was set for the German psychiatrist Emile Kraepelin to write what is regarded as the founding text of modern scientific psychiatry. His *Compendium of Psychiatry*, first published in 1883, established psychiatry as a branch of medicine and developed a classification system of mental illness that rested upon distinguishing 'manic depression' (now classified as a variety of mood disorders) from 'dementia praecox', by which he referred to the rapid cognitive disintegration associated with the various schizophrenic disorders. Kraepelin remained influential well into the twentieth century, with his classifications still familiar to us today. He also saw mental illness as primarily genetic, urging support for eugenics and racial hygiene to enhance the German people.[11]

Yet, even as psychiatrists felt they were making sense of what they saw as the largely innate or endogenous nature of depression, the father of sociology, Émile Durkheim, undertaking a new discipline of study, was looking in the opposite direction. He saw much evidence for social determination of the levels of personal misery that were evident at the close of the nineteenth century. Most famously, in his 1897 study *Suicide*, Durkheim compared the suicide rates of people belonging to different religious and other social groups, concluding that suicidal depression was attributable to what he called the levels of 'anomie', people experiencing conditions where social norms were absent or confusing. This meant that suicidal depression could not be seen as primarily an individual phenomenon, since it was distinctive of groups of people rather than of individual types. For instance, Catholics, Jews and married people were less prone to commit suicide than were Protestants and the unmarried, while overall men were more likely to kill themselves than women. Venturing further, Durkheim claimed that all forms of unhappiness had a social side: 'There is a collective as well as an individual humor inclining peoples to sadness or cheerfulness, making them see things in bright or somber lights. In fact, only society can pass a collective opinion on the value of human life; for this the individual is incompetent.'[12] As Durkheim saw it, it was the unhappiness produced by the rise of industry and the factory system undermining traditional societies which explained the extremes of modern misery.

In the meantime, Freud and the evolving psychoanalytic tradition believed that depression had a very personal history, although definitely a relational one. Freud did not dismiss biological factors, but he emphasized above all the role of grief resulting from the loss of an important relationship, triggering earlier memories of loss of, or rejection by, those first objects of love, the parents and especially the mother.

In one of Freud's most influential essays, 'Mourning and Melancholia', published in 1917, he saw processes of normal mourning (often a period of two or three years) as people registering their loss of, or rejection by, someone or something they have been narcissistically invested in, but eventually managing to let go of their sorrow. However, melancholy or extreme depression occurred when a person could not move on from their bereavement but had internalized the lost object and, especially in cases where there had been repressed ambivalence or anger towards that now absent 'presence', grief and anger could become directed inwards towards the self, establishing relentless and bitter self-reproach: 'In mourning it is the world which has become poor and empty; in melancholia it is the ego itself.'[13]

Working in this tradition, and drawing upon the later work of Jacques Lacan and Melanie Klein, Paris-based Julia Kristeva writes vividly in *Black Sun* (1989) that whether observing melancholia or depression – seeing the two as blurring into each other – 'Freudian theory detects everywhere the same impossible mourning for the maternal object.'[14] However, Kristeva also argues that this lasting desire for the lost mother, the partial refusal to let go of that first maternal identification, can be a source of great artistic creativity. At least it can be in men, in her view, visible for instance in Fyodor Dostoyevsky's writing on suffering and forgiveness. Only the male artist, she believes, can sometimes manage that move of both detaching himself from his early merger with the maternal object, while also succeeding in retaining traces of his former 'feminine' identification, making his melancholia 'the secret mainspring of a new rhetoric'.[15]

This makes such melancholic artists' creations a type of healing therapeutic process, while giving meaning to the hitherto unsayable, thereby producing much cultural beauty and joy, resulting in what Kristeva calls the melancholic 'sublime'.[16] With or without her problematic occlusion of women (who she argues can never similarly both detach from and yet retain vestiges of their early maternal identification), Kristeva's notion of the melancholic sublime is close to what so many philosophers and artists of melancholy have said through the ages, none more directly than Keats in his famous 'Ode to Melancholy', written like all his most famous odes in 1819. Sufferers should not let go of their pain, he urged, but remain attentive and responsive to its mysteries:

Ay, in the very temple of Delight
Veil'd Melancholy has her sovran shrine,
Though seen of none save him whose strenuous tongue
Can burst Joy's grape against his palate fine;
His soul shalt taste the sadness of her might,
And be among her cloudy trophies hung.[17]

Markets of Misery

Whether or not we attribute people's suffering primarily to endogenous, social or early relational disturbances, and whether or not we see possible value in melancholy, there are other puzzles that nowadays are all too prominent when considering the nature and treatment of our sorrows. Today we are encouraged by both the psychiatric profession and also the world at large to see our misery as coming from within. However, questions arise from the extraordinary escalation of diagnoses of major depressive psychosis, or 'endogenous' depression, in recent decades, when it had hitherto remained a relatively rare disease in psychiatric literature and hospital admissions.

Moreover, following the acceleration in diagnoses of depression, a second epidemic soon escalated from another relatively uncommon disorder: Kraepelin's notion of psychotic manic depression was transformed into bipolar disease, and became diagnosed in an ever-increasing number of people, including very young children. In the UK, the Welsh psychiatrist David Healy was one of the first to draw attention to this rapid expansion of clinical miseries and manias, while trying anew to understand their meaning, aetiology and remedies. In his book *Let Them Eat Prozac: The Unhealthy Relationship Between the*

Pharmaceutical Industry and Depression (2004), Healy noted that within a few decades from the introduction of anti-depressant drugs there was 'a *thousandfold* increase' in those diagnosed with serious depression, 'despite the availability of treatments supposed to cure this terrible affliction'.[18]

Going back to the 1950s and 1960s, Healy suggests that there was only a small market in drugs for those diagnosed as suffering from major depression. But since the 1970s, as the medical historian Edward Shorter agrees, there has been a rapid expansion in diagnoses of depression, replacing the earlier emphasis on anxiety disorders.[19] As a result, when the global pharmaceutical company based in the USA Eli Lilly launched Prozac in 1987 as a drug for serious depressive and other disorders, it quickly became one of the bestselling drugs worldwide. And it, or related substances that correct a presumed deficiency of serotonin in the brain, have remained so ever since. Meanwhile, in 2012, the World Health Organization predicted that depression would soon be the second largest public health problem in the world, after heart disease.[20] Given the galloping spread of this disease, which cannot be attributed to any new virus or to increasing life expectancy – since it is now seen as occurring in people of ever-younger ages, including many children – we surely need to wonder what has been responsible for this extraordinary epidemic. How had the handful of melancholic patients in the 1950s mushroomed into the millions evident a mere generation later?

Even within the psychiatric profession, Healy is far from alone in seeing something odd in these statistics. Nor is he alone in observing that the steep rise in diagnoses for serious depression and bipolar disorder had occurred in exact parallel with the discovery and marketing of drugs for treating them. Looking into the history of the launching of Prozac, the British journalist Anna Moore found that Eli Lilly had funded a massive media campaign, including 8 million brochures and 200,000 posters, informing doctors and the public at large about the new wonder drug, stressing its significance and safety for treating people of all ages whose distress might have gone previously undiagnosed.[21]

All this publicity was thus designed to provide 'disease awareness', accompanying new non-stigmatizing understandings for people to identify with, in order to rid themselves of their unhappy emotions. Practitioners, too, were taught to recognize unhappy patients as suffering from an easily rectifiable 'chemical imbalance', as people whose happiness could be restored via the new anti-depressants. It is therefore not so hard to explain why within ten years of the launch of Prozac, around 10 per cent of Americans over the age of six were taking anti-depressants, including almost one in four in middle age.[22]

The monumental success of anti-depressant drugs encouraged the search for a pharmaceutical solution to the now renamed 'bipolar disorder'. Again, despite the hitherto small number of people being diagnosed with 'manic depression', drug companies began suggesting that 'depression is only half the story', with new advertisements encouraging people to log on to a help centre, again sponsored by Eli Lilly, and take a 'bipolar test' so that they might know how to describe their symptoms to doctors.[23] The media were also involved in popularizing this new disorder, and the 'mood stabilizers' necessary for treating it. In 2006 the BBC, for instance, commissioned the very popular TV comedian, Stephen Fry, to interview fellow celebrities who shared his own 'bipolar' disorder.

There were soon scandals surrounding the spiralling marketing of these mood-altering drugs. In the USA, the clinical psychologist Glen Spielmans obtained confidential documents describing the successful legal proceedings against Eli Lilly for misleading advertising promoting the use of the drug Zyprexa for dementia patients. These documents also revealed that Eli Lilly saw Zyprexa, a 'mood stabilizer' developed for the treatment of bipolar disorder and schizophrenia, as the next drug to supplement their anti-depressant range. It too was launched with an advertising crusade that would turn it into the 'most successful pharmaceutical product ever'.[24]

Joanna Moncrieff is another psychiatrist and clinical researcher active in the British Critical Psychiatry Network, set up in 1999, who agrees with Healy and the many critics of this suddenly escalating mood disease. She points out that there is simply 'no evidence for any chemical imbalances in the brain prior to taking the new psychotropic drugs for altering brain function, nor any convincing evidence that there are dopamine or any other biochemical imbalances in bipolar disorder, or that the drugs used to treat the condition work by reversing these'. Like Healy, she concludes that what has been taking place before our eyes is the social creation of a new 'brain disorder', attributing the popularity of the modern concept of bipolar pathology primarily to the vast resources behind its creation and dissemination.[25]

Far worse, however, there was a disturbing lack of reporting of the very serious physical side effects of these drugs, especially in their long-term use: weight gain, involuntary physical movements, possible cardiac injury, cortical brain shrinkage and impotence. This is all the more alarming when drug companies have been targeting young children for the same 'aggressive medication regime', despite 'paediatric bipolar disorder' being previously entirely unknown. This move was strongly

promoted by a particular group of eminent psychiatric researchers at the Harvard Medical School, including Joseph Biederman,
now known to have been receiving significant funding from the
major drug corporations.[26]

There is much more that could be said here, in particular about the failure of pharmaceutical companies and their
researchers to mention the significant placebo effects discovered in the course of trials for their new psychotropic drugs.
One US psychologist, Irving Kirsch, who conducted an overview of research findings on these drugs over a fifteen-year
period, discovered that placebos overall had been found to be
three times as effective as no treatment when tested on patients,
and also that they had proved to be 75 per cent as effective as
any of the anti-depressant medications being tested. It led him
to conclude that the beneficial effects of these new drugs came
primarily from patients' own expectations of cure.[27]

Two long, highly critical articles on the contemporary illusions of psychiatry and the questionable epidemic of mental
illness were published in the *New York Review of Books* in
2011, both written by the American physician and writer
Marcia Angell. She highlighted a range of publications on the
dangers of these new psychotropic drugs, and the risky practices of those promoting them.[28] The publications she reviewed
included the American psychiatrist Daniel Carlat's book
Unhinged: The Trouble with Psychiatry (2010), in which he suggests that his profession was now in crisis since it was so clearly
associated with, and indeed being manipulated by, the giant
pharmaceutical companies. He confessed that like most other
psychiatrists, he had himself received thousands of dollars from
drug companies for conducting research and pushing the benefits of particular anti-depressant drugs to colleagues.[29] In his

own judicious response to Angell's overview, Carlat agreed that the psychiatric profession does indeed over-diagnose disorders today, and is 'fixated on medical solutions to life's problems', as well as pocketing too much money from drug corporations. Yet, showing just how complicated these controversies are, Carlat also defends his colleagues with the insistence that the new drugs are used because they can 'work', even if 'much of this response is undoubtedly due to the placebo effect'.[30]

It is a weak defence, now that we know quite how much money pharmaceutical corporations have poured into changing the climate of opinion to encourage consumption of the drugs they produce. Their success is also tied in with the current pressure to be happy, and especially, as we saw in the last chapter, to be *seen* to be happy. This undoubtedly compels many to imagine that they can and must find a quick cure for their sorrows and misery, whatever form it takes, even if they do know something about the dangerous side effects of the chemical panacea on offer. As the British journalist and author Oliver Burkeman suggests, the pressure we are under to banish all spectres of sadness and failure is one of the reasons many people feel so unhappy in the first place, with many then driven to seek help for their miseries.[31]

Surviving Depression

Whatever the controversies over the nature and treatment of our psychic sorrows, one thing we cannot dispute is the reality of the many adults around the world today who see themselves as suffering from depression. I have never doubted that for many currently diagnosed with depression, the suffering is intense and agonizing. Certainly, in the closing decades of the last century and the opening of this new one, some of the most widely read and highly applauded literature covered its authors' battles with depression. Moreover, these texts offered far more holistic and nuanced descriptions than any self-help literature, or psychiatric adoption of pharmaceutical notions of chemical imbalances.

Andrew Solomon's *The Noonday Demon* (2001) has often been described as 'the definitive text' of this genre, as well as being widely promoted by the best-known mental health charity in England and Wales, Mind.[32] The book takes us through all the unbearable anguish of Solomon's episodes of depression, when his only real desire was for self-obliteration and during which time he was barely able to move or feed himself. Recovering just enough to venture out, but still suicidal, Solomon cruised the streets at night at the height of the AIDS crisis, hoping for a fatal sexual encounter that could hasten his end, sparing the greater anguish he believed he would cause his family and friends by committing suicide. Imagining his sudden death through illness, he recalls, 'I felt such a sense of release and of gratitude'.[33]

The Noonday Demon in no way glamorizes Solomon's dramatic suffering caused by depression – the suicide attempts, catatonia, dangerous weight loss, inability to work and much more, especially the huge burden of care that was placed upon his father, first of all, and on his closest friends. Indeed Solomon tells us that he needs, and intends, to stay on anti-depressant medicine for the rest of his life, though he perhaps reflects the pharmaceutical narratives of our time in suggesting that depression may turn out to be 'the biggest killer on earth': 'Depression claims more years than war, cancer, and AIDS put together.'[34]

Whatever its cause, nature or solution, Solomon is certainly right, sadly, to suggest that according to all statistics being gathered, rates of depression are not only rising but depression is affecting people at ever younger ages.

Nevertheless, Solomon also thinks that it was only through depression that he discovered a part of himself that feels most like his 'soul'. Echoing Spinoza, Solomon notes that the opposite of depression is not happiness, but vitality, reflecting that depression not only obliterates joy, but also teaches us a great deal about what it is we are missing. Thus while he closes his book with the thought that he hated his feelings when depressed, he adds 'but I know that they have driven me to look deeper at life, to find and cling to reasons for living. I cannot find it in me to regret the course my life has taken. Every day, I choose, sometimes gamely, and sometimes against the moment's reason, to be alive. Is that not a rare joy?'[35]

Is that not a rare joy? Other books similarly suggest that facing up to a sense of torment and grief, however painful, can end up as life-enhancing, as well as opening us up to the vulnerabilities of others. Thus, as we saw in discussing the many shades of melancholy, Solomon was hardly the first victim of depression to imagine that something can be gained from such suffering, at least for those who manage to overcome its most devastating episodes.

No one captured depression's intolerable pain and despair more starkly than one of the very first of these memoirs, William Styron's *Darkness Visible: A Memoir of Madness* (1989). Yet Styron did also suggest that there was 'a theatrical quality' about the height of his depression, as though he had a double watching him, such that as he 'went about stolidly preparing for extinction, I couldn't shake off a sense of melodrama

– a melodrama in which I, the victim-to-be of self-murder, was both the solitary actor and lone member of the audience'.[36]

Again, telling us something of depression's strange allure, limning despair and hope, in her memoir, *An Unquiet Mind* (1995), Kay Jamison concluded that it is 'the individual moments of restlessness, of bleakness, of strong persuasions and maddened enthusiasms, that inform one's life, change the nature and direction of one's work, and give final meaning and color to one's loves and friendships'.[37]

Moreover, if these memoirists recording their descent into and recovery from depression were never more popular than in recent decades, they were no doubt assisted by the pharmaceutical promises that a chemical cure was to hand (which most of these writers both believed in and promoted). Taking us on into the twenty-first century, the widespread interest in these misery memoirs has led the literary scholar Jonathan Dollimore, in an article on what he labels 'Depression Studies', to wonder whether depression is 'becoming the focus for the stubborn Western quest for authentic being'.[38]

Moreover, it is Dollimore's critical interest in whether there is anything positive to be gained from surviving suicidal episodes of depression (as he himself has done several times) that I found the most illuminating of all these narratives. As someone finely attuned to both the tragic and the utopian spirit, whether in literature or in life, Dollimore agrees with Solomon that depression sensitizes you to the suffering of others: 'Depression is like that – it attaches to the negative in anything'. Yet, as he qualifies, this is worth rather little when one is depressed, since as he found himself, it also accompanies an overflow of self-pity, usually rendering the depressed person least able to be helpful to others: 'in weeping for others I'm weeping for myself'.[39]

For all the self-pity and sense of impotence, this empathy with the suffering of the world can be important, even when all one can see is that 'the whole world seems to be in pain'. What one learns from depression, he cautions, is much like that which any person might learn from other intense or unusual experiences, such as acute or prolonged illness, all the more so when through them we are forced to confront our mortality.

Finally, however, Dollimore too concludes that surviving acute depression can mean that 'horizons are broadened'. It has led him to try to embrace a certain way of living that at times moves him beyond the noise of the everyday, beyond personal desire and loss, towards something more transcendent, which he calls a 'deeper silence': 'I hear it in the winds of March or in the stillness of a foggy November landscape; even in the stillness of the late morning in any season'.

After three decades of suffering from and reading about depression, Dollimore decides that it still remains for him utterly mysterious in its sudden and overwhelming intensity. That everyone else thinks they understand more about its causes than he does is another mystery, especially given the diversity of aetiologies they suggest. Metaphorically, he understands his own depression as 'an illness of desire driven by memory' – memories of some 'inarticulate feelings of loss'. More mundanely, however, and with an apology for its triteness, he suggests that one solution is simply 'to try and find something, preferably someone, who makes you laugh more'. Laughter is so magnificently contagious, whatever its causes. Thus he concludes that laughter that can be genuinely shared, which must therefore be something deeper than mockery, will always serve as some relief from depression, if not an antidote to it.[40]

Public Feelings

I will be returning in my next chapter to the significance of shared laughter, and the different ways in which we still experience and speak about authentic joy – however corrupted that word has become in the language of the market. Yet, even more than happiness, joy usually arrives unexpectedly and leaves us just as fast, easily overlapping with sorrow. However inflated those figures on depression might be, they tell us that we live in worlds of pain and unbearable sadness. That being so, it is surely possible to try to see beyond personal suffering to suggest that such prevalence of misery might also have a public dimension, and hence a political one.

This is exactly what Ann Cvetkovich proposes in her book *Depression: A Public Feeling*, in which she is dedicated to 'thinking about depression as a cultural and social phenomenon rather than a medical disease'.[41] This kind of shift in thinking is a hopeful start, if only as a route out of the isolation always threatening those experiencing depression and similar afflictions. Along with a group of primarily queer scholars, Cvetkovich is active in the Public Feelings Project, a feminist collective largely based in the USA but including others elsewhere also interested in exploring the place of feelings in public life. The collective was formed in 2001, in the shadow of 9/11 and the subsequent US invasion of Iraq. Those in the project were interested in trying to understand just why people might have voted for Bush and assented to war.

However, in ways that seem more urgent than ever today, they also wanted to work out how to overcome or learn to live with the negative feelings, sense of failure, disappointment, depression, anxiety and shock experienced by people shattered by these events, by those on the left who had tried so hard to prevent the election of George W. Bush and then the subsequent military invasions, beginning with Afghanistan in October 2001. This, they concluded, meant acknowledging feelings of apathy and despair, while trying not to be overwhelmed by them. Accordingly, one activist cell linked to this project, calling itself Feel Tank Chicago, began discussing 'political depression' and initiating novel ways of addressing it communally. They named one of their events, the 'International Day of the Politically Depressed', inviting people along in their bathrobes, or whatever, and distributing T-shirts and refrigerator magnets carrying the slogan 'Depressed? It Might Be Political!'[42]

In her account of the Public Feelings Project, Cvetkovich stresses the work of those earlier HIV/AIDS activists and theorists who had politicized that disease over two decades earlier. Those living with AIDS assertively rejected the victimization so routinely accompanying fragility and disease, a stigma which was never harsher than when AIDS had been primarily sexually transmitted and was (for several decades at least) mostly fatal. Gay men living with AIDS not only insisted on their own agency, but were often the recipients of significant love and support from their communities, who publicly celebrated and mourned their lives when they died. Cvetkovich also acknowledged earlier legacies of second-wave feminism, with its politicizing of personal life, stress on mutual dependency and the importance accorded caring work (both personal and collective) as distinct from market rules and individual career advancement, which also fed into work on public feelings.

Above all, Cvetkovich embraced what has become known as the 'affect theory' associated with the much loved and influential queer scholar Eve Sedgwick. This line of thinking prioritizes public feelings – how we affect, move, touch each other, through our feelings, operating as visceral forces outside conscious knowledge or verbal communication. It was while living for eighteen years with breast cancer from the age of forty that Sedgwick refined her distinctive 'reparative' writing – a term she borrowed from her reading of Melanie Klein – a strange mixture of the graphic, the tender, the poetic and the abstract, all rolled into one.

This writing enabled her to express and work through a life often lived with excruciating feelings of loss, depression and shame, especially bodily shame. Thus in one books of poems, *Fat Art, Thin Art* (1994), she began by recalling her enduring blues as a large, lonely, unattractive child, born 'Colicky, pre-mature/not easy to supply, nor fun to love'. Then later, in one of so many glowing passages, she refigures fatness in terms of plenitude and generosity:

> I used to have a superstition that
> there was this use to being fat:
> no one could come to harm
> enfolded in my touch.[43]

As well as her intricate, intimate writing, Sedgwick took up weaving and worked with textiles and fibre installations, and also immersed herself in the study of Buddhism. Her engagement with these comforting material objects and differing texts helped Sedgwick surmount her fear of mortality and, initially, her even greater fear that her illness might mean she lost the capacity to like and desire the world around her. She describes all this in her short, dense book *Touching Feeling* (2003), its title capturing exactly what she hoped to do. Here, too, she expresses her debt to her gay friends who had already lived with and sometimes died from AIDS, now that she herself had to face 'a "female" cancer whose lessons for living powerfully I found myself learning largely from men with Aids'.[44] However, what Sedgwick most wanted to share were the many ways she found of expressing the affection and humour she experienced with all those she most loved, often gay men, and also with the therapist she started to see after she developed cancer. She described these healing love relationships in her book *Dialogue of Love* (2000).[45]

Cvetkovich is just one of many scholars, especially queer scholars, who have drawn inspiration from Sedgwick in finding words for their own experiences of depression. For instance, a remarkably impressive and wide-ranging anthology on the significance of enduring narratives of shared pain and loss was edited by the gay literary scholar David Eng together with his American colleague David Kazanjian, *Loss: The Politics of Mourning* (2002). What these writers emphasize is the lack of attention paid to the social influences on those most vulnerable to depression and despair, when, as Eng notes, all the evidence shows that 'women, homosexuals, people of color, and postcolonialists seem to be at greatest risk for melancholy and depression in contemporary society'.[46] Nevertheless, drawing on Freud's writing on melancholia, with the addition of Walter Benjamin's reflections on history, the collection also explores how loss can function as a potentially creative, productive force in history, providing support and meaning for new forms of activism and refashioned identities. Understanding the lineages of loss, whether from war, genocide, exile, migration, AIDS or any number of past traumas, can supply the tools for pondering what remains afterwards, and hence for both a possible 'rewriting of the past as well as the reimaging of the future'.[47] This is exactly what Cvetkovich hopes to achieve in her depathologizing of depression, both personal and collective, through her belief that seeking ways of sharing painful experiences might sometimes pave the way for collective action.

Importantly, she does not minimize the difficulties of overturning the anguish and inertia caused by depression. On the contrary, she tries to capture just how distressing long-lasting despair can be, dividing her book on depression into two parts: the first is a memoir of her own suffering over a two-year period between 1989 and 1991, when she was struggling to complete her doctoral dissertation, grieving the loss of her grandmother, and finding it increasingly hard to get up in the morning to face yet another day. Like Sedgwick, she sees her writing as 'reparative', and is also eager to summon up 'bodily states and sensations rather than reflections on their meanings'.[48] As a result, she wants to distance her writing from those of Solomon, Jamison or Elizabeth Wurtzel, with their strong endorsements of psychotropic drugs for rebalancing brain chemistry.

Like Eng and Kazanjian, Cvetkovich, in the second half of her book, seeks out new public forums for sharing negative feelings. This means that she goes looking for all manner of healing communal spaces and activities for dealing with shared pain. She describes the different forms of consciousness raising where people come together to discuss and act upon the significance of their common injuries from the past that feed into their depression. As she says, this experience of deep injury is most vivid for those living in the long shadow of racism, sexism and colonialism in the USA, issues which remain unresolved, even expanding to significant degrees and in various forms in the present. More soothingly, she writes of communalizing the everyday, with women coming together in a diversity of creative endeavours. Indeed, her book moves from an experience of feeling overwhelmed by daily pain and apathy to modest proposals for utopian practices in the here and now, including all those skills that women have long been the most proficient in practising. These are ideas about the utopian everyday that I will return to later in this book.

Attempting to politicize depression can therefore be seen as a project that is both grand and uncertain, as Cvetkovich writes: 'A political analysis of depression might advocate revolution and regime change over pills, but in the world of Public Feelings there are no magic bullet solutions, whether medical or political, just the slow steady work of resilient survival, utopian dreaming, and other affective tools for transformation'.[49]

More generally, we need again to understand that the emphasis on happiness, and the smiley culture we occupy, is the wrapper around a world full of pain. However, with the World Health Organization, as we've seen, identifying depression as the major health hazard of the century, the question remains how might we connect the social and cultural regimes of the present with what is being documented as the dramatic rise in depression. 'Depressed? – So, you should be!' is the 'joke' on the billboard in one drawing by the popular Australian cartoonist, Michael Leunig. The quip merely illustrates Freud's thought from a century ago that, among other things, the depressed person might have 'a keener eye for the truth' than the non-depressed.[50] It is a view backed up by the empirical research of those cognitive psychologists otherwise usually dismissive of Freudian poetics.[51] It perhaps explains why Munch's painting, known as *The Scream*, with its agonized face against a lurid, tumultuous background, has proved one of the most resonant

54

images of modern times, cited, parodied, copied millions of times over.[52]

However, it will never be easy or indeed possible to separate out what might be realistic anger about shared mistreatment or pessimism over the sorry state of the world, from the accumulation of personal losses and private distress. It is clear that the same history and general situation will elicit different responses in people for numerous idiosyncratic reasons, even in those who are thought to inherit a vulnerability to depression.

Reflecting on this, Will Davis notes that today's emotional politics is the reverse of that formulated in the 1960s. Then, people were 'coming to define themselves by their pleasures', sexual and otherwise, whereas today 'many are coming to define themselves by their pains: past traumas, mental illnesses and chronic health conditions'. The search for pleasure led women and others to politicize the obstacles we saw as standing in our way to more fulfilling lives. So today, Davis suggests, we need similarly to attempt 'the repoliticisation of social troubles', however difficult and messy, wondering how distress can be directed outwards, 'turning private pain into protest'.[53]

The problem, of course, is that there are very different, diametrically opposed ways of doing this. It might, as above, involve connecting our own pain to that of others, near and far, or it could mean turning our hurt and anger onto those more vulnerable than ourselves. The latter is the precise flare used so successfully of late by the torch-bearers of right-wing populism, most spectacularly by Donald Trump and his ilk. It is only when people's distress can be turned into solidarity with others who are vulnerable, with anger directed at the injurious practices of those dictating the conditions that make our lives more precarious, that politicizing depression might connect us with any collective practices of resistance or utopian dreaming.

This requires a huge amount of reflection and work, which is only likely to have any success if it also involves some levels of joy, playfulness and the fostering of communities, small and large, where we take more responsibility for each other. There is much for us to build on. It is not only feminists and queer theorists who continue to show a persistent creativity and energy in developing their vision of a society that could prioritize rather than marginalize or medicate the needs of distressed people, young and old, including ourselves.

There is also another significant shift harking back to '60s talk of personal liberation, and that is what remains of the anti-psychiatry movement, when some psychiatric patients started taking things into their own hands for the first time. In the UK it began with the formation of the Mental Patients Union by a tiny group of psychiatric hospital inmates, ex-inmates and their friends at the close of 1972, with Andy Roberts (then as now) prominent among them.

In line with the zeitgeist, the tone of pamphlets back then was left libertarian, with the labelling of mental illness seen as one of the most cunning conspiracies of the capitalist class. Over the years, mental patients' groups in Britain mutated into PROMPT (People for the Rights of Mental Patients in Treatment) and CAPO (Campaign Against Psychiatric Oppression) in the early 1980s. Since then, there has been the formation of the Mad Pride and Hearing Voices groups, which as part of what is known as the 'survivor movement' have all been significant in shifting attitudes to mental health.

So, too, have charities, such as Mind, which played a critical role in supporting those in need of psychiatric support, as well as more structured and unstructured, assisted and alternative, therapeutic communities. The British magazine *Asylum*, established in 1986 as an anti-psychiatry resource, and relaunched in 2010, is a hub for mental health workers and service-users, carers and others, aiming to promote more collective, democratic and egalitarian ways of furthering mental health and dealing with distress.

Yet even here there are dangers. As Healy shows, the pharmaceutical companies have themselves been involved in setting up patient groups as part of their market development programme for new drugs, with such groups being encouraged to put pressure on doctors for costly treatments. Hence, Healy notes, at times 'groups that were formerly hostile to physical as opposed to talking therapies in psychiatry have been brought onside'.[54] There can also be an awkward association between collective self-help groups and government rationalizations justifying cuts in the spurious name of 'self-reliance', the mantra of neo-liberal rationality.

Thus, any collective efforts at repoliticizing depression, or mental health generally, need to be part of a very broad project that not only analyses the concrete ties between mental stress and what are right now only ever-increasing social hazards, but works to provide more caring support in a multitude of ways. It will never be possible to eliminate sadness from our lives, even in its most acute forms, though many more of us could more usefully be supported in managing to live with our everyday unhappiness while dreaming of better lives. As we'll see throughout this book, dreaming of happier lives overall begins from careful attention to, not disavowal of, the pain of the world, whatever combinations of anger, love and shared responsibility for changing things this attention generates.

3

Where Is Joy?

If happiness can prove elusive or fleeting over a lifetime, joy itself is not often mentioned at all today, except glibly. In his scholarly history of joy in the Western tradition, Adam Potkay affirms that 'joy is a word we don't use much anymore, at least not in secular contexts ... And while joy has grown less common, still less do we now "rejoice."'[1] From my earnest search through the indexes of all the books I have read over the last five years, including those on utopian thinking, I can see he is right.

Yet, despite this, I think we can frequently discern joy's hovering presence somewhere on the horizon of possibilities, if only in those experiences we think we are missing out on. Of course, it will always be difficult to pin down any feeling of joy, seeing how easily pleasure mixes with sorrow. However, at the very least, I think we can agree that what is most distinctive about moments of joy is that, tending to arrive unexpectedly, they raise us altogether above our routine concerns.

Moments of joy usually break down the distances between people, bringing us together at least with those able to share the same delight. Such collective sentiment explains joy's traditional ties with things that are larger, better and more exciting than we are individually. How could there not be a certain delight and freedom in escaping that gloomy tyrant – ourselves – forever brooding over or blocking out our own feelings of failure, shortcomings, neediness, neglect or isolation? Thus, the expression 'tears of joy' describes the compelling reality in which our strongest emotions seem to overflow and become quickly contagious when normally stifled feelings are released.

The Fading of Communal Joy

Given her biting wit and political tenacity, I often seek out that remarkable American writer and activist Barbara Ehrenreich when pondering contemporary affairs. From her, however, we are used to reading about the evils of poverty, inequality and brutal exploitation, as documented in her bestseller *Nickel and Dimed* (2001).[2] Some years later she warned us about the dangers of America's relentless promotion of optimism, cheerfulness and the power of 'positive' thinking in the new 'science of happiness'. At the personal level, Ehrenreich notes, this can lead to self-blame and a morbid preoccupation with avoiding any acknowledgement of loss, sorrow or anger (thereby undermining the courage to resist abuses and exploitation). At a national level, this kind of thinking assisted the reckless blindness that resulted in financial disaster as well as war.[3]

More pertinently for me now, however, her book *Dancing in the Streets* (2007) explores the origins and decline of communal celebrations, public feasting and fervent dancing. Never frightened of encompassing the broadest historical sweep, Ehrenreich traces the clashes between rapturous merrymakers and righteous moralizers right back to Greek mythology, with the dramatist Euripides portraying the tragic fate of Pentheus, the king of the Thebes, when he tried to ban the worship of the pleasure-loving Dionysus. Dancing and revelry seem a perennial theme from earliest times, evident even in the rock paintings before written history, as well as a common theme in the surviving vases of ancient Greece. Yet it is the mythic Pentheus, and the many puritans in his wake, who would in the end prevail in 'civilization'.

Illustrating this, Ehrenreich researches the altogether horrified encounters between Europeans and the indigenous peoples of the non-Western world. Everywhere they went, whether to islands in the Pacific Ocean, to India, Africa, the Caribbean or the Americas, Europeans were invariably shocked by what they depicted as the 'savage' communal celebrations of those they came across – jubilation expressed through drumming, dancing and diverse festive practices, often culminating in joyful sexual embraces. We can read about Captain Cook's repulsion while surveying revelries in Tahiti at the end of the eighteenth century, or Darwin's similar revulsion when glimpsing the noisy corroboree rites of natives in western Australia a few decades later. Around the globe, European missionaries, enslavers and other visitors venturing, for instance, into Africa from the 1700s onwards would record their expressions of fear, dislike and repugnance. As Ehrenreich notes: 'Well into the twentieth century, the sound of drumming was enough to spook the white traveller, suggestive as it was of a world beyond human ken'.[4]

No one depicted and embodied the typical Victorian racist mentality more vividly than Joseph Conrad in his *Heart of Darkness*:

We were wanderers on a prehistoric earth ... We could have fancied ourselves the first of men taking possession of an accursed inheritance, to be subdued at the cost of profound anguish and of excessive toil. But suddenly as we struggled round a bend, there would be a glimpse of rush walls ... a burst of yells, a whirl of black limbs, a mass of hands clapping, of feet stamping, of bodies swaying, of eyes rolling ... The prehistoric man was cursing us, praying to us, welcoming us, who could tell? We were cut off from comprehension of our surroundings; we glided past like phantoms, wondering and secretly appalled, as sane men would be before an enthusiastic outbreak in a madhouse.[5]

As Ehrenreich also notes, the traveller did not have to go far for such encounters. The celebrated American administrator and social critic Frederick Law Olmsted, travelling to New Orleans in the 1850s, observed the echoes of African heritage expressed in black Christian services in the Southern states of America. He later reported having been swept up by the 'indescribable expressions of ecstasy – of pleasure or agony', finding 'his own face "glowing" and feet stamping, as if he had been "infected unconsciously"'.[6]

Elsewhere, other authorities noted the ties between non-Western rituals and the medieval and early modern carnivals in Europe, when participants wore fancy dress, danced boisterously through the night, and shared other forms of unrestrained merriment. Such collective exuberance, especially when exhibited by peasants or the urban poor, soon became subject to long battles waged by the Church and other public authorities. Before long, many parallels would be drawn between lower-class Europeans and tribal 'savages', with the outcome that over the centuries 'respectable' folk learned that they needed to protect themselves from the seductions of the barbarous follies of the 'primitive' and the poor.[7]

Thus, throughout the Middle Ages, from the thirteenth to the fifteenth centuries, festive religious celebrations continued outside the churches across Christian Europe, providing opportunities for enjoyment and revelries, which included the mocking of authorities of every kind. As Edward Thompson later suggested, such festivities in Britain were a time when food, drink and all manner of courtship flourished: 'These occasions were, in an important sense, what men and women lived for; and if the Church had little to do with their conduct, then it had, to that degree, ceased to engage with the emotional calendar of the poor'.[8]

This meant that, although there were times of buoyant collective joy that occurred as part of Christian holidays, especially just before Easter, on Shrove Tuesday, the Church had ever less to do with them. Jews, of course, also stayed aloof from these Christian festivities, although they have always had the public celebration of Purim, usually in March, involving feasting, masquerade and other playful revelry.[9] However, from the seventeenth through to the twentieth centuries, even the Christian carnivals and other festivities were systematically suppressed, as both the Church and the state worked together to curtail most exuberant celebrations, especially after the rise of Calvinism and related Protestant sects.

Max Weber, one of the founding fathers of sociology, saw the development of the Protestant ethic occurring alongside the growth of capitalism, especially during the eighteenth and nineteenth centuries, as responsible for a rising sense of disenchantment in the world at large (Weber's word *Entzauberung*, meaning the elimination of magic).[10] The evolving bourgeoisie needed to invest and save, so workers were required to remain sober and disciplined for work all year around. In Weber's memorable words on the formation of capitalist manhood:

> Man is dominated by the making of money, by acquisition as the ultimate purpose of his life. Economic acquisition is no longer subordinated to man as the means for the satisfaction of his material needs. This reversal of what we should call the natural relationship, so irrational from a naïve point of view, is evidently as definitely a leading principle of capitalism as it is foreign to all peoples not under capitalistic influence.[11]

In the same period as well, contempt for working-class lives and cultures would began to merge with rising imperialist racial denigration as prominent features of Western culture.

Thus in France, the historian of peasant life Eugen Weber opened his book *Peasants into Frenchmen* by quoting a mid-nineteenth-century Parisian traveller in rural Burgundy writing that 'you don't need to go to America to see savages'.[12] In her classic text on racist fantasy and framings at the height of European imperialist expansion in the nineteenth century, Ann Stoler also details the merging of racial and class denigration with contempt for the rowdy amusements of the poorer classes, and especially the Irish who were depicted in the British magazine *Punch* as 'the missing link between the gorilla and the Negro'. Within Britain, the English journalist and reformer Henry Mayhew (one of the founders of *Punch*) compared the moral degradation of the British urban poor to that of 'savage tribes'.[13]

Interestingly, at much the same time as Weber was addressing the promotion of self-denial and disdain for hedonism with the rise of Protestantism and emergence of capitalism, the French father of sociology, Émile Durkheim, was introducing the notion of 'collective effervescence', which he used to describe the traditional communal festivities of non-Western societies. He saw these moments as the glue necessary for binding communities and at times also changing them. Drawing upon work with Australian Aborigines, Durkheim wrote of the dual function of religious ritual and festivities: while they served 'to strengthen the bonds attaching the believer to his god, they at the same time really strengthen the bonds attaching the individual to the society of which he is a member, since the god is only a figurative expression of the society'.[14]

Moreover, with the general rise of the social sciences, anthropology and the impact of psychoanalysis, in the early twentieth century there was a greater interest in studying both non-Western cultures and the shifts in or remnants of pre-industrial societies in the modern world. Critiquing the earlier Western horror at so-called 'primitive' societies, by the 1950s the celebrated Oxford anthropologist E. E. Evans-Pritchard had begun arguing that ethnographers 'rarely succeeded in entering the minds of the people they studied', instead ascribing to them motivations which were either thought to match their own thinking and culture, or brusquely labelled as its antithesis.[15]

With even greater impact, the illustrious ethnographer Clifford Geertz fundamentally changed anthropological thought, noting in so many persuasive ways: 'It is no more possible to escape the situational immediacies of ethnographical knowing, the thoughts and occasions one is trying to intrude upon, than it is to escape its temporal bounds, and it perhaps is even more mischievous to pretend to do so'.[16]

Thus, whether in the books of the Britain-based Max Gluckman or his ex-pupil Victor Turner, anthropological interest in non-Western ritual now viewed the collective rituals of all pre-industrial societies as complex ways of expressing and relieving underlying social tension, while finally serving to reinforce social bonding.[17] They had also begun to address more seriously the possible ties between the euphoric rituals in distant lands and the lower-class revelries of the European carnival that had been so determinedly suppressed since the seventeenth century.

However, no one offered a more comprehensively positive, and ambivalently subversive, analysis of carnival, celebrating its earlier delights and mourning its enforced loss, than the Russian literary scholar Mikhail Bakhtin. He saw in what he called the 'carnivalesque' the construction of an alternative or 'second world of folk culture': 'It is to a certain extent a parody of the extra-carnival life, a "world inside out" ... Folk humor denies, but it revives and renews at the same time'.[18] Although his landmark book *Rabelais and His World* (completed in 1940) was itself for decades suppressed in the Soviet Union (suspected of perhaps mocking Stalinism), it became an iconic text once translated into English in 1968, especially with the blooming of cultural studies at the close of that decade.

As Bakhtin presents the words and images of the sixteenth-century French Renaissance monk François Rabelais, he showed that carnival was a time when everyone behaved as 'equals', with barriers of caste, property, profession and age all collapsing in the collective ridicule of high culture and officialdom. With its dancing, music, masks and costumes – peasants dressed as lords, lords as peasants, women as men, men as women – the general jollity, derision and displays of flesh promoted a joyful inversion of hierarchy, decorum and bodily discretion. According to Bakhtin, all these festivities constituted a separate reality from the harshly enforced social norms of everyday life, enabling people to transcend routine fears and woes, indulging their physical desires, impulsively exhibiting what he labelled the 'grotesque body', especially its 'lower' parts and functions.

All that was usually hidden would be displayed as visible sites of enjoyment and excess during the public feasting, coupling, drinking and dancing of carnival. In Bakhtin's words: 'The death of the individual is only one moment in the triumphant life of the people and of mankind, a moment indispensable for their renewal and improvement'.[19]

Bakhtin had always been interested in 'the politics of laughter', which he believed provided the vital ingredient for the fearlessness that rendered festive moments subversive. Describing collective laughter as both joyful and triumphant, and simultaneously mocking and derisory, it should also be seen, he suggested, as a possible way of addressing general problems. Bakhtin viewed laughter as a medium that should be taken as seriously as high culture itself.[20] Addressing the functions of collective laughter some years later, and trying to make a distinction that I suspect is very hard to uphold, Bakhtin again contrasted the 'joyful, open, festive laugh' during carnival, with 'the closed, purely negative, satirical laugh' that replaced it in modern times, where no sense of collective liberation was on offer.[21]

Despite its significant impact in the Anglophone world, Bakhtin's work has been criticized or amended by later literary scholars. The well-known literary historian Stephen Greenblatt, for instance, cautions that it would be wrong to simply equate Rabelais's highly crafted 'brilliant aesthetic representation' of carnival motifs, indulgence and communal laughter 'with the festive mayhem of a largely illiterate populace'.[22] Bakhtin has also been censured for his loose historical periodization of carnival, though not for his argument, echoed by many others, that the new bourgeois order would end up either suppressing carnival or else largely assimilating it to the private sphere.

More significantly, Bakhtin has been criticized for his nostalgic, overly optimistic account of folk humour, in which his explicitly anarchistic and utopian celebration of the carnivalesque all but ignored the manifestations of physical violence, anti-Semitism and contempt for women and their bodies usually evident in carnival.[23] As the British cultural historian Peter Burke argues, Bakhtin's focus on symbolic violence overlooked instances of actual physical aggression, neglecting the ways in which ritualized insult could also spill over 'on to objects that could not easily defend themselves'.[24] Moreover, the Canada-based literary critic Ken Hirschkop suggests that Bakhtin had a cultural but not a political theory of social transformation. He represented Russian populism as 'a tradition of parody, farce and plebeian laughter far removed from reactionary images of a pious, backward and stolid "folk"'.[25]

Thus, while Bakhtin emphasized the scandalous subversiveness of carnival, however briefly enjoyed, others have suggested that its pleasures served more as a safety valve than as any genuine rebellion or renewal, divorced as it usually was from any form of actual socio-economic struggle. The Marxist literary scholar Terry Eagleton, for one, argues that since the authorities of the day largely tolerated carnival, it should best be seen as merely a 'permissible rupture of hegemony, a contained popular blow-off as disturbing and relatively ineffectual as a revolutionary work of art'. In agreement, another well-known literary critic Umberto Eco even suggested that carnival's mockery could have a conservative function, reinforcing the very codes it so exuberantly violates![26]

Nevertheless, there are reasons for holding a more open view of the potential challenge that dissident, collective festivities sometimes offer. Others studying the regular cross-overs between low and high culture, such as Peter Stallybrass and Allon White in *The Politics and Poetics of Transgression*, emphasize that while over the centuries carnival and other related subversive practices may have generally had few transformative effects, they also provide many examples of particular conjunctures in which carnival *did* sharpen political antagonism and serve 'as *catalyst* and *site of action and symbolic struggle*'. They add: 'Carnivals, fairs, popular games and festivals were very quickly "politicized" by the very attempts made on the part of local authorities to eliminate them ... even when no overt oppositional element had been present before'. Thus, while concluding that there are no necessary links between carnival and politics, Stallybrass and White cite many other historians who are in agreement with their position on the significance of outbreaks of political revolt coinciding with carnival: 'On the one hand, carnival was a specific calendrical ritual ... On the other hand, carnival also refers to a mobile set of symbolic practices, images and discourses which were employed throughout social revolts and conflicts before the nineteenth century'.[27]

Moreover, whether or not carnival's ecstatic moments of freedom tied in with more enduring social revolt, there is no doubt about its routine significance as a joyful affirmation of collective existence. Such moments of radical happiness were effective precisely when they overcame the individuating principles that have become so prominent in modernity. Bakhtin is right to insist that joy most easily resides in the release from egotism and self-importance, overturning the weight of high culture and its cerebral sublimations and thereby escaping that never-ending project of self-invention and self-improvement that nowadays rules our lives.

It was Sigmund Freud, writing just before Bakhtin, who argued that the evolving process of 'civilization' makes people unhappy because it confines and restricts our instinctual libidinal desires. Interestingly, the memorable opening pages of *Civilization and Its Discontents* (1930) begins with Freud's repudiation of that 'oceanic feeling' he has heard described by others as a 'feeling of indissoluble connection, of belonging inseparably to the external world as a whole'. For Freud this is a 'strange and incongruous feeling', which he saw as completely at odds with the sense we each have and struggle to maintain of our very own separate selves, our unique 'ego', which we think of as something quite separate from the outside world, however unknowing we remain about our equally distinct 'unconscious' life.[28]

Unsurprisingly, with his suspicion of group behaviour and the dangers of mass psychology, Freud himself shed little direct light on any celebrations of collective joy, however liberating or erotic. Indeed, as Ehrenreich comments wryly: 'It is doubtful that [Freud] ever witnessed, much less experienced, anything in the way of collective ecstasy'. He dismissed the lower-class revelries of the European carnival as 'neither pleasant nor edifying' compared with other pleasures, such as those of 'reading a book'.[29] With few exceptions, contemporary scholarly consensus agrees upon the decline of collective festivity in modernity. The increasing reverence for 'rationality', as the distinguished sociologist Peter Berger concludes in his book

Redeeming Laughter, 'did away with much of the enchantment that medieval man still lived with', while 'the counterworld of folly began to recede'. However, Berger does close his book by suggesting: 'As long as modern man can still laugh at himself, his alienation from the enchanted gardens of earlier times will not be complete'.[30]

Passion in a Secular World

Freud was notoriously hostile to religion of any variety. He thought it essential to expose the infantile illusion at its root in order to promote the gains of rationality that result from a strictly scientific world-view. Freud described religious belief overall as a neurotic defence against feelings of helplessness, expressing our childhood desire for some all-encompassing protection and love, a desire which we first invested in our parents and above all in the authority of the father. It was precisely this infantile longing for a strong father that in Freud's view was easily displaced onto something larger, attaching people to particular groups and leading them to form identifications with whole societies and their dominant beliefs: 'Religion would thus be the universal obsessional neurosis of humanity ... it arose out of the Oedipus complex, out of the relation to the father'.[31]

He was surely right to stress that in adulthood we long to find again the parental protection and love we had, hopefully, once known in childhood – with religion being one of the most prominent of the illusions we construct to further this end. However, the obvious failing here is that in his almost exclusive focus on the F/father and the F/family, the distinct social, cultural, ethical structures and traditions sustaining religion are all muted. So, too, is the place of religion itself in giving meaning to our lives, consolidating social bonds by encouraging adherents to express their love and support for each other, while also finding guidance for, and securing, shared ethical ideals or commandments.

'I don't believe in God, but I miss Him,' Julian Barnes wrote, opening his vivid meditations on his fear of mortality and reflections on religion, *Nothing to Be Frightened Of*.[32] The question of how we face the turbulence of our mortal lives without the consolations of religion, and how we find that sense of 'fullness', is one the Canadian philosopher (and practising Catholic) Charles Taylor has often addressed. In his monumental *A Secular Age*, Taylor follows Weber in suggesting that in modernity there is a general nostalgia for the enchantment of earlier times: 'There is certainly a widespread sense of loss here, if not always of God, then at least of meaning.'[33] Secularists are usually presented as cherishing only rational self-development, autonomy and choice, as distinct from acceptance of any higher force or meaning to existence. This suggests to Taylor that it must be hard for secularists to escape some sense of personal futility, facing the capricious, ephemeral nature of a godless life.

However, there are many ways of challenging the supposed link between secularism and joylessness. First of all, it was the monotheistic religions themselves, and not only Protestantism, which were responsible for opposing the belief in 'magic' and instead emphasizing obedience, submission and sacrifice. Indeed, the puritan aestheticism of much religious practice might at times be seen as the very antithesis of joy.[34]

Secondly, the very idea that we live in a purely secular society is problematic, even if we reduce secularism to the uncoupling of religion from the state and other social institutions. Far from religious practices fully disappearing from Western cultural spheres, many have noted the fluid relations between the secular and the theological, their continuities evident across the cultural spectrum: 'including civic forms of religion, transcendental forms of political engagement as well as acts of resistance that are infused with the logic of sacrifice and religious beliefs'.[35]

Indeed, it is the upsurge of fundamentalisms, both secular and anti-secular, that has led many today to call themselves 'post-secular', opposing the certainties both of religion and of anti-religion while noting numerous ties between the secular and the sacred.[36] On the one hand, it is evident that religious fundamentalism, whether Christian, Judaic or Islamic (to name only the three major monotheistic faiths), focuses on literal readings of only certain sections of 'sacred' texts, usually those admonishing against sin and sexuality, leaving them deeply at odds with any recognition of the body and its potential pleasures.

On the other, the reigning voices of evangelical non-belief, headed by the militantly atheistic Darwinian fundamentalist Richard Dawkins, pay no heed to ancient religious warnings against literal Biblical readings, or to the true scope of contemporary theological debate, which remains far more open to celebrating joyful diversities.[37] Indeed, it is even possible to question the basic narrative underpinning Charles Taylor's account of the move from firm religious faith to contemporary agnosticism: 'Why is it so hard to believe in God in (many milieux of) the modern West, while in 1500 it was virtually impossible not to?'[38] For instance, in their accounts of religion in medieval Europe, historians such as John Arnold and Susan Reynolds suggest that there may well have been religious scepticism and dissent in earlier times, but it could not easily be expressed given the vigilance of heretic hunters.[39] In the same way, today there may be those who declare themselves secular but have various spiritual inclinations.

Nevertheless, few would question Taylor's account of the gradual growth of secular humanism from the eighteenth century onwards, at least in the sense of the increasing separation between Church and state in the ordering of Western societies.[40] Historians of religion, also, emphasize the distinct significance of shifts in religiosity associated with the emancipatory movements of the 1960s.[41] Certainly, as Callum Brown's study of religion in Britain shows, there was indeed a sudden and dramatic decline in religious conformity, with lowered church attendance, baptisms and similar activities from the middle and especially latter part of the twentieth century.[42]

The '60s also saw an Anglican archbishop, John Robinson, write the scandalous, bestselling *Honest to God* (1963), which questioned all orthodox religious tradition by rejecting the very notion of the existence of any separate supernatural being. He drew upon the existentialist theology of Paul Tillich to describe the existence of God inside everyone, as 'the Ground of our very being', such that whenever we act ethically, compassionately and lovingly we are reaching towards God.[43]

Thus, while the '60s and post-'60s generation – my generation – were indeed often hostile to mainstream religious institutions, many went in search of alternative, often more individualized, spiritual practices. They searched for their very own form of mystical wellbeing, at least for a while usually in criticism of the acquisitive conformities of Western capitalism. Such personal journeys in search of salvation were frequently fragile and fleeting, as in the celebrity visits made by the Beatles, Mick Jagger, Donovan, Mia Farrow and even Clint Eastwood to learn transcendental meditation from the Maharishi in Madhya Pradesh. Some of my own '60s friends settled in and around Pondicherry at the close of that decade, impressed by and to this day remaining attached to the compassionate teachings of a French spiritual leader known as The Mother (Mirra Alfassa), who had created a retreat or ashram with her Indian spiritual collaborator, Sri Aurobindo.

I never shared my friends' hankering for spiritual revelation, having been raised austerely atheistic, and never straying far from my roots except to drop the disdainful dogmatism I once imbibed. Characteristic of much of the mid-twentieth-century professional classes, especially those of Jewish background, my parents revered such secular prophets as Bertrand Russell, who argued that it was necessary to 'slay the dragon' of religion which had always stood in the way of full human progress and inflicted needless cruelty.[44]

Gradually, I did see the crude reductionism of their naïve faith in the magnificent potential of science to deliver Russell's 'golden age'. I grew more sympathetic, as well, towards those who cited their favourite '60s gurus, such as Aurobindo, however neat the fit seemed to me between such forms of Indian mysticism and the latest emphasis on expressive individualism. Despite its apparently anti-Western stance, this new spirituality shared many features with Western Enlightenment. Its primary characteristic was no longer moral purity or religiosity, but rather, as Aurobindo emphasized, an 'awakening to the inner reality of our being'.

For those of us not drawn to the spiritual, we need to account for our own forms of intense and lingering exultation, to understand the feelings we have that propel us beyond our routine ways of coping with the vicissitudes of everyday life.

Our first problem is how to find an adequate language of joy. Here, perhaps, we can learn something from those versed in the rhetoric of religion and the sacred, even if believing, as I do, that religions emerged to help maintain communities and provide comfort in the face of the perils of life, especially of loss and mortality. This is presumably why correlations are often found between religious practices and happiness, and also why the notorious atheist Karl Marx called religion the 'opium of the people'.[45] If we are to reframe rather than ignore some of the communal strengths of religion, a helpful place to start is with the compelling arguments of one of the chief religious scholars of our time, the former leader of the Church of England, Rowan Williams. In his sermons from when he was Archbishop of Canterbury, Williams often spoke of joy. Even without the resplendent robes and elevated ritual on display in the delivery of these sermons, I find his arguments relevant for understanding secular moments of collective joy.

In his Christmas 2009 sermon, Williams argues that 'a truly fulfilled existence means accepting joyfully our dependence on one another'. He then castigates the way in which the whole notion of 'dependence' is nowadays seen as weak and deplorable, as if the goal of life is attaining complete independence as soon as possible: 'Turning you into a useful cog in the social machine that won't need too much maintenance'. Marx could not have put it better, though Williams, unlike Marx, added something we feminists have always stressed: 'Embracing and celebrating our own dependence gives us the vision and energy to make sure that others have the freedom to make the most of their dependence too.'[46]

It is, of course, not only children who are dependent, as, among others, Judith Butler's recent writing on 'precarious lives' emphasizes. Butler knows that accepting the fragilities of life, however fit and vigorous we may be in the moment, is what it means to be fully human.[47] Such acceptance suggests that we have an ethical responsibility to pay as much attention as we can to the lives of others, though never for purely instrumental reasons, which might serve primarily to advantage ourselves. It is because of our mutual dependence, Williams notes emphatically in one of his Easter sermons, that joy 'comes from the outside, from relationships, environment, the unexpected stimulus of beauty'.

As something that jolts us out of the ordinary, this joy usually arrives unexpectedly. It is not something that can be easily pursued or reproduced or reliably summoned, even when we attain goals we have been seeking most of our lives. The same can be said about intense happiness: 'It doesn't take away the reality of threat or risk or suffering', Williams notes, 'it's just there'.

Like Freud, as we shall see, emphasizing the contradictions of strong emotions, Williams notes that it is possible to experience a certain sense of joy even in the presence of grief. For instance, when with a dying friend, you can still feel completely grounded in doing exactly what you are doing, 'an overwhelming sense of being where you should be, being in tune with something or someone'.[48]

The obvious point about all this for me, however, is that there is no need to include any religious parables here, even if I am trying to describe something that feels like 'a blessing'. Joyful feelings of gratitude, wonder or awe can simply arrive from the sense of being fully alive to the world we are in at the moment, whatever triggers that heightened state of affirmation in the time and space we occupy. This is exactly what

William Wordsworth celebrated on visiting Paris in the early years of the French Revolution, when hopes rose for an end to poverty and for the spread of reason, love and kindness around the world, and the Church had nothing to do with it:

> Bliss was it in that dawn to be alive,
> But to be young was very Heaven! O times,
> In which the meagre, stale, forbidding ways
> Of custom, law, and statute, took at once
> The attraction of a country in romance![49]

Being able to share the joy of being alive is exactly what the American literary scholar George Levine expresses in a buoyant introduction to his anthology *The Joy of Secularism*. He stresses that secular pleasures need to be celebrated as an affirmation of the world we occupy which, despite all its pain and losses, exploitation and brutality, can also be joyful. Moreover, Levine affirms that along with enjoying and recalling the sporadic satisfactions of our corporeal desires and other physical pleasures, it is the pondering of moments of human or natural wonder that can in itself assist our hopes for creating better futures for all. Levine himself finds special delight in contemplating the collective beauty of flocks of birds in flight.

Hence, in this secular outlook, it is precisely our desire for sharing moments of worldly joy that resonates most closely with religion in its goal of building and binding communities: 'It is not that the world is beautiful just for me, but that it is, simply, beautiful ... The world counts first and we can take advantage of our luck to watch the stooping hawk and the flocking of starlings as we learn more about it and make it better'.[50] It is not just beauty and the joy it brings us that lift our spirits, but also the joy of sharing it, of sensing something far bigger than ourselves to communicate to others. 'Grief can take care of itself', Mark Twain once wrote, 'but to get the full value of joy you must have someone to divide it with.'[51] As the often troubled poet Anne Sexton wrote in one of her last poems, 'Welcome Morning', joy can be found in anything, as when she hears 'laughter in the morning', but she quickly adds:

> The Joy that isn't shared, I've heard,
> dies young.[52]

As did she. It is this sharing of joy, or at least the potential that it could be shared, that is so often celebrated in verse, as when Auden wrote, in his usual memorable way: 'In times of joy, all of us wished we possessed a tail we could wag.'[53] We can hardly get more basic than that!

Consuming Pleasure

The joy not shared may be fleeting, but for some considerable time we have been everywhere encouraged to associate pleasure with acquiring all the things that we need or want, whether as gifts or, far more often, by purchasing them ourselves. Yet debates around 'consumption' – including its meaning – have always been with us, with their range and variety mirroring the expansion of commodities themselves. Thus, while many applaud the choices increasingly available to advance our human health, happiness and wellbeing, others warn of consumer addiction, anxiety and wretchedness, with the added drama of full-blown environmental catastrophe drawing ever closer.

Looking back at the *longue durée* of consumption, we could once more return to Plato's *Republic*, with its disdain for the 'luxuries and idleness' of the governing classes, or, four centuries later, notice in early Christianity St Paul's Biblical warning that avarice is 'the root of all evil'.[54] However, in his prodigious survey *The Empire of Things*, the Britain-based historian Frank Trentmann traces the significant emergence of worldwide networks of consumption back to the 1500s, when, with the rise of cities and the emergence of modern banking in Renaissance Italy, new economic patterns began to emerge around the globe.

Nevertheless, the possibilities for expanding the acquisition of varied commodities only began appearing with new manufacturing processes from the eighteenth century in northwestern Europe.[55] This was when the philosopher Adam Smith, a key figure of the Scottish Enlightenment and pioneer of political economy, in his landmark text, *The Wealth of Nations* (1776), first used the notion of 'consumption' in something like its modern sense. And only with these new historical conditions could a growing minority of individuals begin to aspire to possessions as luxuries rather than as necessities for survival and define their relation to the world in terms of property and possessions.[56]

During this period, the consumption of imported sugar, tobacco, tea and coffee arriving in Britain and elsewhere from slave-based labour on plantations in the Caribbean increased twenty-fold.[57] As the cultural theorist David Bennett notes in *The Currency of Desire*, 'the Industrial Revolution had created high volume, standardized production which in turn produced a pattern of high volume, standardized consumption, driven by social imperatives of fashion'. The wealthy and the burgeoning middle class could now indulge what later economists came to see as the infinite elasticity of demand, noting that 'desire was endlessly renewable'.[58] Desires are, indeed, endlessly renewable, and also dangerous, as many critics have mourned. 'Getting and spending, we lay waste our powers', that true Romantic William Wordsworth wrote back in the early years of the nineteenth century. He echoed arguments over the relationship between consumption and happiness that had by then already been rumbling for over a century and continue to this day.[59]

However, it was only at the very close of the nineteenth century that the increase in wages in working-class homes enabled the beginnings of greater access to manufactured goods for people overall. This occurred mainly in households where men's labour could pay for a full-time housewife attempting to meet the needs and tastes of her husband and family – even though resources in working-class families still remained scarce.[60]

In contrast, in middle-class homes, those who could aspire to be 'ladies of leisure' had the benefits and freedoms of roaming the newly emerging department stores. Such stores quickly became icons of modernity, even as detractors feared these new 'cathedrals of commerce' were replacing the worship of God with the worship of goods, while simultaneously destroying family shops and corrupting or destabilizing women. The large department stores, with their elegant tea-rooms and focused attention, contributed greatly to women's sense of autonomy and sophistication in the cities of the Western world at the close of the nineteenth and early twentieth centuries. This was not least by the provision of public toilets for women, which in Victorian times had largely only been available for men, but also in the offering of all manner of visual gratifications, cafés and other amusements for women.[61]

Despite the acclaimed delights and the moralizing fears surrounding the explosion of department stores, genuine mass consumption, and indeed the very notion of the 'consumer society' itself, only truly took off in the Western world from the post-war era. This was the moment when the renewed proliferation of consumer goods enabled a vast expansion of household equipment as well as diverse hobbies, entertainments and other leisure activities across all classes. This whole-sale increase in private consumption was only made possible through the increase in public spending by the state – whether directly through child benefits, pensions and the vast exten-sion of welfare provisions, or indirectly through state spending on infrastructure, including on transport, roads, housing, edu-cation, libraries and more.

This rapidly rising tide of consumption, however, triggered even deeper anxieties over the invasion of commercial inter-ests into people's private lives. Vance Packard's *The Hidden Persuaders* (1957) became a runaway bestseller in the USA and well beyond, suggesting that commercial interests were using subliminal messages to take over and manipulate consumers' purchasing decisions, based on experiments to discover the best techniques for persuasion: 'Typically they see us as bundles of daydreams, misty hidden yearnings, guilt complexes, irrational emotional blockages', Packard wrote.[62] Deploying a kind of popularized version of Freud, Packard declared it was just these unconscious yearnings that were being incited and manipulated.

The pioneers of marketing practices in the USA were indeed eager to bring psychoanalytic ideas to advertising in the early twentieth century. This move began with Freud's nephew,

Edward Bernays, employing the analyst Abraham Brill to assist in his forceful marketing campaign for the American Tobacco Company. As one result, cigarettes were quickly branded 'torches of freedom' and became iconic of women's liberation.

Bernay's determination to call upon 'depth' psychology, hoping to trigger repressed sexual desire for marketing commodities, was expanded further by Ernest Dichter, another émigré who would make his fortune in the advertising industry. Dichter was responsible for the slogan 'Put a Tiger in Your Tank' for the petrol company Esso. He saw his task as using persuasion to 'liberate' desire, hence moving the economy forward and, at the very same time, engineering happiness: 'Trying to reach a goal but having that goal recede is the real mystery of happiness,' he wrote. In Dichter's outlook, it was fortuitously the era's very combination of booming profits and proliferating desires that generated both social and personal wellbeing, conjoining the ideals of free enterprise and freedom.[63] Dichter was a key target of Packard's censure, portrayed as responsible for invading individual privacy and triggering self-destructive desires – a condemnation which ironically served only to increase his fame and fortune as an advertising guru.

Echoing Packard, many prominent post-war academics stressed the dangers of consumerism for raising anxieties and undermining people's genuine happiness and sense of community. These included many of the most prominent names in the fast-flourishing social sciences, such as C. Wright Mills, David Reisman, Herbert Marcuse and Kenneth Galbraith. Thus while the USA was diligently setting the pattern and pace for the rest of the Western world in the 1950s, with money spent on advertising increasing six-fold and the consumption of luxuries five-fold in the period, many of its public intellectuals were at the very same time delivering some of the most trenchant criticisms of this market evolution.[64]

Mills wrote that consumerism was creating alienated, 'cheerful robots'. Reisman, in *The Lonely Crowd*, similarly depicted Americans as status-obsessed, anxious conformists, while in the early '60s Herbert Marcuse stressed that the market creates political apathy and 'false needs', alongside waste and, presciently, environmental destruction.[65] Perhaps most influential of all, in 1958 the left liberal North American economist and public figure J. Kenneth Galbraith published his long-lived bestseller, *The Affluent Society*. Here again we can find anxieties over the enticements to excessive private consumption, although one of Galbraith's main concerns was the continuing existence of significant pockets of poverty in the USA. In his view, public spending had not kept abreast with individual consumption, creating 'an atmosphere of private opulence and public squalor', where 'private goods have full sway'.[66]

Highlighting a gender bias in the machinations of the incitement of desire, Betty Friedan's *The Feminine Mystique* (1963) addressed all the ways in which advertising targeted women as full-time housewives, urging them to find meaning and purpose in what she saw as their largely lonely and frustrated domestic lives through, and only through, unbroken consumption of all that was depicted as essential for creating ideal homes and healthy families. Indeed, when Friedan began writing for women's magazines herself in the 1950s, she recalled listening to editors announcing, as if it were an immutable fact of life, that women 'were not interested in the broad public issues of the day … not interested in national or international affairs', unless it could be packaged as of immediate importance in the home, 'like the cost of coffee'.[67]

None of these critics were classical Marxists, although their views had a certain resonance with Marx's contempt for consumerism. Marx, however, was far more concerned with the alienation of workers whose labour was exploited in their production, thereby turning labourers themselves into commodities and rendering them 'consequently exposed to all the vicissitudes of competition, to all the fluctuations of the market'.[68]

However, those twentieth-century American fears of commercial indoctrination via mass communications mirrored more closely the post-Marxist suspicion, especially that stemming from the Frankfurt School in the 1930s and 40s, which had described the speedy growth of mass production of their day as turning citizens into passive victims of the communications industry, inciting false and unnecessary desires through ideological control and manipulation.[69]

Yet, especially after the spread of cultural studies in academia from the late 1970s, it was the Frankfurt School in particular that was later rejected by social theorists for its high-culture elitism, censoriousness and economic reductionism, which was seen as expressing a central European pessimism. A new line of enquiry initiated by cultural studies brought different understandings of the complexities of everyday cultural life. Addressing how meanings are created, disseminated and contested, cultural studies explored the more active and varied forms of agency, identifications and pleasures that are evident in many consumer practices, especially in their collective articulations.[70] In particular, cultural studies was interested in alternative or dissident subcultures, querying the notion of consumers as intrinsically passive and conformist. In his now-iconic survey of British punks, for instance, Dick Hebdige depicted their creative and critical appropriation of fashion, music and style, which he

85

described as enabling working-class youth to construct their own identities and sense of belonging in defiance of dominant norms and structures.[71]

More generally, cultural studies came to emphasize the paradoxical nature of mass culture. As Stuart Hall, the most charismatic founding figure of the field, would sum up the main purpose of this new transdisciplinary domain, on the one hand mass culture enacted and legitimated the power relations of capitalism; on the other, however, it managed to serve the symbolic interests of those subordinated by it. Hall's work provided the tools 'to enable people to understand what [was] going on', while also applauding 'strategies for survival and resources for resistance'.[72] He showed how decoding class, gender and other symbolic practices of domination can help us challenge what is accorded or denied cultural value, significance or even intelligibility.

Influenced by this tradition, cultural ethnographers from the 1980s were publishing a constant flow of research on the densely textured, symbolic nature of things, and our differing relations to them. One of the more recent and most prolific, the British anthropologist Daniel Miller is always eager to emphasize how profound our relationship to material things can remain, however mass-produced and consumed they may be. Indeed, he even maintains that 'usually the closer our relationships with objects, the closer our relationships with people'.[73] This sentiment is reflected in a lovely long poem by the Chilean poet and diplomat, Pablo Neruda, 'Ode to Things', where he celebrates touching simple objects, from pliers or scissors, to cups or rings, because they

bear
the trace
of someone's
fingers
on their handle or surface,
the trace of a distant hand
lost
in the depths of forgetfulness.[74]

Whatever the market forces involved, what is always emphasized in these appraisals is that the buying, giving, receiving, cherishing and discarding of goods are social acts, *not* just individual matters, perhaps serving as confirmations of identity and belonging, or sometimes securing our ties with others. In her book *Adorned in Dreams* (1985), the British socialist feminist Elizabeth Wilson was one of the first to reject earlier feminist disapproval of women's interest in fashion, which had been generally seen as keeping us in thrall to the male-dominated clothing industry and dressing to please men. She suggested instead that women also dress for each other, and to express ourselves in diverse ways. Nevertheless, with her communist leanings, Wilson also understood the ambiguities of fashion:

We live, as far as clothes are concerned, a triple ambiguity ... the ambiguity of capitalism itself, with its great wealth and great squalor, its capacity to create and its dreadful wastefulness; the ambiguity of our identity, of the reflection of self to body and self to the world; and the ambiguity of art, its purpose and meaning.[75]

Rather differently from the above, in critical marketing scholarship today we can read an explicit belief that 'objects and commodities can themselves serve political ends'.[76] Indeed, in a recent edition of the marketing journal *Ephemera*, Olga Kravets draws our attention to the iconic Russian revolutionary constructivist Alexander Rodchenko, who asserted in 1925, still at the height of revolutionary creativity after the emergence of Soviet Russia: 'Objects will be understood, will become people's friends and comrades, and people will begin to know how to laugh and enjoy and converse with things'.[77]

In this opening period of revolutionary hope, many believed that the goal of communist Russia was to build a world of cooperation and peace between all people and nations, one in which workers' needs were sovereign. Thus, far from commodities here being used to manipulate desire, in the early constructivists' dream revolutionary art and design could help inspire the masses in the creation of the new society.

As Kravets elaborates, it was thought that social transformation grew from the solidarity between workers in the production of goods, while consumption practices as well could also be shared and linked to collective goals. As we know, the constructivists' dream was defeated by many factors, including Russia's weak economic situation, confrontations from within and without, together with the Communist Party's focus on the speedy modernization of heavy industry, creating huge economic antagonisms between rural and urban areas.

However, Kravets still sees real value in the constructivist notion of a more sociable, friendlier and responsive relation to material things. Others in the same issue of *Ephemera* look at similar views evident in William Morris's notion of the commodity as comrade and his belief, as explored by David Mabb,

'that interior design had a fundamental role to play in the transformation of everyday life', especially following the encounter
between Williams and the Russian constructivist artist Liubov
Popova in the 1920s.[78]

Other forms of radical consumer practices have emerged in
recent times, such as those in Exarcheia in Athens following
upsurges of street protests and political mobilization against job
losses and a sense of youth disenfranchisement, especially after
the street riots in 2008. These have involved solidarity trading
initiatives, freeshops, collective kitchens, and the liberation
of public spaces which become, at least for a while, occupied
areas for creativity, play and the maintenance of comradeship,
hope and shared energy. As Greek marketing scholar Andreas
Chatzidakis has explored, in such moments objects themselves
'become an indispensable part of social and political struggles',
acquiring their own 'comradely' dimensions.[79]

Getting and spending our powers, in contexts such as these,
can therefore become part of the resistance to commodification
itself. But, as Chatzidakis also notes, over time capitalism has
always proved to have an extraordinary ability to draw back
into the competitive market even practices of resistance. Indeed,
that is precisely the nature of the beast: regularly finding ways
to repackage those disobedient, comradely objects as ersatz
badges of resistance, as when that Zapatista T-shirt hits the
shopping malls.

Yet the strength and significance of consuming differently
as part of building alternative spaces of power, resistance and
collective belonging remain important. For example, throughout the 1970s until well into the 1980s, much of the furniture in
my own collective household was dragged in from skips, most
of our clothes came from jumble sales, and we always seemed

to prefer the second-hand over the new. Remarkably, some of those objects still remain in their corners, or even occasionally on my shelves, along with stray badges and old magazines, especially *Spare Rib*. They provide an enduring trace of the shared joy we often had at those fundraising jumble sales, benefits, discos, always organized or attended to support or maintain specific radical productions, causes or activities of the moment.

We didn't articulate this as an anti-consumerist politics exactly. It was simply part of the alternative landscape in which 'capitalism', or the practices of business corporations, along with the patriarchal, authoritarian aspects of the state seen as protecting them, was the 'enemy'. A type of lifestyle politics, expressing the ideals of caring for others and sharing as much as we felt able to, were the alternative ideals we practised, trying to live our politics in the present as diverse socialists and feminists. However, any shared vision of the future remained incredibly vague once extended outside our own enclaves.

Such lifestyle practices often occurred alongside engagement in some forms of more traditional political activism, whether in trade unions or, especially at least for a while at the close of 1979, the Labour Party. However, as I have explored often before, alternative ways of living and consuming were easily diluted or abandoned once circumstances changed, and busier lives of everyday survival or the disillusionment of collective defeats left little time or space for the more 'inspirational' acquisition and sharing of things.[80] Before too long, with the evident reversal of possibilities for greater social equality and mutuality, what remained of alternative domestic or working lives was often only a few of those comradely objects as mementoes, once the human variety had departed from shared households or resource centres. This hardly means, however, that such practices will not emerge anew. Indeed, as we have seen, they constantly reappear, as I explore later in this book.

In the meantime, despite sophisticated rethinking of consumption as tied in with identifications and belongings (occasionally alongside dissident distribution practices), other critics were emerging to highlight the dangers of the heightened individualism unleashed since the 1980s by newly unregulated, ever-accelerating global corporations. A few were survivors from earlier Marxist traditions, such as the sociologist Zygmunt Bauman, who died in 2017, one of the fiercest critics of the anxious insecurities of contemporary life. He saw consumer values as becoming ever more entrenched and responsible for sidelining popular interest in the possibilities of a fairer world. In Bauman's view, a multitude of personal, yet patently similar, commodities are always promising instant gratification.[81] *Does Ethics Have a Chance in a World of Consumers?* is just one of his books looking askance at a life he labels 'liquid modernity'. In all his books, Bauman writes of the dangers of the relentless market emphasis on choice, updates and technical innovation: 'the consumerist rendition of freedom', with its excess and waste, weakens any sense of the ties between personal freedom and collective responsibility for the welfare of others, and the world itself.[82]

Some of this sentiment is echoed by a host of other well-known social critics. Nowadays, though, it is less common for critics to frame consumers simply as passive victims of market forces than for them to register their dismay at the increasing social polarization bred by the unrestricted market logic of neo-liberalism, as well as its environmental costs. While many indeed enjoy the instant visual gratification of the very latest iPhones and apps, or any number of branded products with the

click of a finger, others lose visual acuity or fingers in the production of them.

The formidable sociologist of global networks Manuel
Castells has also written extensively about the deep contradictions of this ever-accelerating networked economy, with
its mantra of individual consumption.[83] Amid weakening social
infrastructures and welfare provisions, a wealthy financial elite
has grown massively richer from the debts of the poor and the
wealthy alike. What most well-known critics of contemporary marketing and consumption practices now all emphasize,
including Don Slater, Douglas Holt and Juliet Schor, is that
the cultural amplification and significance given to individual
choice, in contexts where credit and borrowing are made readily
available, have fuelled desires for all that is new, modern, exciting and fashionable, making consuming itself 'the privileged
form (or site) of identity construction'.[84]

Put simply, the very notion of 'consumers' has been substituted for critical thinking about public life generally, as
notions of choice (however unequal) and of expanding markets
(however destructive) have pushed aside concerns with a
greater provision of public goods and the possibilities for
a more equal distribution of commodities overall. In the words
of the British social historian Matthew Hilton, surveying state
spending and consumer patterns since the Second World War:
'In more recent decades, the politics of consumer society based
upon access and the collective has been eclipsed by a politics
that emphasizes choice and the individual.'[85]

Any notion of shared joy is thus largely disappearing from
serious reflection on our world of consumption, one in which
market principles seem to have invaded all aspects of our ever
more precarious lives. It is a world that British broadcaster

Charlie Brooker satirizes in his sci-fi TV series *Black Mirror*, where everyone is busy the whole day long posting selfies of themselves looking happy and being good, all the while consumed by anxieties about their status and other people's reaction to them. In one episode, soldiers are employed who enjoy hunting down and slaughtering the shrieking zombie-like 'roaches' in their midst, the implants they have received preventing them from seeing that those they pursue are not monsters at all, but rather social casualties who deserve compassion. Commenting on the series, Brooker's fellow journalists Sam Wollaston and Owen Jones insist that this is hardly the future, but rather (with only slight exaggeration) a depiction of what is actually happening right now – whether in our ubiquitous Facebook postings or our treatment of refugees![86]

Marx's old notion of commodity fetishism can thus be given a slightly new twist nowadays: not only are workers turned into commodities in their production of things, since the real cost of their labour goes unrecognized, but consumers, too, become commodities, competing to improve their personal value and significance through tireless investment in themselves. Meanwhile, the possibilities for collectivized forms of consumption, mutuality and engagement in the world are downplayed or ridiculed in the mainstream media. Lenin once predicted that capitalists would sell the people the rope with which to hang them; today, radicals fear they are selling us the rope with which we hang ourselves. Echoing this thought, today's most popular Leninist, the Lacanian scholar and scatological joker Slavoj Žižek, insists that in our time the super-ego is dominated by what he calls the 'injunction to enjoy that permeates our discourse', making consumption as much a duty as a pleasure: 'elevating my striving for pleasures itself into my supreme Duty'.[87]

I am not altogether convinced by these dystopian reflections. I would agree, however, that in looking at consumption patterns today we have indeed drifted a long way from those moments of collective joy I described in the earlier sections of this chapter. If we seek our fulfilment in strictly individualized consumer behaviour, whatever the immediate gratification or enhancement of our market value, we are indeed heading away from helping to forge communities that foster the resources to enable all of us to enrich our ties to each other, and to the world at large. But many would already agree about this, which is why critiques of consumerism are popular in Green politics, and well beyond. Moreover, there are certain continuities in collective resistance and democratic engagement in political life clearly re-emerging today, whether inside or outside political parties and movements.

David Graeber is just one of many alternative voices of affirmation:

The human imagination stubbornly refuses to die. And the moment any significant number of people simultaneously shake off the shackles that have been placed on that collective imagination, even our most deeply inculcated assumptions about what is and is not politically possible have been known to crumble overnight.[88]

Individual consumption patterns will certainly not crumble overnight, nor would we want them to. However, the potential for the unleashing of collective action in almost any form, and along with that the moments of shared joy collective energies easily foster, are always reappearing on the social horizon. This is why breaking down distances between people remains possible, at least some of the time, when we are working together for happier futures. Before returning to any utopian dreaming, however, I want to linger a while in our most intimate spaces, seeking out personal bliss.

4

The Perils of Desire?

I can hardly write a book on happiness without venturing into the dreamland of love. Yet, if joy and woe are woven fine, they have never been more tightly stitched than in tales of love. Likewise, philosophical puzzles reflecting upon the nature of happiness and sorrow proliferate endlessly when considering the nature of love. Love is intangible, ineffable, mysterious, and this hardly scratches the surface of its many dimensions. Shakespeare captured this, writing one of the most iconic love stories of the last 400 years: *Romeo and Juliet*. In the first act, Romeo tries to convey love's essence to his cousin:

> Love is a smoke made with the fume of sighs
> ... a fire sparkling in lovers' eyes
> ... a sea nourished with lovers' tears.
> What is it else? A madness most discreet,
> A choking gall, and a preserving sweet.
> Farewell, my coz.[1]

People have been aware of the pains of love, at least of romantic love, throughout time, as is evident in legendary tales from across the world. Yet, in our time, it is precisely this form of love that is seen as the only route to happiness – even as its provenance is questioned at every turn. 'Haven't they suffered enough?' was the joke that some of my lesbian friends often repeated from a cartoon depicting the response of a wife in bed being told by her husband, reading the paper, that gay marriage would be legalized.

It is not just that love, sanctioned or not, is nowadays seen as the basis of happiness, but that sexual satisfaction is expected to accompany adult love. Indeed, Lawrence Stone, the eminent historian of family life, announced in the mid 1980s that in no previous society known to him had 'sex been given so prominent a role in the culture at large, nor … sexual fulfilment been elevated to the list of human aspirations – in a vain attempt to relieve civilization of its discontents'.

If Thomas Jefferson were updating the Declaration of Independence today, Stone teased, 'the right to total sexual fulfilment' would have to be added to the natural right of American citizens to 'Life, Liberty and Human Happiness'.[2]

Is Love Real?

'Is Love real?' was the question one young woman asked the *Woman's Own* agony aunt back in the 1940s. She wrote that her boyfriend, although doing nothing 'wrong', seemed to have to spend his life trying to resist temptation. This troubled her greatly: 'Are all men like this? It makes me feel that love is nothing but desire.'[3]

A few decades later, and no agony aunt would be publishing such a letter. Sex before marriage has since become the norm, though perhaps there might still be anxieties over whether

a young woman should be waiting for an engagement ring
or some other sign of commitment before moving in with an
amorous boyfriend.

Throughout popular culture, love, understood as the fulfilment of our erotic desires, is widely treated as the pivot of our
existence: love is life and life is love. Less romantically, some
such as Diane Akerman and Helen Fisher, rehearsing a now
familiar narrative of neurological explanation for social phe-
nomena, are committed to maintaining a true 'science of love'.
They believe we can learn all we need to know by emphasizing what they call the biology of love, looking in particular
at four basic hormones (adrenaline, dopamine, serotonin and
oxytocin) as the chemical constituents of all our emotions.[4] Yet
there is not now, nor will there ever be, any scientific account
of exactly how, when, where and why these hormones have
generated, or failed to precipitate, the occurrence and course of
romantic attachments or erotic engagements. This is because,
like all complex emotions, 'love' has a complex history.

Indeed, each love has both an intricate cultural and personal
history, even a geography, relating to age, gender, ethnicity,
religion, status and much more. The whole weight of the past,
public as well as private, is condensed into the fears and hopes
we bring to thoughts of love. What will be recognized as love
in one place may be seen quite differently in another; whom and
how we love is equally part of the understandings we bring to
the world of our desire for others, and the attachments we can
secure with them.

Once again, some researchers seek a more historical explanation for love. They look back through time, returning for
wisdom to the reputed origins of Western civilization, to
ancient Greece, over two thousand years ago. Others might

rightly point to other ancient civilizations or religions for guid-ance, but I am too ignorant of those to venture on such a quest.

Plato, in his *Symposium*, provides the first detailed reflec-tions on love in Western philosophy, describing a banquet at which Socrates is present with friends and various guests give speeches in praise of Eros, the god of love. What we see as sexual passion today, now popularly taken as the foundation of happiness, is described here as merely the beginning of love, or *eros*, the physical desire for a beautiful body – with all its jeal-ousy, anger and neediness, as displayed at the end of the text by a drunken Alcibiades. Such carnal passion, however, is declared only the first step on the way to a more exalted spiritual love for beauty and goodness: 'Love more than anything (more than family, or position, or wealth) implants in man the thing that must be their guide if they are to live a good life', says Phaedrus at the start of the text.[5]

However, there is more than one aspect to *eros*, as other diners make clear, and Socrates himself points out that desire is the need for the very thing we feel we *lack*: 'the man who desires something desires what is not available to him … what he doesn't already have in his possession'.[6] The often elusive object of desire being referred to in these pages is usually a beautiful boy. Men's education in love is said to be 'like a ladder; as he climbs from the love of one person … to love of all physical beauty'.[7] Plato then goes on to refer to other forms of love, especially to *philia*, the joys of friendship, the recip-rocal, non-sexual love between equals, providing intimacy and inspiration. This is the love between men who become friends and wish to be together for life. It is this friendship-love that Aristotle celebrated in his *Nicomachean Ethics*: 'for friends the most desirable thing is living together … spending their days together in whatever they love most in life'.[8] Two further terms for describing love traced back to ancient Greece include *agape*, God's unconditional love for man, extended to embrace the essence of spiritual or caring love, and *storge*, the upright loyalty to family.[9]

These forays into the nature of love by the ancient Athenian aristocracy, who could insouciantly rely upon both their slaves for performing all menial tasks and also their submissive, house-bound wives for procreation, provide just one illustration that what we see as 'love', and to whom we direct our passion, changes across time and place, along with what troubles us about it.

We also know that from the days of ancient Greece, right through to the present, although to varying degrees, there have always been more constraints and prohibitions surrounding women's entitlements to express desire, at least in the form of erotic love. Moreover, the weight of history has been one in which people's bodies, especially those of women and black people, but in actuality those of any group of people designated 'inferior', have been objects for the projection of guilt, anxiety and above all fear over any violation of sexual, racial or class boundaries, threatening to disturb what at any time is seen as the natural order of things.[10] Thus, non-sexual relations of power are always firmly, usually harshly, located within the sexual.

As we saw in the last chapter, the arrival of Christianity saw the heightening of negative attitudes towards sex in general. The historian of love and sexual passion, Anna Clark, is just one of many who point out that early Christianity tended to fear sex in any form as potentially polluting, a distraction from religious devotion. This meant that even while sanctioning marital love, early Christians positioned celibacy as superior to marriage.[11] Similarly, the harshest policing of sexuality mostly targeted women and especially accompanied times of social crisis, whatever its cause – outbreaks of plague, wars, national conflicts and, above all, military defeat.

Thus, the peak of the long, barbaric medieval witch-hunts occurred at the height of the lengthy religious wars in Christendom, between 1550 and 1650. These witch-hunts caused unprecedented levels of cruelty and suffering, with the tortured bodies of impoverished older women the primary victims in most places, accused of sexual pacts with the Devil.

In 1487, two German clerics of the Dominican Order, Jacob Sprenger and Heinrich Kramer, had broadcast their chilling incitement to hatred and disparagement of women in *Malleus Malificarum: On Witches Who Copulate with Devils*. Declaring all women feebler in mind and body than men, they further insisted that 'she is more carnal than a man, as is clear from her many filthy carnal acts'.[12] It was women's intrinsically weaker nature that made her a conduit for the Devil to enter. These revered Church authorities believed that it was women's frustrated sexual passions and secret longings for power that made them such easy prey of Diabolical intent.[13]

Although never without their own shifting complexities, for the most part the writings of the Christian Church suggested that it was only divine love, *agape*, and people's love of God, which could bring them true happiness. For centuries, the ascetic words of the Epistle of Paul to the Colossians were widely quoted: 'Set your minds on things that are above, not on things that are on earth', parishioners were told, while awaiting their eventual union with God. Thus, throughout the Middle Ages clerical texts suggest that 'dying to the world' had become the ideal way for Christians to live their lives on earth, as Simon May concludes in his compendium of love.[14]

Tales of women's dirty and contaminating bodies inciting men to sin or debauchery have cast a hideously long shadow right up to the present, their flickering and malignant ghosts forever dancing across landscapes of misogyny while inviting contempt for signs of 'effeminacy' in men. Christianity may have endorsed marital bonds – the German Protestant reformer, Martin Luther, stressed the importance of marriage and the place of the home as the centre of the universe – yet the residual dread and disapproval surrounding the display of women's sexual bodies continued: 'The female sex, so very, very weak, joined by nature or rather by God to the other, perishes when cruelly separated.'[15]

Hypocrisy, however, was ever present, and so it is hard for us to grasp the actual nature of medieval sexual conduct. Despite the Church's fulminations binding sex to sinfulness, there is plentiful evidence of priests seducing women during confession, of liaisons between nuns and priests, and of same-sex activities among the religious, as well as knowledge of wealthy men keeping mistresses, extensive prostitution, peasants copulating behind the bushes, and much evidence of rape – which was rarely mentioned in any documents of the time, let alone prosecuted.[16] Nevertheless, chastity remained the ideal in medieval Christian thought. This was hardly a recipe for personal happiness, least of all for women of whatever age, left anxious and shamed over their bodies against which these Christian ideals were most energetically enforced.

The Church's authority over human affairs only began to be questioned towards the end of the seventeenth century, with the beginning of the European Enlightenment's belief in rationality and its search for universal truths, promoting notions of democracy, liberty and human rights. Thus there were attempts, too, to reinstall sexual life as one of nature's sweetest pleasures, such as the publication of a sex advice book, *Aristotle's Masterpiece* (1680–1735), which recommended that women should experience sexual pleasure as part of the reproductive process: 'Perform those rites nature and love requires, / Till you have quench'd each other's am'rous fires'.[17] At the same time, the remarkable British playwright, novelist and poet Aphra Behn dared to join the libertines of the Enlightenment, writing bawdy poetry celebrating women's sexual pleasures.[18]

Accordingly, much of the popular art of the eighteenth century began to object to the harsh demands for women's chastity, while also focusing on the perils of human desire, as seen in Samuel Richardson's first epistolary novels, *Pamela* (1740) and *Clarissa* (1748). Nevertheless, even in these works, women were for the most part still correctly represented as imperilled by men's pursuit of pleasure. Thus, gender and racial differences remained heavily marked. Both came to be seen to draw fundamental distinctions between the 'civilized' West/male and 'primitive' rest/female, as Gayatri Spivak and other postcolonial theorists have noted.[19]

Moreover, accompanying the new emphasis on pleasure in the eighteenth century, women's sexual wiles were regularly depicted as tricks used to manipulate men. The truth was in fact far more grim, when so many impoverished women, forced into surviving as street-walkers or prostitutes, or occasionally as wealthier courtesans, remained the most visible sign of sex in society. For the most part, these women's lives were bleak, rather than conforming to male fantasies like those of John Cleland's popular *Fanny Hill: Memoirs of a Woman of Pleasure*

(1749), in which a young woman makes her way up the social ladder through her seductive powers.[20]

The Enlightenment thus reopened the space for discussing sexual activity. And, although routinely excluded from the record, women played a significant part in its intellectual life as essayists, novelists, polemicists, poets and philosophers, as has been explored by the feminist historians Barbara Taylor and Sarah Knott.[21] In Britain it was the provocative thoughts of Mary Wollstonecraft that were the most remarkable, evident in her passionate *Vindication of the Rights of Woman* (1792), in which she denounced those men who created only misery for women through the neglect of women's education. In particular, she criticized the radical philosophy of Jean-Jacques Rousseau on the 'natural' but contrasting education necessary for boys and girls (where girls would be taught modesty and how to become perfect wives, forever busy in their homes). This was an 'education' which Wollstonecraft saw as continuing to 'degrade one half of the human species, and render women pleasing at the expense of every solid virtue'.[22] Thus, far from gaining any autonomous rights to happiness, women still existed as men's property or sexual prey.

Worse, however, was that by the close of the eighteenth century, notions of sexuality as a destructive force were once again being reinforced due to new fears of population growth. The advent of the Industrial Revolution and improved medical knowledge, accompanied by a fall in mortality and rise in fertility rates, led to an almost doubling of the population in England and Wales in the second half of the eighteenth century.[23] The influential English clergyman and scholar, one of the most prominent voices of the time, Thomas Malthus, warned that increased procreation could unleash the end of civilization in his ground-breaking *An Essay on the Principle of Population* (1798). Malthus stressed the need for greater chastity, moral restraint and self-denial, especially for the working classes, whom he saw as biologically inferior, urging the abolition of poor relief for the destitute.[24]

The Birth of Modern Sexuality

Although it had never been completely uncontested, the policing of sexuality increased throughout the nineteenth century in Britain and other European countries. Erotic advice books such as *Aristotle's Masterpiece* disappeared, while social purity societies intent on suppressing vice and rescuing prostitutes proliferated. The first punitive Contagious Diseases Act, passed in 1864, victimized women but ignored men, allowing the arrest of any woman suspected of being a prostitute, and subjecting all such women to compulsory checks for venereal disease while making no checks at all on men. This was also a time when masturbation was fervently condemned, birth control information forbidden and women denied access to sexual knowledge. In the writing of leading physicians of the time, such as Alexandre Mayer in France or William Acton in Britain, women were declared largely devoid of sexual feelings. The entire essence of womanhood was efficiently reduced to procreation.[25]

As historians Catherine Gallagher and Thomas Laqueur argued, it was only in the nineteenth century, in what they called 'the making of the modern body', that the paradigm of male and female as innately opposite yet complementary was introduced. Hitherto, the female body had been seen as similar to the male body, albeit a weaker, inferior version of it.[26] This was the view expressed in *Aristotle's Masterpiece*:

For those that have the strictest searchers been,
Find women are but men turn'd outside in:
And men, if they but cast their eyes about,
May find they're women with their inside out.[27]

But this was about to change.

The control of sexuality at the close of the nineteenth century was shifting from religion to science. Nonetheless, these supposed scientific advances insisted that women were completely at the mercy of their menstruating bodies, a claim that relied entirely upon metaphor rather than any physiological evidence. As Laqueur concludes: 'In a world in which science was increasingly viewed as providing insight into the fundamental truths of human creation ... a biology of incommensurability became the means by which differences could be authoritatively represented'.[28]

Officially, women were seen as inherently incapable of genuine lust, being constitutionally frail and vulnerable. Yet their very existence could arouse the fiercest of passions in men, which it was *women's* job to control. Indeed many, though far from all, first-wave feminists at this time advocated chastity as the route to women's autonomy, including Christabel Pankhurst, the leader of the activist Women's Social and Political Union. Claiming that most men had some form of venereal disease, she called in 1913 for 'Votes for Women and Chastity for Men'.[29]

If love was real, men and especially women still needed to be very wary of it. Yet the notion of romantic love was becoming ever more tightly woven around sexual passion, with sexuality now viewed as the moving force in both personal and public life. This is clear in the foundational text of sexology, *Psychopathia Sexualis*, by the Viennese psychiatrist Richard Krafft-Ebing, who declared in 1886 that 'love unbridled is a volcano that burns down and lays waste all around it; it is an abyss that devours all – honour, substance, and health'.[30]

For nineteenth-century sexologists, love was now firmly tied to the sex instinct, stemming from the biological imperative for breeding. Yet, in complete contradiction with their belief in the teleological bedrock of reproduction, sexologists were in actuality busy recording all manner of non-reproductive sexual activities, which they insisted were anomalies and labelled 'perversions'. Moreover, it was the precise sexual proclivity, however anomalous – whether fetishism, masochism, homosexuality, transsexuality or any other type of sexual act – which was thought to reveal the very essence of the person: 'since upon the nature of sexual sensibility the mental individuality in greater part depends'.[31]

In contrast with the pleasures of those classic Athenian citizens, what was significant about the birth of modern sexuality in the closing years of the nineteenth century was the very centrality of its focus on desire as tied to potential depravity and guilt, and the need for restraint. These early sexologists proposed sex as a natural force, even an overpowering one, at least in men, and yet as potentially corrupting and dangerous. As a result, just like the medieval interpretation of religious love, this new sexual science also displayed a deep suspicion of most aspects of sexual desire as any source of happiness. Once again it condemned all sex outside marriage, while creating much misery within it. This is clear from records held in the Mass Observation Archive in Sussex, as one housewife born in 1887 reflected sorrowfully in 1939:

My husband accused me of being 'cold' but little knew the passionate longings I experienced if only he had made love to me instead of using me ... Now, at fifty-two, I feel the whole business is nature's great joke of which we are the victims.[32]

Almost forty years later, the influential French philosopher Michel Foucault scorned the idea of the extended, repressive 'Victorian twilight', by pointing out that Church and state were singularly ineffective at regulating private sexuality. Doubtless they were. Moreover, Foucault goes on to argue that the multiplying discourses surrounding sexuality, from sexologists, psychiatrists and criminologists, not only helped to shape individuals' understandings of themselves as sexual people, but also served to stimulate desire: 'The nineteenth century and our own have been the age of multiplication: a dispersion of sexualities, a strengthening of their disparate forms, a multiple implantation of "perversions". Our epoch has initiated sexual heterogeneities'.[33]

Nevertheless, Foucault's disdain for and apparent demolition of what he called the 'repressive hypothesis' constraining desire in Victorian and Edwardian times is questionable. The punitive treatment so often inflicted upon women pregnant outside wedlock or accused of prostitution was in fact both cruel and oppressive, as was the threat of and frequent occurrence of incarceration of men for homosexual encounters in the late nineteenth and early twentieth centuries, stemming from the paranoid fear that the existence of the homosexual could seriously undermine 'normal' society.[34] There were also abundant anxieties unleashed by the professedly baleful effects of masturbation.

As the rigorous British social historians Roy Porter and Lesley Hall suggest, Foucault's reasoning was misleading when – despite all the sexual activity actually occurring and the erotica circulating – sex in actual daily life remained everywhere muffled, 'furtive and shameful, as was the body itself', and sexual behaviour of any sort was rarely mentioned in any of the working-class autobiographies surviving from that period.[35] London was also notable in that *fin-de-siècle* for having more religious and moral organizations determined to save prostitutes than any other European capital.[36] Repressive? I think so!

Of course, Foucault was right that during this period there was abundant writing about sexuality in all its diversities, which did have an impact in unintended ways. The scientific birth of 'the homosexual' did assist some men in identifying themselves as distinct and different in their enjoyment of the illicit pleasures of same-sex behaviour – whether they felt guilty about doing so or not. Moreover, as Matt Cook's vivid historical research on late Victorian London shows, however illegal the pursuit, there were networks of places for men to 'hook up' in clandestine intimacy, whether in theatres, music halls, clubs, churches, railway stations, museums, army barracks, cafés or parks. Homosexual behaviour in private was thus not so easily policed, while the existence of 'the homosexual life of the city was rarely out of the eye and the newspaper-reading public had consistent reminders of it'.[37]

The late nineteenth century also saw the rise of homophile groups and writers in Europe and elsewhere, such as John Addington Symonds and Edward Carpenter in Britain, who began the long battle against punitive legislation, supported by Havelock Ellis and other social radicals of the day. Carpenter was one of those inspiring radical figures who, finding himself culturally disdained as homosexual, could link his own struggle for sexual pleasure and mutuality in loving with a broader interest in all forms of democratic socialist and anarchist thought, supporting workers' rights and women's rights, and opposing the misrule and condescension of the powerful wherever he saw it. He was also one of the first voices to oppose capitalism as a social and economic system, in favour of greater self-sufficiency and a 'simple life'.

In the 1880s Carpenter managed to establish a type of utopian community of mutual aid and sexual openness in the property he bought in Millthorpe, outside Sheffield. For the next forty years and more, Carpenter travelled, speaking on free love and socialism, and zealously wrote his many books, including *Towards Democracy* (1883), *Love's Coming of Age* (1896) and perhaps his most famous, *The Intermediate Sex: A Study of Some Transitional Types of Men and Women* (1908). Carpenter also lived openly with his working-class lover, George Merrill, declaring: 'Eros is a great leveller. Perhaps the true Democracy rests, more firmly than anywhere else, on a sentiment which easily passes the bounds of class and caste, and unites in the closest affection the most estranged ranks of society'.[38]

As Sheila Rowbotham captures in her eloquent, exhaustive biography of Carpenter and his friends, Millthorpe became a haven for visits from diverse sexual radicals, labour activists, feminists, politicians and writers, including E. M. Forster, Siegfried Sassoon and Robert Graves. Graves later wrote that his 'doubts and suspicions' as a schoolboy had been much relieved by reading about Carpenter's advocacy of Platonic attachments.[39] Other radicals, such as Lytton Strachey, with his ascetic notion of 'Higher Sodomy', openly 'disdained the Carpenterian simple life nearly as much as heterosexual copulation'. The younger socialist George Orwell, in *The Road to Wigan Pier* (1936), was eager to defend 'proletarian' manliness against 'readers of Edward Carpenter or some other pious sodomite', with their 'vegetarian smell, who go about spreading sweetness and light'.[40] Overall, however, Rowbotham believes that Carpenter 'possessed a knack which helped to prod the modern world into being', even if we might still say today that some have yet to catch up with it: 'Carpenter's personal life became ineradicably connected to his politics ... Being a homosexual man and a left-wing sexual rebel in a period of moral panic, he had limited space in which to manoeuvre. Yet manoeuvre he did.'[41]

Elsewhere the Criminal Law Amendment Bill passed in 1885, outlawing all forms of male homosexual contact, was ensnaring other men, most spectacularly through the trial and incarceration of the celebrated but notorious Oscar Wilde in 1895.[42] The law may indeed create 'a desire for what it forbids', as the well-known psychoanalyst Adam Phillips writes, when 'the act of forbidding intrigues us and distracts us'.[43] However, that does not in itself create a less repressive milieu.

Nevertheless, the movement of sexual reformers objecting to the punitive spirit of the purity movement expanded significantly in the twentieth century, first of all during the 1920s among those determined to present conjugal sex as the best route to happiness.

And no one sought harder to overturn Victorian reticence than Marie Stopes, whose passionate, romantic idealism in *Married Love: A New Contribution to the Solution of Sex Differences*, was apparently written when she was herself still a virgin, following the end of her first unconsummated marriage.

Married Love promised to provide 'the key to happiness', overcoming 'years of heartache and blind questioning in the dark', with its bold advice on contraception and sexual technique.[44] After suffering rejections from most publishers, *Married Love* was finally distributed by a very small press in 1918 (and remained banned as obscene in the USA for well over a decade). As often happens with anything declared forbidden, the book sold at once in tens of thousands, outstripping the most popular fiction of the era. With its account of the technicalities of erection, the beauty of the naked body, and above all the need for men's and women's mutual sexual pleasure, the publication of *Married Love* resulted in Stopes being bombarded with innumerable letters from both sexes, seeking advice on how to find that hitherto elusive sexual pleasure – simultaneous orgasm no less – that Stopes insisted was both obtainable and necessary for any successful marriage.[45]

Stopes, who would later be condemned for backing the powerful Malthusian eugenics of her day, organized teatime talks on married love, helping to fund the 'Mothers' Clinics' that provided contraceptive advice for women, especially working-class women. Years later, one grateful reader of *Married Love*, the celebrated Scottish writer Naomi Mitchison, commented in her own autobiography on the 'marked increase of happiness' generated by Stopes's guidance: 'It seems incredible now that this book was such an eye-opener. Why had none of these elementary techniques occurred to either of us before?'[46]

From the 1920s, Naomi Mitchison, Dora Russell and a few other prominent radical women, including the Canada-born Stella Browne, all of them interested in socialism, all peace activists and vocal feminists, went on to campaign for birth control and women's sexual rights, while hoping that companionate romantic love could not only change people for the better but be the catalyst for a new and healthier society. Russell, most of all, combined the joys of motherhood with belief in mutual sexual freedom: 'For whence can come love, compassion and understanding if not out of the relations of men and women and of them to their children?' Russell later wrote in her three-volume autobiography, *The Tamarisk Tree*, written in her eighties.[47] She had devoted much of her life from her twenties on to campaigning for birth control, later battling, with huge levels of frustration, to influence the British Labour Party to pay more attention to women's happiness. This meant, she argued, understanding women's bodies and their requirements for sexual pleasure and also for desired motherhood. 'Woman loves sex and loves children', she wrote as a young woman in her book *The Right to Be Happy* (1927), having even earlier called for 'a trade union of lovers … to conquer the world', in *Hypatia; or, Woman and Knowledge* (1925).[48]

This was certainly laying it on the line, especially from someone who would end up so disappointed by the men in her life, including Bertrand Russell, with whom she had four children and who treated her harshly when they divorced. As one contemporary male historian surveying her life and times commented: 'Most importantly, what gave life to Russell's work in disparate spheres was the fervent belief that the female body was political.'[49] In the late 1970s, the then young socialist feminist Sheila Rowbotham went to speak with 'Dora' in a London café, where the older socialist feminist from almost two generations earlier startled her, along with other diners, by announcing in her loud, patrician voice: 'The trouble with men is they just don't understand the female orgasm.'[50] Russell may have ended up disillusioned about men, but it was the maternalist, utopian thinking of these radical women from the 1920s that led to the eventually successful campaigns for public provision of birth control and state endowment for motherhood – though these have been contested in different ways ever since.[51] In this framework, the happiness to be found in mutual love and companionship was predicated upon what was seen as the basic contrast between women and men, which later feminists would challenge.

Yet, while changes in attitudes to sexual pleasure seemed to come fast in Western countries in the twentieth century, they were hampered by the projection of all manner of cultural fear and hostility towards thoughts of 'filthy', feral sexual practices. The economic and political crises during the Depression of the 1930s, for instance, led most radicals to see the sexual concerns of the 1920s as unimportant and selfish, firmly reinstalling the Victorian ideal of the male head of household and his dependent wife. This was revived as well following the familial and sexual disruption of the Second World War, when celebrations of the male breadwinner and women's stay-at-home domesticity once again resurfaced around the Western world. Surveying personal life throughout the 1950s, scholars of British history, such as Peter Mandler and Susan Pederson, conclude: 'What was radical in the Edwardian age of the 1920s seemed hedonistic, even retrograde in the 1950s'.[52] Yet, a mere decade on, things would rapidly evolve once more.

Sex as Liberation?

It was only in the closing three decades of the last century that notions of sexual pleasure began shifting for the majority of people. This battle, still ongoing, involved renewed assaults on many fronts. The goal was to untangle the increasingly contested ties between desire, gratification and personal happiness, issues so often entwined with the questioning of assumed gender differences. Until well into the 1960s, the persisting condemnation of sex outside wedlock, alongside contempt for unmarried mothers and their 'illegitimate' children, kept most young – or unmarried – women anxious, fearful and largely ignorant about their bodies, especially in relation to sexual pleasure.

The 1960s became emblematic of the 'sexual revolution', but the term was in fact older than that. It had been Wilhelm Reich in the late 1920s who wrote of the need for 'sexual politics'.[53] At the same time, in the early years of the Russian Revolution, the Bolshevik Alexandra Kollontai, People's Commissar for Social Welfare, called for greater sexual freedom.[54] But if the 'swinging '60s' was indeed a revolution, it did not come with a bang at the start of the decade, though by its close, a host of different social, economic and legislative changes meant that many women were having more sex than ever before, especially premarital and outside marriage. Meanwhile, the possibilities for diverse sexual pleasures were multiplying, with less apportioning of shame than ever before. In Britain, attendant legislative changes occurred only in the late '60s, beginning with the Sexual Offences Act (decriminalizing sex in private between men over twenty-one), the Family Planning Act (making contraception available on the NHS for married women), plus the Abortion Act (legalizing abortion under certain conditions) all in 1967, followed by the Divorce Reform Act (permitting divorce following irretrievable breakdown of marriage) in 1969. In the USA, legal reforms came more slowly, varying across state lines, although the 1973 *Roe v. Wade* ruling on abortion – still fought over today – was a landmark moment.

Many, however, remained sceptical of the changes, perhaps agreeing with the ageing Dora Russell that there was now 'a very great deal more sex ... but a decrease in the volume of love'.[55] In contrast, others would soon suggest that it was love itself, and especially the continuing ideal companionate marriage that Russell supported, which was very much part of the problem.

Certainly, a greater permissiveness wafted around throughout the '60s and early '70s. In Britain, the decade kicked off with the unbanning of D. H. Lawrence's *Lady Chatterley's Lover,* widely available for the first time since its appearance in 1928. Soon, rock music was getting raunchier, with much borrowing from American blues. Women's hemlines were rising, and recreational drugs were easily obtainable, as many of us entered our teenage years, including myself, during the hedonistic '60s: our numbers were 20 per cent higher than usual due to the postwar baby boom. Money was flowing into many more pockets in what was later seen as a 'golden age' of capitalism, the expansion of the consumer-driven economy that continued from 1945 up until the early 1970s.

Nevertheless, just as with legislative reform, the radical impact of the decade was only consolidated in the final years of the '60s, with ever more deliberate provocation in underground magazines and other 'alternative' products of the counterculture. At the same time, there were more resolutely militant civil rights and anti–Vietnam War demonstrations taking place around the Western world, as well as the formation of the Black Panthers in the USA, and students everywhere occupying their universities to demand more control over courses. Above all, a new spirit of egalitarianism and class-consciousness was in the air, when by 1970 a working-class hero was something to be, and not only in the Cavern Club in Liverpool.[56]

Along the way, young women's sexuality was feted and made visible, with most indications suggesting that women were for the most part enjoying their greater sexual freedom. This was especially possible after the contraceptive pill became available in 1963, although it was quite a few years before it could be officially prescribed for unmarried women on the NHS.[57] It meant that women were now supposedly freer to flaunt and enjoy their sexual desire (though certainly not yet any unwed pregnancies). But it helped to be young, indeed very young, for any such display – 'sweet little sixteen' being around the right age for some men's fantasies: in Britain it was Twiggy, at just sixteen, insect-thin, resembling a child in adult drag – typically displayed mouth open, thumb sucking, holding a balloon, chasing butterflies or riding a baby scooter – who became the leading London fashion icon in the second half of the 1960s. Her waif-like sexuality was clearly little threat to older men's fantasies of control. This stick creature retired on reaching the grand old age of twenty, only to make a partial return to fashion some forty years later, post-feminism, when the world had grown up – just a little!

Thus, if to be young and female in the swinging '60s was 'very heaven', it had many hazards, and not just that youth – especially women's – was so fleeting. For sure, many just like me were eager to partake of the new sexual freedoms that came along in that decade. As I have written before, having sex and refusing to hide it was one way for women then to rebel against parental and bourgeois norms – although my own parents were rarely bothered about their daughter's sex outside wedlock, just not wanting the neighbours to know. According to the radical psychiatrist R. D. Laing, admired by the New Left and counter-culture alike, girls who were forbidden to rebel might be driven mad by their over-controlling, manipulative families, headed up, in his version, by depressed and frustrated mothers, with whom he had little sympathy.[58]

However, as many a budding feminist later testified, women's sexual confidence then was paper-thin, my own included. Despite and because of all the pageant around young women's naked bodies, the 1960s remained quintessentially a male decade. As soon as women left their swinging 'teenage' years behind, they might find their hedonistic male peers viewing their growing maturity with alarm. It was the association of fully grown women with motherhood and the domesticated conformity of family life that men in this permissive, distinctly pre-feminist, '60s moment often abhorred. Certainly, those so-called 'Angry Young Men' of the day, first visible in the late 1950s, revered the tough, amoral, anarchic *male* hero, as he battled any and all constraints of domesticity or family responsibility.[59]

I have written in *Making Trouble* of my own young adulthood among a gentler version of such male rebels, the all-permissive, peaceful, pessimistic anarchists from the Sydney Push, which formed in the 1950s. I read all the publications and attended all the meetings, parties and gatherings of their intellectual wing, the Sydney Libertarians. However, given the stifling authoritarianism and conformity of Church, state and family life in post-war Sydney (continuing well into the 1960s), their notoriety came not so much from their anarchist outlook or atheism, but rather from the promotion of 'free love' – a non-possessive, Reichian version of it. These leftish Libertarians, who briefly welcomed the Melbourne graduate Germaine Greer into their midst in the early '60s, were rigorously anti-utopian in relation to any form of institutional power, seeing all formal structures of authority as inevitably corrupting. Yet they were thoroughly utopian in imagining that sexual freedom was both intrinsically good and also a route to social emancipation.

Having formulated this view in the 1950s, at the very height of the strictest anti-permissive cultural conformity, these anarchic agents of dissent and 'free love' were just slightly ahead of their time in expressing a view which would become commonplace in the '60s counter-culture. Meanwhile, like so many women of the '60s, I soon grew slightly sceptical of the emancipatory potential of love, especially when reduced to sexual pleasure. Knowing how easily I could feel unbearably jealous and rejected in relationships, and seeing the difficulties women faced around questions of motherhood, the only time I ever ventured to speak on a libertarian platform in the mid 1960s was to endorse Freud's pessimistic belief in the inevitability of everyday sexual sorrows, rejecting Reich's utopian notion of the 'genital character' free from psychic misery. Later, I read with some incredulity, in letters from my old libertarian comrade Michael Taussig, about the graffiti in Paris, where occupying students had daubed on the walls of the Sorbonne in May '68: 'The more I make love the more I want to make revolution. The more I make revolution, the more I want to make love.'[60] It no longer seemed so simple, at least for women.

Yet women, wherever we were, certainly participated in the more joyful moments and increased personal freedoms of the '60s. It was just that the tensions around love, desire and sexual pleasure, not to mention the dilemmas surrounding maternity, emerged more clearly by the close of the decade. Victorian legacies dividing us into 'virgins' or 'whores' had far from disappeared, their residue clearly visible in the wide-ranging double standards that left us prey to accusations of being either 'frigid prick-teasers' or 'sluts'.

Some of the most cavalier and defiant of the new radical women tried gallantly to ride the tigers of sexual liberation.

Most prominently, leaving behind her Sydney libertarian mates, by the mid '60s Germaine Greer was living in the UK and eagerly celebrating what she saw as women's new freedom as a form of 'Pussy Power', and later 'Cuntpower', even declaring it the beginning of the end of patriarchy in *Oz* – the underground magazine that now, like her, had been transported from Sydney to London. She briefly helped to edit the pornographic magazine *Suck*, though left swiftly after finding she was the only one of the editors in 1972 prepared to expose her naked genitals.[61] Such bravado and gritty sexual agency seemed also to be what Erica Jong was celebrating in her bestseller *Fear of Flying* (1973), in which she described her protagonists' joyful desire for the 'absolutely pure', speedy and anonymous 'zipless fuck', because here the 'man is not "taking" and the woman is not "giving"'.[62] It was never clear to me why this particular fantasy would offer any route to women's sexual liberation.

However, most radical women of the day, especially those about to begin meeting together to build our own autonomous movement, were much more troubled trying to become sexually 'free' women. We often shared mutual affection with men while also confronting the projection of men's anxieties onto us, alongside our own conflicts and uncertainties. In Britain, it was my friend Sheila Rowbotham who when still in her twenties first and most eloquently summed up these hazards, in *Woman's Consciousness, Man's World* (1973):

> We lumbered around … in borrowed concepts which did not fit the shape we felt ourselves to be … We clowned, mimicked, aped our own absurdity. Nobody else took us seriously, we did not even believe in ourselves. We were dolly, chick, broad.[63]

Only in hindsight, she said, was she able to find the words to explain her sense of 'the tragedy of the sexual divide and the way it had hobbled me'.[64] Just a few years earlier, on the eve of the formation of the women's liberation movement, she was the sole woman on the radical left paper *Black Dwarf*. It was in that journal that Sheila named 1969 the 'Year of the Militant Woman', appealing to all her male comrades to abandon their sexism and forgo their use and enjoyment of the pin-ups of lubricious women, which some male comrades wanted to place in *Black Dwarf*. She wrote:

> Men will have nothing to lose but their chains ... You will no longer have anyone to creep away and peep at with their knickers down, no one to flaunt as the emblem of your virility, status, self-importance, no one who will trap you overwhelm you ... who will wrap you up and SMOTHER you ... [just women] who will understand you when you say we must make a new world in which we do not meet each other as exploiters and used objects. Where we love one another and into which a new kind of human being can be born.[65]

Here can be found the early utopian spirit of second-wave feminism. Women could share love and find happiness with men, but only by building a new egalitarian world, in which the sexes would be no longer seen as so very different or complementary, but instead be able to share the promise and burdens of domesticity, labour and power.

In the USA, another early women's liberationist, Ellen Willis, who helped found New York Radical Women in 1967 and Redstockings the following year, wrote: 'Feminism is a vision of active freedom, of fulfilled desire, or it is nothing.'[66] Certainly, women's liberationists in those early years were having more fun, were blooming and cheerful, whether declaring themselves members of WITCH (Women's International Conspiracy from Hell) and invading the New York Bridal Fair wearing black veils, or racing around the London Underground (as one friend was later told, like demented nuns) posting up stickers on ads objectifying women's bodies declaring 'this exploits women'.[67]

At much the same time, black lesbian feminist Audre Lorde, writing in *Sister Outsider*, proclaimed: 'The sharing of joy, whether physical, emotional, psychic, or intellectual, forms a bridge between the sharers which can be the basis for understanding much of what is not shared between them, and lessens the threat of their difference.'[68]

Such were the first passionate years of women's liberation when, we, mostly young women, joyfully took to the streets pushing against the ubiquitous landscape of sexism we inhabited. It was clear at once to us that there was a distinction to be made between sexual liberalism and sexual liberation, when all the discourses and iconography of sex, as well as women's experiences of it, showed that women were neither seen as nor felt ourselves to be free agents in the same way as men often could.

Indeed, even sexologists such as Alfred Kinsey in 1954 and, more insistently, Masters and Johnson in 1966 had argued that women were not getting their fair share of orgasms in coital sex, compared to men. However, feminists wanted to broaden the focus, to talk about sexuality and pleasure, but also about care, comfort, and the diverse trappings of intimacy so often missing from men's talk about sex and revolution. This included, among other issues, reproductive control, shared childcare, financial independence and overall respect and equality, which, as we saw it, required nothing less than a cultural, political and sexual revolution.

This feminist interest in personal life was a product of the '60s counter-culture, and also a reaction against it. I described all this in the opening of *Straight Sex*, pointing to a time when women's saying YES to sex was seen as part of our liberation, even empowerment. But it had to be a feminist or 'liberated' type of sexuality with – or without – a man.[69] A liberated sexuality, there's the rub! How on earth do we really talk about that? It grew harder, not easier, as the years passed. Women's liberation began confidently enough, but quickly hit a million snags, entrenched in the very language, iconography and affect of sex itself. We struggled to change this, of course: 'Think Clitoris' was how the American feminist writer Alix Kates Shulman summed up the then rather behaviouristic feminist thinking on sexuality in 1971, drawing heavily upon the work of sexologists, soon including the feminist Shere Hite, who had much to say about women's orgasms, and their independence from coital sex.[70] Shulman's popular second novel, *Burning Questions* (1978), a few years later, covers the rise of the women's movement, in which she has one young feminist detailing the three non-negotiable conditions for good sex: 'plenty of dope, three hours minimum and cunnilingus'.[71] Nice try!

Over a period of three years in the mid 1970s in the UK, the most popular feminist magazine, *Spare Rib*, published a series of articles by Eleanor Stephens, similarly drawing upon the research of Masters and Johnson, to stress the importance of women taking charge of their sexuality, without embarrassment or shame, to find their favourite pathway to orgasmic satisfaction.[72] In the footsteps of the iconic essay by Anne Koedt in 1968, 'The Myth of the Vaginal Orgasm', many feminists argued that women must define their sexuality for themselves. They proposed that understanding the diversity of women's sexual pleasures and attachments, while learning the art of sexual satisfaction, was learning how to love oneself and hence in itself empowering: 'The Moon Within Your Reach', as Stephens's article was entitled.[73]

Doubtless, such writing did help provide both the words and the resolution for many women who wanted to talk more openly with their lovers, and encourage some men to ponder their own sexual practices – especially when the importance of affirming women's sexual pleasure was then mirrored in certain mainstream magazines, such as *Cosmopolitan* under Helen Gurley Brown. Thus, whereas Kinsey in the 1950s had found well under 50 per cent of women regularly having orgasms in coital sex, that figure had risen to 81 per cent in a US survey by 1975. Another *Cosmopolitan* survey in 1980 described American women as 'the most sexually experienced and experimental group of women in Western history'.[74] Furthermore, there was more confidence and bravado in lesbian writing by the close of the 1970s. Lillian Faderman, Sarah Schulman and others later noted with glee that there had never before been so many women coming out as lesbians – though this soon became a source of significant contention.[75]

However, I was far from the only feminist who remained a little dubious about the extent of the emancipatory potential of sexual satisfaction on its own to assist women on our voyage to greater power and authority in the world at large. This is despite my thinking, then and now, that fighting for and achieving sexual rights is important, and far from irrelevant to women's level of confidence and wellbeing, while also attracting many women to feminism in its early years. Alix Shulman herself reported that when some of her friends met in New York in the late 1970s to discuss the changes a decade of feminism had made in their lives, most agreed that the sex had improved – when they had it – while agreeing sadly that they had not found love.[76]

It was not just that finding the supportive, enjoyable physical relationships women wanted could be difficult, but that feminists were soon falling out, too, over any notion of women's sexual liberation in heterosexual contexts. Crucially, by the late '70s, the heightened visibility of some men's persistent sexual aggression and harassment of women was designated as *the* overriding feminist issue, marginalizing any talk of heterosexual pleasure, let alone empowerment, or women's changing relationships with men. All feminists agreed on the significance of opposing men's violence against women, while stressing its historic prevalence as one intolerable aspect of women's subordination and sorrows – although this was for many of us, including me, seen as far from the sole foundation of gender hierarchy. Nonetheless, we objected to the rhetorical reductionism of leading anti-violence campaigners, especially Andrea Dworkin and Catharine MacKinnon, whose American voices on behalf of this movement soon became the loudest and best known. Their lurid prose condensed male sexuality into male violence, presenting these as the essence of masculinity and men's power over women, while targeting 'pornography' as the chief cause of men's sexual coerciveness.[77]

The fact that more women were actually then enjoying their relationships with men was altogether muted in this account of feminism, for a focus instead on women's role as victims in what was fast emerging as the more morally conservative '80s. The painful irony of this is that it was economic and social parity that remained most elusive for Western women, even as more of us were actually achieving greater sexual equality with men, as Barbara Ehrenreich and others have noted.[78]

This view of straight sex as ineluctably oppressive coincided with the politicization of lesbian sexuality, or at least one view of it, now seen as a revolt against patriarchy rather than as an enthusiastic expression of sexual desire for women. As some prominent lesbian feminists objected at the time, including Gayle Rubin, Joan Nestle, Amber Hollibaugh in the USA, and Mandy Merck and Elizabeth Wilson in the UK, such idealization of lesbian desire promoted a prescriptive version of lesbian practice, since it had to symbolize what was being celebrated as exemplary 'feminist sexuality'. It meant 'foreplay as all-play': Hollibaugh mocked the disavowal of the existence of power, passion or any desire for penetration in lesbian encounters, if you were to avoid being accused of having a 'male-defined' sexuality. In scornful agreement, Rubin added that lesbians were expected to imitate what she called 'the missionary position of the women's movement', which was what straight women regarded as 'good' sex: it had to be 'very gentle' and undertaken only 'in the context a long-term caring relationship'.[79]

Hollibaugh and Rubin, with Deirdre English, came together to discuss and subsequently publish their view of sex in the USA at the start of the 1980s, all equally troubled by what they saw as a new moral puritanism arising within the women's movement. The only straight woman in the conversation, Deirdre English noted that women seemed to occupy 'a strange transitional time': no longer so repressed, but with few available images of women's 'healthy, assertive sexuality. Or lust'.[80] For Rubin, feminist theory at the time only seemed able to consider women's sexuality in terms of problems of sexism and gender hierarchy, lacking 'a language for sexual desire and wants'.[81] For a while it was only lesbian feminists who dared openly to mock this new prescriptiveness, and who would lead the search for new ways of portraying female desire.[82]

Ironically, before long, in the mainstream it was the capitalist market itself drawing upon feminist language to offer its own mellow version of sexual emancipation, suggesting a young woman could feel strong and empowered donning her 'liberty' bra or sporting a teasing thong. The sociologist Angela McRobbie was just one of many older feminists voicing her criticism of this turn, in *The Aftermath of Feminism*, arguing that young women donning the sponsored trappings of a sexually liberated 'femininity' did nothing to undermine continuing masculine hegemony. [83]

Nevertheless, if some feminists were still unsure how to combine love, happiness and desire with their continuing struggle for equality with men, this was far from the end of our engagement with the story of love.

5

The 'Truth About Love'

If feminists, particularly straight feminists, lacked an adequate language for their pleasures and practices of sexual desire in the 1970s and '80s, this was also because in the post-war Western world, sexual desire and its satisfaction had become the primary focus for thoughts of 'love'. Few things in history are more troubled or contentious than the nature of love, even more so at a time when there are always newer technologies for making profit from commodifying love and desire, the market selling us back promises of romantic triumph by feeding whatever erotic fantasies it comes across.

The Flaws in Love

Such promises are made to be broken: 'To be creatures who love, we must be creatures who can despair at what we lose, and depression is the mechanism of that despair', Andrew Solomon pointed out at the start of *Noonday Demon*.[1] But Solomon was hardly the first to highlight the perils of love. Rather, those trying to understand the ambivalences and pains of love, observing how easily it can switch over into feelings of resentment or even hatred, have often turned to Freud, some-times without actually meaning to, since his enduring thoughts have been repudiated quite as much as they are recycled. Yet, acknowledged or not, it is psychoanalytic thought that has left its mark on Western culture over the last century, at least when addressing the hazards of the heart.

We know that Freud placed libido, or the sexual instinct, at the very centre of human existence and the search for happi-ness, as did the sexologists emerging at much the same time, in the late nineteenth century. However, steadily over the next century but especially in the wake of the 1960s, the increasingly accepted science of sexology was stressing the diverse pleasures of sex, now seen as essential to human fulfilment and happi-ness in adulthood – just as soon as women and men learned to overcome their inhibitions and acquire the right techniques for giving and receiving orgasmic satisfaction.

In recent times, sexologists have provided expedient forms of cognitive behavioural sex therapy to facilitate the techniques of finding satisfaction in relationships, while also working hand in glove with the pharmaceutical industry. In striking contrast, Freud, and his psychoanalytic legacy right up to the present moment, impart a more pessimistic vision of the ineluctable ambivalence, difficulties and disappointments in our search for love and sexual fulfilment. This resulted from the unknown and uncontrolled forces Freud saw as impeding that search for love, a pursuit that always took us back to the residue of physical satisfactions and inevitable frustrations of all our early inter-actions with the world, when the body and its needs were part of every move we made, without our conscious awareness of them. Indeed, in Freud's view, our very sense of self is formed through the residue of those we have loved and lost, the anguish of loss leading us, unconsciously, to internalize the presence of those we desire.[2]

As no one will be surprised to learn, for Freud this applied above all to our very first object of attachment, usually our mother, who cared for us in infancy and whose original nurture provided us with 'an unending source of sexual excitation and satisfaction', as he wrote in his pivotal text, *Three Essays on Sexuality*, in 1905.[3] It is why 'mother' remains 'the prototype of all later love relations – for both sexes'.[4] She was the first person we desired, whose absence we immediately internalized in erotic fantasy. It was she whom we once vainly wanted to keep for ourselves alone, hating all rivals for her affection – whether our siblings or her own sexual partner (usually our father) – but whom we had to learn first to share and then to relinquish as our primary object of desire, journeying to autonomous adulthood.

For Freud, the 'finding of an object is in fact a re-finding of it'.[5] It is also why loss, whenever it occurs, stirs up all previous losses, right back to infancy, easily evoking a sense of total abandonment. Yet, despite and because of its entanglement with all our past losses, Freud always insisted that the ability to love, as well as to work, was essential for a healthy life: 'In the last resort we must begin to love in order that we may not fall ill, and must fall ill if, in consequence of frustration, we cannot love'.[6]

The psychoanalyst Julia Kristeva begins her *Tales of Love* by asserting that the nature of love is inevitably 'a crucible of contradictions and misunderstandings', which for her suggests at once 'the abyss separating the sexes'.[7] Her mentor Jacques Lacan, who also made sexual difference foundational in language (the symbolic order) and hence the formation of selfhood, argued that it 'was not possible to say anything meaningful or sensible about love'.[8] He then proceeded in his subsequent writing to provide his very own 'precise', if provocative, 'meaning and sense about love': which was to say that it is always illusion.

What happens in love is that one imagines one has found an ego ideal, an object to love, which at least for a while facilitates the narcissistic gratification of how one likes to see oneself: 'That's what love is. It's one's own ego that one loves in love, one's own ego made real on the imaginary level.'[9] Lacan's position is that in love you have to recognize your own lack, which he and his followers are certain is more difficult for a man, since according to Lacan 'to love is to give what you haven't got'.[10]

As Lacan's leading representative in Paris, Jacques-Alain Miller explains:

> Every man in love has flashes of pride, bursts of aggressiveness against the object of his love, because his love puts him in a position of incompleteness, or dependence. That's why he can desire women he doesn't love, so as to get back to the virile position he suspends when he loves. Freud called this principle the 'debasement of love life' in men: the split between love and sexual desire.[11]

Lacan's best-known and most provocative partisan, Slavoj Žižek, adds, 'What one often forgets is to add the other half which completes the sentence: "to love is to give what you haven't got, to someone who doesn't want it."'[12] Here, then, we could hardly be further from the view of romantic love as a source of happiness. Spelling this out, Žižek elsewhere responds with characteristic melodrama, but equally Lacanian precision, to the question of what it feels like to be in love: 'like a great misfortune, a monstrous parasite, a permanent state of emergency that ruins all small pleasures'.[13]

Far less sensationally, one thing that I find useful in Freud or Lacan is something most of us can easily recognize about love, which is that there is a narcissistic element in romantic love, as we project onto the object of our desire attributes we would like to see in ourselves. This does indeed make us vulnerable, since it is all too easily shattered – either by the rejection of our love or by the one we have passionately desired disappointing us.

This helps to explain what Adam Phillips calls 'the lure of violence in human relations', which is that those we most love and desire are always 'beyond our control', and likely to prove rather different from how we imagined them to be.[14] Elsewhere, exploring the certainty of ambivalence in love, he adds, 'Ambivalence is the way we recognise that someone or something has become significant to us ... wherever there is an object of desire there must be ambivalence'.[15] The poet Adrienne Rich similarly captures these contradictions:

> But among the dualities that lend love both its electricity and its exasperation – the interplay of thrill and terror, desire and disappointment, longing and anticipatory loss – is also the fact that our pathway to this mutually refining truth must pass through a necessary fiction: We fall in love not just with a person wholly external to us but with a fantasy of how that person can fill what is missing from our interior lives.[16]

As I've already suggested, added to the dangers of love's potential to generate jealousy, anger and other hostile fantasies, as well as subsequent remorse, we face the issue today of its commodification at a time when everything is for sale. We are sold 'love' along with innumerable products from chocolates to racing cars or even soap powder. Still others, most routinely men, can be more directly serviced via sex workers, foreign brides or others apparently 'happy' to satisfy any manner of fetishized wants and desires. The very finding of love nowadays is itself as likely as not to involve the technologically mediated social interaction of some virtual 'lost object'.

Thus, the more things have shifted towards apparently greater sexual permissiveness, the more we find fresh questions, obstructions or incitements to trouble or erode the joys or consolations we might seek in intimacies with others. For instance, the arrival of online porn streaming and sex phone-lines creates endless opportunities for profit, mostly from the production of sexist, misogynist objectification of women's bodies, with all its tired, racist cliché and sexualization of young girls' bodies.

Yet, within its money-spinning possibilities, there is also potential for more positive, queer, women-friendly images of shared passion, even community building or, as we'll see below, narratives of love that may have little or no erotic component.[17] For decades now, some feminist scholars and women in the adult sex industry have looked at how women have actively engaged in producing, performing and consuming porn while working to overturn its routinely sexist, racist and other demeaning categorizations of women.[18]

Nonetheless, even as women, queers, and trans women and men find new ways of asserting their agency, love remains a battleground, sometimes literally, of fatal encounters. According to the United Nations, 35 per cent of women worldwide are reported to have experienced violence from their partners, and three or more women are murdered by their boyfriends or husbands every day in the USA alone.[19] Yet, relative to their number, it is black trans sex workers who are probably the most endangered people around the globe.[20] Nowhere are these battles of sex, love and violence more sharply etched than in the USA.

As the self-styled global champion of democratic rights, with over one hundred different LGBT advocacy groups across the country, the USA can rightly be seen as the site of the largest, most remarkable, in the end often successful, political struggles for the recognition and theoretical understanding of non-normative relationships and sexual pleasures.[21] However, equally and perhaps even more significantly, especially at this moment, the USA remains the home of the globally influential far-right Christian movement, which has remained a key force in both the Republican Party and American politics more broadly since the late 1970s. It was in 1979 that the late Republican senator and Baptist minister Jerry Falwell founded the Moral Majority, determined to restore conservative, Christian sexual values to the USA. In the process, Falwell helped to get Ronald Reagan elected in 1980 and achieved another of his central goals: to get the Equal Rights Amendment rescinded two years later.[22] Espousing a morality totally opposed to sex outside marriage, even to sex education in schools, Falwell's influence was at its height in the 1980s. This was also precisely when there was the most exuberant flaunting of sexual dissidence from the other side of the fence, evident in campaigns such as ACT UP (AIDS Coalition to Unleash Power) demanding more state funding to combat the pandemic of HIV/AIDS then decimating gay men and triggering lethal homophobia.

Right-wing Christian fractions have proliferated ever since the demise of the Moral Majority in the late 1980s, with its demographic core coming from Evangelical Protestantism and forms of Roman Catholicism, also supported by politically conservative Jews and Mormons.[23] Other prominent far-right Christian

Republican polemicists include Reverend Pat Buchanan, who insists that no pregnancy should ever be terminated, whatever the circumstances, nor should sex education in school ever be made available.[24]

Today, the election of Donald Trump as president both strengthens, and partially originated from, all those far-right, misogynistic, homophobic forces. Not long ago, Trump had declared himself a supporter of women's reproductive rights, but in campaigning for the presidency he switched sides, promising to fight to criminalize abortion, a promise he is keeping with his appointment of 'pro-life' judges to the Supreme Court, beginning with the anti-choice, anti–LGBTQ rights Neil Gorsuch. Going further, Trump has appointed Jerry Falwell Jr. to lead his taskforce on higher education reform – the man who heads the world's largest Christian college, where Biblical creationism is taught alongside the theory of evolution.

This is all the more frightening in the context of the ferocious grass-roots anti-abortion campaigning that for decades now has been targeting abortion clinics in the USA, not just with leaflets and pickets, but with incendiary bombs and murder, resulting in the deaths of several doctors and attempted murders of other staff at abortion clinics. The firebombing of abortion clinics has also occurred in other Western countries, from Canada to Australia and New Zealand.[25]

Tragically, we can see materialized the insights of French anthropologist Maurice Godelier, from over three decades ago: 'It is not so much sexuality which haunts society, but society which haunts the body's sexuality'.[26]

It thus remains as challenging as ever for those of us still hoping to turn that combat zone into a space for genuine empathy, allowing both the potential delights and the despair trailing our contradictory needs for love, commitment and physical pleasure. It is important to note that there are socially orchestrated reasons for the obstacles we face when, as we have seen so often before in history, intolerance is encouraged by the uncertainties of the moment.

For over three decades, social mobility has stalled, with wages declining and jobs disappearing across much of the USA and Europe, even as we also witness populations of desperate people on the move following regional struggles, Western military interventions, and the suppression of democratic uprisings around the globe. To say we live in uncertain times hardly does justice to any of this. Rather, it indicates the level of change needed to beat back the reactionary mindset – one always threatened by unruly bodies and the joys of others, which challenge the brittle certainties of some people's identities, especially around masculinity.[27]

Where Love Resides

How can love flourish in such a climate? Quite apart from its inherent fragilities, commercial exploitation, and targeting by moral crusaders in paranoid times, second-wave feminists were from the beginning especially sceptical about 'true romance', seeing it as wedded to men's traditional patriarchal power. 'Don't Do It, Di!' we warned the future Princess of Wales in the late 1970s, appropriately as it later turned out. We wore badges that said, 'It begins when you sink into his arms and ends with your arms in his sink.' Yet, despite sexism's cunning persistence, it is surely true we have since seen the ever more rapid decline of the patriarchal family in the West, much to the horror of orthodox conservatives determined to maintain men's dominance as breadwinner and boss, especially in the home.

Women's greater reproductive control and financial independence have enabled more of us to leave marriages or relationships we found oppressive or unsatisfactory. It is interesting to note that while both men and women are equally likely to end a 'dating' relationship, it is women who initiate most divorces in the USA, Europe and Australia.[28] More importantly, the change in the whole climate of opinion means single, widowed or divorced women are no longer the objects of pity or disdain that they were in former times. Indeed, living on one's own today need not entail the absence of erotic ties, let alone close intimate ones.[29]

In her droll polemic *Against Love*, the American cultural critic Laura Kipnis delights in mocking the treadmill of coupledom, describing it as an endless catalogue of tedium and rules, while recalling how recent is the whole idea of romantic love as the foundation of marriage: 'Domestic coupledom is the boot camp for compliant citizenship: a training ground for gluey resignation and immobility.'[30] Refusing to give up on the delights of desire, though, she sings the praises of adultery, or following one's sexual interest wherever it leads.

Kipnis, of course, was offering a deliberate provocation to mainstream reflections on love over the last twenty years, a period when sociologists had finally begun writing about love, almost for the very first time. They stressed its increasing ideological primacy accompanied by its growing personal hazards in a changing world. Thus, Ulrich Beck and Elisabeth Beck-Gernsheim, soon followed by Anthony Giddens and Zygmunt Bauman, all cautioned that the greater the choice and variety in relationships, the less any true commitment could be taken for granted, leaving partnerships, whatever their nature, perpetually open for renegotiation or dissolution.[31] Moreover, coinciding with exactly the period in which relationships became less dependable and divorce or separations routine, the rising individualization of contemporary life meant that ever greater value was placed on the search for love, 'forcing people into an endless cycle of hoping, regretting and despite everything trying all over again'.[32]

Bauman's metaphor of 'liquid love' captures the tension between this desire for personal freedom and the need for security, as does Giddens's notion of 'active, contingent love', which he sees, somewhat controversially, as more egalitarian, less gendered and power-ridden than traditional notions of romance.[33] However, a few of their peers, such as Carol Smart, have suggested that the theme of insecurity and lack of commitment has been exaggerated in these sociological texts, with Smart pointing to the lasting bonds and commitments that often remain in personal life, even when people live apart: 'This means that there is more open conceptual space for families of choice, same-sex intimacies, reconfigured kinship formations and so on.'[34] Nevertheless, as I covered in *Out of Time*, more people today are indeed troubled by fears of loneliness, which has a particular significance for ageing women, when they constitute 70 per cent of those living alone over the age of sixty-five.[35]

What remains paradoxical for ageing women is that we are often negated as objects of desire, even though it was our traditional ties to the labours of love that contributed to our marginalization in the world at large. This is why many feminists remain as suspicious as ever of love's domain, and the symbolic place of women within it, noting that we live in a cultural climate that more than ever places so little value (least of all any satisfactory state support) on the work of love, caring and commitment, the responsibilities for which still fall disproportionately on women's shoulders.

Thus, the British feminist scholar Mary Evans suggests that in the harsh world of neo-liberalism, the word 'love' has become so devalued that it is better simply not to use it. In these times, when we are encouraged to be relentlessly aspirational and competitive at every turn, love is reduced to self-gratification, and has become 'as meaningless as the kisses on the emails between strangers'.[36]

Less pessimistically, others hope to bring meaning and enchantment back to our notions of love, while fearing that the very glut of internet messaging and online dating merely provides token substitutes for it, while undermining people's ability to hold fast to the frailties and challenges of love.

The social studies scholar Sherry Turkle suggests in her latest book, *Alone Together: Why We Expect More from Technology and Less from Each Other*, that we are nearing a 'robotic moment' when it will soon be machines rather than people performing the 'caring' roles that our social fabric has been undermining. Since its inception in the mid 1990s, Turkle has been carefully scrutinizing the social and psychological impact of living in 'cyberspace', noting that today pet robots are already available to comfort lonely residents of care homes, mechanical nurses are on the way, and the old sex toy is being superseded by recreational sex robots.

She is well aware that social media have also served to enhance friendships, family ties, knowledge and entertainment, alongside their personalized targeting of each us for commercial ends and surveillance. Notwithstanding these convolutions, from her interviews with people of all ages about their increasing, often constant, use of instant messaging, iPads and Facebook, Turkle joins others in pondering the danger that our huge reliance on technology to mediate human relations might be making simulated life more alluring than the messiness and challenges of actual human relationships. What she fears is that we are 'increasingly connected to each other but oddly more alone: *in intimacy, new solitudes*'.[37]

However, from the perils of love I have already explored, I would suggest that any addictive resort to technology is as much symptom as cause of the increasing alienation, atomization and potential loneliness that many people complain of today. At a time when the boredom and stress of long working hours, insecure accommodation and other pressures of life make finding the time and space for creative sociability harder to organize, some still manage to use the internet precisely to organize such contacts.

Turkle may be right to suggest that 'insecure in our relationships and anxious about intimacy, we look to technology for ways to be in relationships and protect ourselves from them at the same time'.[38] Yet, as she concludes, there is nothing about the technology itself that necessitates that we should expect more from it and less from each other. There are still very real possibilities for intimacy and delight, if we choose to put down our gadgets, at least some of the time, and begin listening to and connecting more directly with those around us.

Nevertheless, the Israeli sociologist Eva Illouz remains pessimistic throughout her book *Cold Intimacy*, seeing online dating as especially damaging for women, threatening disenchantment and destruction of the emotional glue that binds us to others.[39] She explores this further in her next book *Why Love Hurts*, adding a far tougher feminist inflection to the mainstream sociological literature of Beck, Baumann and Giddens. In it, Illouz argues that the current social geography of erotic life, encouraging complete freedom of choice, while locating self-worth in our sense of desirability, leaves everyone, women especially, particularly vulnerable in what is still an unequal marketplace.

The quest for love is an 'agonizingly difficult one', when for women above all, it remains love, and love alone, which is not just a cultural ideal, but 'a social foundation for the self'. The rituals of love remain cemented to gendered power relations in our heteronormative world, as women hope for children and committed relationships, but enter a competitive sexual arena that places a high value on men's sexual practice and autonomy: 'Men's emotional detachment and commitment phobia are thus an expression of their position in sexual fields, created by a new ecology of choice.'[40]

Disappointment, and the managing of disappointment, Illouz concludes, is thus the most distinctive feature of love today, at least for straight women. Her solution for greater gender equality, indeed for greater happiness overall, is not for everybody's equal detachment but rather for their equal commitment to relationships that are less about sexual prowess and more about offering focused attention on one another 'in a way that is self-forgetful (as in models of parenthood or friendship, for example)'.[41] Her hope is thus to rejoin masculinity with passionate commitment.

Illouz's call is not unlike that of the philosopher Alain Badiou, who in his short text *In Praise of Love* suggests that love today is threatened by internet dating sites, which offer relationships and sexual satisfaction, free from emotional risk or long-term commitment. 'Real love', Badiou insists, 'is one that triumphs lastingly, sometimes painfully, over the hurdles erected by time, space and the world.'[42] Moreover, he adds, since it is the capitalist world that tries to pull us apart with its threat to love through the marketing of every form of impulse gratification, it is possible to see enduring romantic attachment as a form of political resistance. Seeing love as that which overcomes the selfishness of mere individual satisfaction, Badiou suggests, makes it possible to see it as a form of 'minimal communism'.[43]

While sharing Badiou's horror about the individualism of our times, I find his suggestion that online dating is free from emotional risks unconvincing. Equally unpersuasive, in my view, is his hope that support for romantic commitment can be seen as a form of political resistance to capitalism. It is more often political and moral conservatives who advance this view, such as Badiou's fellow French philosopher, the centre-right politician Luc Ferry, who similarly believes that love – by which he clearly means love of family – can save the world.

However, undermining the view of upholding love as any sort of anti-capitalist triumph, the world Ferry wants to save is precisely the contemporary neo-liberal world of minimal government and laissez-faire economics, which, as he wrote in 2012 (the year Badiou's text appeared), he proclaims the best world there is, or ever could be: 'I must insist on this point: nowhere else and at no other time have people taken more care of each other'.[44]

Finally, after surveying these diverse and shifting thoughts on love over the years, this alluring notion that is itself the receptacle for so much yearning, hope, fear and suspicion, I think I am finally beginning to see some sort of pattern emerging to help me tie up a few threads. Putting to one side for the moment its ubiquitous shadows of jealousy, envy, resentment and loss, at its most hopeful the language of love embraces just some of the possible combinations of desire, pleasure, intimacy, care, admiration, familiarity and commitment. This means that love is best seen as a project, although not always the same project, when both our understandings of and relation to 'love' differ across a lifetime.

Pondering all that is said and done in the name of love, it is clear that sexual difference has always loomed large where love resides, both seductively and, quite often, menacingly. Menacingly, because sexual difference is an inevitable issue of contention for feminists. The shifting understandings of sexual difference have been entwined with normative patterns of desire and reproduction that underpin the long history of gender hierarchy: representing the life of the sexed body in ways that have traditionally circumscribed women and empowered men.

'Happiness Is a Warm Gun' is the title of a song John Lennon wrote in 1968. He had just been shown the cover of a gun magazine with those words on its cover (twelve years before he was shot by just such a hot lethal weapon).[45] Whatever really inspired the allegedly pacifist Lennon (the riff itself lifted from a gentler one-liner in Charles Schulz's comic strip *Peanuts*: 'Happiness in a warm puppy'), Lennon later confirmed that it referred to his early sexual desire for Yoko Ono: 'That was the beginning of my relationship with Yoko and I was very sexually oriented then'.[46] You 'cock' a gun, reflecting the massive power invested in the iconography of men's penises – all of which serves to conceal just how frail and wilting they usually are, but connects with the coerciveness endemic in some men's sexual practice. Maddeningly for women, this is what has for so long been iconic of sexual desire itself: male erection.

As Jacqueline Rose says, the scandal of feminism was daring to challenge notions of masculinity and, above all, in that moist and intimate sexual domain.[47] Understandings of sexual difference have subordinated women, even as they have also often troubled men – for not being manly enough. The young British gay poet, Andrew McMillan, captures this beautifully in his poetry, writing of all those men left

> weeping in the gym
> using the hand dryer to cover
> their sobs.

These are the men, he continues, pretending

> that they don't hear
> the thousands of tiny fracturings
> needed to build something stronger.[48]

In innumerable ways, the ties made between gender and sexuality have also menaced, and often murderously destroyed, sexual dissidents. These are many people who found they could not slot into what proved for them the torments of gender or heterosexual expectation and coercion, whether they were lesbian, gay, or in what we now know as the plethora of transsexual, asexual or polyamorous proclivities. Such dissidents, including today those who identify as non-binary, have always been vulnerable in the house of love, as we witnessed in the grotesque murder of forty-nine people and the wounding of as many more, in an Orlando gay nightclub in the USA in June 2016.

Yet, contrary to the position of certain feminists, most notably the French materialist Christine Delphy, we cannot just eliminate gender from our language or practices of love and desire.[49] How could we, when so much of desire rests upon fantasies cemented onto what we have understood, or perhaps resisted, around sexual difference, knowingly and, largely, unknowingly? Indeed, given the place of gender in culture, our initial and abiding sense of ourselves can only be constituted through our acceptance of or need to contest how we have been placed in the world as sexed creatures, with men especially facing a constant pressure to reaffirm their masculinity. As Jonathan Dollimore says in his recent memoir *Desire*, 'I think one's sexuality corresponds to the sex in relation to which one feels complication, loss, distress, because these things are intrinsic to love, to desire.'[50]

It doesn't end there, of course, when our gendered attachments always interlace with those other positions of power or diminishment we confront along lines of class, race, ethnicity, religion and more. Gay men or lesbians, for instance, may be seen as gender dissidents in one way, because they uncouple the orthodox ties between gender and sexual preference. Yet, in their distinct desire for men or for women, they are quite as gender-focused as any straight person. Leo Bersani captures this paradoxical resistance and reassertion of gender elegantly in pointing out that gay men's desire, despite and because of its threat to straight men, is not so much a 'subversion' as a 'worshipful tribute' of socially pervasive definitions of masculinity, indeed a '*yearning* toward' them.

Nevertheless, gay men do menace male jocks, just because, in their intense identification with masculinity, 'they never cease to feel the appeal of it being violated.'[51] Same-sex desire also subverts the heterosexual paradigm by exposing its shaky and bizarre foundations based upon a fantasized male active/ female passive binary, supposedly condensed into 'the' sex act. As I argued in *Straight Sex*, it is the absurdity of this polarity itself that is the problem: who is active, who passive, in fellatio? Much the same question could be asked of any other consensual sexual encounter, depending upon how it is performed, and the fantasies involved. Think about it!

In the realm of desire, what has been liberating about queer theory over recent decades is precisely its emphasis on the complex and shifting ways in which we occupy our gender and our sexual lives. Our understanding of love and sexuality does become richer when we see gender less rigidly. Yet it seems to me unlikely that we will ever live in a world where sexual difference is entirely unmarked, or where related notions of gender completely disappear. For gender identity is not only tied up with selfhood but, as the leading instigator of queer theory, Judith Butler, noted recently:

> If gender is eradicated, so too is an important domain of pleasure for many people ... Some want to be gender-free, but others want to be free really to be a gender that is crucial to who they are.[52]

Curiously, however, one dismal way in which the place of gender in relation to the wider terrain of love, care and commitment has shifted in our times is in its outsourcing in richer countries to low-waged, usually female, service workers. Financial need and career pressures have meant more women as well as men spending much of their time away from home in ever more demanding workplaces, leaving them unable to devote time providing the necessary love and care to those who need and want to see more of them, even when they might want to. The American sociologist Arlie Hochschild suggests that, for women and men alike, 'the more anxious, isolated and time-deprived we are, the more likely we are to turn to paid personal services' to provide for our needs for comfort, care, sex or companionship. Moreover, she notes that the greater our reliance on market resources for care, the less confidence we have in our own capacities, or those of friends or relatives, to provide comfort and love.[53]

Love's Lasting Residue

As I have said, part of our problem in rethinking our need and desires for each other, and the impediments to our realizing them, is that it is sexual intimacy, with all its hazards, that has loomed so large as the primary substance of love, and the main route to happiness in adulthood. Yet this is a narrow view that does not encompass all forms of love, care and commitment that influence our lives. Other forms of love – familial, friendly, comradely and many more – remain distinct and significant, with their own pressures, rhythms and demands, all woven around our need for each other.

Yet, despite their substantial differences, what *all* forms of love have in common is our dependence on each other, and the differing ways in which our need both to give and to receive love, at any age, can leave us vulnerable. 'We must all make do with what rags of love we find flapping on the scarecrow of humanity,' the British novelist Angela Carter once said.[54] Where there is hope and possibility, there is also despair, boredom or exhaustion.

Sex is certainly not an aspect of all relations where there is love, but risks and anxieties are rarely absent from love. Again, it is Judith Butler who expresses this well: 'Love is not a state, a feeling, a disposition, but an exchange, uneven, fraught with history, with ghosts, with longings that are more or less legible to those who try to see one another with their own faulty vision.'[55] This is the drama of love. Personally, I realize I am falling in love with someone, or just that love enters the picture, when I start to grieve at this person's absence and usually have to control feelings of jealousy about their closeness to others, their enjoyment of others. Sexual intimacy may have nothing to do with it, even though I suspect some sort of physical attraction is relevant.

Apart from the feelings of vulnerability that always enter with love, attending any dread of being ignored by someone we care deeply about, there are other characteristics I am aware of in those to whom I could easily say 'I love you', though most often will not. Such is the force, and what many would perceive as the demand, which arrives with such words. Unsurprisingly, given that idealization is usually a part of the attachments we cherish, what I see in the people I love, or perhaps what I project onto them, are just those things I most admire and would like to possess myself.

For me, this includes kindness, an intellectual sharpness, left political commitment, and other ways of responding to and being in the world that I want to cultivate in myself – an idealization that also consists of what I hope to learn from those I care about. There is also, simply, the physical comfort of being near someone I find attractive, for whatever reason that I do. In trying to please or amuse those I love most in the world, I am also trying to make myself a better, more lovable person.

I see some of my own thoughts reflected in Eve Sedgwick's writing shortly before her early death, in *A Dialogue on Love*, which documents, often in poetry, her tender exchanges with her therapist, Shannon. As she had hoped, Shannon enabled

Sedgwick to overcome her fears that her illness might revive the depression of her teenage years, which would have prevented her from being able to keep liking, desiring and knowing the world right up to the end. Soon after her diagnosis with breast cancer at forty, she wrote: 'My own real dread has never been about dying young but losing the people who make me want to live.'[56]

Sedgwick's subsequent discussions with Shannon are mainly about love, of differing kinds. In one encounter she mentions the centrality of her passionate attachment to her gay friend and housemate, Michael Moon. It would be true to say, 'I'm in love with him', she reveals, explaining that this friendship had changed her in so many different ways, providing her with endless laughter and joy: 'It preoccupies me a lot; it's very physical, though we don't have sex'. I identify with Sedgwick here, and all the more so when she mentions the many other passionate friendships she has experienced throughout her life, mostly with gay men: 'By now I feel almost promiscuously skilled in such intimacy'.[57]

I could say much the same, looking back on my own life as I age – although having married a gay man, my son's father, I guess at times there was even less separation between love and sexual encounter. Overall, Sedgwick expresses my thoughts on broadening out the meaning of love, when she writes:

I keep forgetting, for lots and lots of people in the world, the notion of 'falling in love' has (of all things) sexual connotations. No, that's not what I think is happening. For me, what falling in love means is different. It's a matter of suddenly, globally, 'knowing' that another person represents your only access to some vitally

transmissible truth
or radiantly heightened
mode of perception,

and that if you lose the thread of this intimacy, both your soul
and your whole world might subsist forever in some desert-like
state of ontological impoverishment.[58]

For all that, I agree it can be all the more exciting, for a while,
when sexual contact enters the encounter; more exciting, but
usually, more hazardous. Few people wrote more vividly about
the risks of love than Gillian Rose, writing *Love's Work*, in the
year before she died. Having always got love wrong, she con-
fesses, she would determinedly keep doing so until the day she
dies. Rose knows that: 'Love-making is never simply pleasure',
but she lives with the longing that she may at least continue
to desire: 'To grow in love-ability is to accept the boundaries
of oneself and others, while remaining vulnerable, woundable
around the bounds. Acknowledgement of conditionability is
the only unconditionability of human love'.[59]

Talking in Lisbon to celebrate the twenty-fifth anniversary
of her iconic feminist text *Gender Trouble*, Judith Butler echoes
this theme on the limits of sexual love: 'satisfaction, bodily
satisfaction' is this what we need, she wonders. 'I don't do satisfaction', she reflected. 'No, I do survival, liveability, perhaps
the Lacanian desire to desire. We need that.'[60] I agree, we need
that – the desire to keep desiring – but how we do it, with whom
or with what, when, where and how we desire, that can surely
stay open if we manage to remain where love resides. And if
we can continue to desire, throughout our lives, how lucky
we are!

It remains open also because it is clear that love persists when erotic passion weakens, and who knows, it might even deepen. You only have to look at some of the writing from people in old age to get a sense of this. We find it here, in this poem by Thom Gunn, at sixty-five, expressing the delight of presence and absence, contemplating the mutuality of long-time love. Gunn was recalling what happened after his drinking late, staggering home, barely making it to bed with his partner of over forty years, in his poem 'The Hug':

> I dozed, I slept. […]
> My sleep broke on a hug
>   Suddenly from behind
> In which the full length of our bodies pressed:
>   Your instep to my heel,
> My shoulder blades against your chest.
> It was not sex, but I could feel
> The whole strength of your body set,
>   Or braced, to mine,
>   And locking me to you
> As if we were still twenty-two
> When our grand passion had not yet
>   Become familial.
> My quick sleep had deleted all
> Of intervening time and place.
>   I only knew
> The stay of your secure firm dry embrace.[61]

Lines like this can make me weep, at the description of such chaste, physical pleasure. Or here is Seamus Heaney, at seventy-two, presenting a more reserved image of the mutuality of love in old age in his final collection of poetry:

Too late, alas, now, for apt quotation
About a love that's proved by steady gazing
Not at each other but in the same direction.[62]

Where love resides will also be a place where we must also expect to find loss and pain, which may also include shame. It is where hopefully we are able to keep hold of our desires, keep looking out for love, and when lucky, not looking entirely on our own.

Fortunately, love also extends beyond human encounters: many fall in love with animals, having the most rewarding relationships with their domesticated pets. The impressive Californian historian of science Donna Haraway, for instance, writes beautifully in her own uniquely feminist, trans-humanist way of those forms of love and intimacy that extend from humans to include animals. Considering especially those animals interacting most closely with humans, and here above all, dogs, in her *Companion Species Manifesto* (2005), Haraway writes lyrically of how she and her two dogs have been mutually training each other, in what sounds like a type of therapeutic interaction:

We are training each other in acts of communication we barely understand. We are, constitutively, companion species. We make each other up, in the flesh. Significantly other to each other, in specific difference, we signify in the flesh a nasty developmental infection called love. This love is a historical aberration and a naturalcultural legacy.[63]

This reminds me also of the significance of the love and intimacy the gay American poet Mark Doty experienced with his dogs as together they seemed to share the grief of his lover dying of AIDS, in his poignant memoir *Dog Years*. Only years later, and at the time in a new happy sexual relationship, does Doty come to find his anguish hardly bearable, when facing the death of his most beloved dog.

Knowing also that we can, in different ways, fall in love with ideas, ideals, places, sounds, anything that inspires and uplifts us, I cannot possibly do justice to all that we might call 'love', if I am ever to conclude my thoughts on the subject. It is often because people we have loved have introduced us to other aspects of life that those particular objects or experiences retain their power over us. Love is obviously not one thing, but a set of emotions that takes many forms depending on its object; indeed, it may be easy, some have suggested even easier, to keep loving the dead and feel them still beside us, years after they have departed.

In his long and extraordinary memorial to the friend of his youth, Arthur Henry Hallam, who died at only twenty-two, which Alfred Tennyson spent seventeen years writing, *In Memoriam*, the poet not only mourned his friend but urged him to remain near him till the day he too died: 'Be near me when my light is low'; 'Be near me when I fade away'. It is a familiar sentiment, the love that remains from successful mourning, expressed wonderfully by the Scottish poet Jackie Kay in her poem 'Darling', imagining sitting beside a dying mother, singing quietly to her as she died:

> And what I didn't know, or couldn't see then,
> Was that she hadn't really gone. The dead don't
> go till you do, loved ones. The dead are still
> here holding our hands.[64]

Thus, what I think we can conclude about love is not just that the perverse lies at the beating heart of normality, but again as that queer poet Auden suggested with all his distinctive wit: there is no 'truth about love', however we conceive it.[65] All we can know is that desire connects us to the world, and that to stay alive to it, as Jonathan Dollimore writes in his memoir, is to admit that 'complication, loss, distress … are intrinsic to love, to desire. To be alive is to desire, and to desire is, sooner rather than later to be deeply, subjectively confused'.[66]

And yet that is still not all there is to say, when there is joy also in sanctioned love, in simply affirming commitment, as gay theorist Jeffrey Weeks notes – controversially, for queer theorists who prefer to remain forever outside the normative. For some gay men and lesbians affirming their love in civil partnerships and now marriage, Weeks says, 'was like a second coming out, better seen as a struggle for recognition than a ruse of power.'[67]

Love, I would conclude, although often fraught, is what helps us feel more at home in the world, helps us shore up our sense of who we think we are or would like to be, making us inclined to love those people, places, creatures or experiences that support us in this endeavour.

The British philosopher of the emotions Simon May agrees, suggesting that we will love 'only what can inspire in us a promise of ontological rootedness', what seems to confirm our own existence, enabling us to feel more at one with the world.[68] This is why loving, of some sort, is essential for happiness, but it is crucial to realize that, fortunately for all of us, love is infinite in its variety.

6

Inventing Utopias

Acts of love may be infinite in their variety, their expressions shifting across time and place, yet they remain a risky foundation for personal happiness. Still, love offers us the potential to think about different worlds, communities or, more recently, spaces, of hope and resistance imagined or created for promoting greater social harmony, justice, political education and enjoyment of life. They are places envisaged specifically to bring meaning and creativity as well as recognition and pleasure into the lives of those who occupy them. Yet, almost by definition, few impulses or activities have been more mocked and dismissed in contemporary times than those labelled 'utopian'.

'Utopia is the most self-undermining of literary forms', cultural theorist Terry Eagleton noted two decades ago, before proceeding to devote significant time to defending such endeavours. 'The last thing we need is more utopian visions ... dreams of heaven that could never exist on earth', Immanuel Wallerstein begins his account of what he called 'utopistics', seeking 'the face of an alternative, credibly better, and historically possible (but far from certain) future'.

'Utopias have something to do with failure and tell us more about our own limits and weaknesses than they do about perfect societies', says the prominent Marxist 'anti-anti-Utopianism' scholar Fredric Jameson, while elsewhere concluding that the value of the utopian text lies 'in its capacity to generate new ones, Utopian visions that include those of the past, and modify or correct them'.[1]

'The utopian has a bad reputation in many circles, especially radical intellectual ones', the feminist sociologist Avery Gordon agrees. She attempts not only to convey 'the visions, passions, and longings' that motivate today's forms of collective resistance, but also 'to encourage those of us who see ourselves as politically engaged radical intellectuals or social-change activists to be a little less frightened of and more enthusiastic about our most scandalous utopian desires and actions'.[2]

Meanwhile, the anthropologist and anarchist activist David Graeber in his erudite essay 'A Practical Utopian's Guide to the Coming Collapse' moves from embracing utopian visions to concluding that they must 'be kept in their place': 'We cannot really conceive of the problems that will arise when we start trying to build a free society. What now seem likely to be the thorniest problems, might not be problems at all; others that never even occurred to us might prove devilishly difficult.'[3] Once more I find myself wading through a bog of all-too-human desires and delusions, hopes and disappointments to map the political paradoxes in any proposal for better futures alongside the now more familiar portents of worse.

Engineering Happiness

Dreams of a better world have a long and complex history. We can learn something if we again time-walk back over two millennia into the Athenian agora (to a city at the very site of so much hope and fear today) and ponder Plato's *Republic*. Plato describes a gathering where his mentor, Socrates, dines with friends and followers, when the conversation turns from love to address, instead, society and notions of the ideal or just city (*kallipolis*), while addressing the relation of justice to human happiness (*eudaimonia*, more strictly translated as 'flourishing'). There are differing interpretations of the texts, but it is clear that this Republic was to be ruled by wise men, the philosophers, known as guardians, who would be carefully educated for their role, acquiring both wisdom and a certain harmony of the soul. No peaceful and just society will ever be possible, Socrates taught: 'until philosophers rule as kings or those now called kings and chiefs genuinely and adequately philosophize, and political power and philosophy coincide in the same place'.[4]

This Republic was depicted as a more peaceful and equal society than any in existence: all residents of the city would be provided for with appropriate jobs to fit their abilities, while women (in a proposal quite at odds with the time) would receive an education equal to that of men and play a full role in society. Moreover, their meticulously educated wise rulers would possess no special privileges, sharing everything in common in a world where money, and hence greedy accumulation, have been abolished, thereby increasing the happiness of all.

Significantly, the ruling organization of this model city had little interest in 'democracy', despite the enduring legacy of the 'direct democracy' first practised in the Athenian polis. Instead, this Republic was to be governed by reason and reason alone, and our now revered democratic ideals of 'free speech' and 'majority rule' could not be depended upon to deliver this, Socrates argued. In his view, the populism of a democratic government cannot reliably counteract mob rule, since a clever demagogue can exploit it to take power and indulge his tyrannical tendencies, hence undermining the basis for the truly just society: 'the democratic party gives way to the oligarchic'.[5] Even poets, with their wild, undisciplined imaginations, were seen as potentially disruptive in a sensible and judicious republic, since – like Hesiod and Homer – they 'composed false tales for human beings', tales all the more dangerous when finely told.[6]

Plato's illustrious student Aristotle agreed with his teacher, also suggesting in his *Politics* that rule by many, as distinct from the few, was most prone to distortion, since poorly educated people were more susceptible to demagogues.[7] Nevertheless, although this rejection of majority rule has rendered Plato's model Republic unacceptable in modern Western eyes, it is not only the classic Greek scholar Martha Nussbaum who suggests that many of the dilemmas those ancient Greek philosophers expressed remain with us to this day, 'posing disturbing questions about democratic freedom'.[8] How 'democracy' unfolds, and its capture or stranglehold by vested interests, means that the problem of just what is meant by 'democracy' haunts us still. Indeed, all the more so nowadays, when as I write Donald Trump's regressive populism has been victorious, and 'democracy' itself is a term frequently used, or abused, to dismiss as 'utopian rubbish' any hope for more equal societies in a less divided world.

However, it was not Plato, but a British writer and statesman who first coined the term 'utopia', five hundred years ago, to describe that place he dreamed of where everyone would be happier than in any previously known society. In his short text *Utopia* (1516), the word encompassing the two Greek words *outopia* (nowhere) and *eutopia* (a good place), Thomas More wrote of a peaceful, tolerant island community. It closely resembled Plato's Republic, since it too had eliminated private property, and was educating all its people, including women, to work hard in their various jobs: 'Everyone gets a fair share, so there are never any poor men or beggars. Nobody owns anything but everyone is rich – for what greater wealth can there be than cheerfulness, peace of mind, and freedom from anxiety?'[9]

Here, again, not democratically elected but wise, elderly patriarchs ruled, with able scholars forming its official leaders and priests, and educating their community in such a way that they had 'rooted out of the minds of their people all the seeds, both of ambition and faction'. One is hardly surprised to learn, however, that More's *Utopia* had strict moral codes and rather quirky rules, with adultery punished by celibacy for life, and potential brides to be exhibited stark naked to prospective bridegrooms.[10]

In subsequent centuries, it was often scientists rather than philosophers who assumed centre stage in ideas of the good society, deploying all their technological knowledge and inventions in the wake of Britain's scientific revolution in the seventeenth century. Seen as the founder of our modern 'scientific method', Francis Bacon exemplified the new and since that time prominent belief that only scientific progress could be the motor for the material abundance necessary to enable better lives for all in society. This he illustrated in what is seen as the first scientific utopia, *The New Atlantis* (1627).

Here, Bacon sketched out the pleasant and pious life that was lived by all on his ideal island, named Bensalem, a place where knowledge alone ruled and scientific advances had eradicated chance, along with scarcity, thereby removing any need for money or commerce. The workings of government were largely dictated by a scientific priesthood, living in the state-sponsored research laboratory Salomon's House, where researchers tirelessly conducted experiments for the betterment of society: 'The End of our Foundation is the knowledge of Causes, and secret motions of things; and the enlarging of the bounds of Human Empire, to the effecting of all things possible.'[11]

It is not merely Bacon's leaden and repetitive prose which suggests some of the dangers of placing scientists at the helm of government. One critique is that Bacon's own vision of a better world, like most subsequent scientific dreams, not only allowed certain forms of knowledge to be kept secret, but also routinely embraced techniques of population control and 'enhancement' to assist the maintenance of overall social happiness.

One keen observer of scientific utopias, the English scholar Patrick Parrinder, among many others, notes that even before the birth of modern science, the possibility of some sort of eugenic improvement had been invoked by all utopian thinkers, including the later, more romantic ones: 'Not only are the ideal societies of the utopian tradition full of handsome and healthy citizens, but both Plato and Thomas More supplement their accounts of political organization with ingenious mechanisms for selective breeding.'[12]

Unsurprisingly, this has fed many fantasies of the dangers of the demonic scientist, whose overweening ambition morphs into menacing horror – whether in the more compassionate image of the grotesque monster in Mary Shelley's *Frankenstein: The Modern Prometheus* (1818) or later in H. G. Wells's *The Time Machine* (1895), warning against any complacency when imagining that the evolution of mankind would necessarily follow an upward curve.[13]

Struggles for Citizenship

As the utopian vision moved from philosophical to scientific speculation, more popular hopes for social change were also taking shape. Rather than proposing new forms of rule by the few, these new dreamers of a better future placed their hopes in reimagining the involvement of the majority: the people. Modern notions of citizenship are associated above all with the impact of the French Revolution of 1789. The resulting National Assembly passed the Declaration of the Rights of Man and of the Citizen within its first few months, turning France into a modern, secular society, officially devoid of all forms of religious or ethnic discrimination. The Republic was proclaimed in 1792, with the Paris Commune further radicalized as the Jacobins took over the daily running of the city from central government, culminating in the Reign of Terror under the leadership of Maximilien Robespierre.[14]

Visiting Paris in the early years of the revolution, Mary Wollstonecraft had been inspired to write *A Vindication of the Rights of Woman* (1792). Her text at the time, and for quite some time after, was almost completely ignored in comparison with Thomas Paine's *Rights of Man* (1791). With just a few exceptions, most radicals then had only ridicule for Wollstonecraft's 'unfeminine', 'unsexed', insistence that *if* it was acceptable to assert the rights of man, 'respecting the rights and duties of woman seem to flow naturally from these simple principles'.[15] However, for Paine as for so many radical men of his day (and as some see it still in ours), radicalism 'was a staunchly masculine affair', an endless celebration of the 'political virility' of the ordinary man.[16] This made Wollstonecraft's now very ordinary feminist desire appear, in her day, the most whimsical of utopian yearnings, as when she wrote: 'A wild wish has flown from my heart to my head, and I will not stifle it ... I do earnestly wish to see the distinction of sex confounded in society, unless where love animates the behaviour.'[17]

It would take well over a hundred years for women to be formally recognized as equal citizens, with the right to vote. However, there have been many studies of the far-reaching legacies of the uprisings in France in 1789. As one of its official historians, Rogers Brubaker, argues, the French Revolution is generally seen as the turning point for the invention of the modern nation state, and the corresponding rights and responsibilities of national citizenship.

It was a bourgeois, democratic, national revolution that helped to build and strengthen the structures of the state as against the absolute power of the monarchy and feudal privileges of the aristocracy and the Catholic Church. Although it did not ensure any stable system of government for quite some time, the revolution had set out the rights of citizens as equals before the law, along with the legal right to private property.[18] Many at the time, such as the classic English conservative Edmund Burke, would famously condemn the revolution as a mistake, leading inevitably to violence. The French scholar Gustave Le Bon, claimed in his classic *The Crowd: A Study of the Popular Mind* (1895) that it epitomized the irrationality and viciousness of the crowd, stressing the dangers of any universal principles of human rights upon which the revolution was founded.[19] Nonetheless, however embattled the route, the revolution was carried out in the name of democracy and the rights of citizens, thereby spreading the message to the world that the people are, or ought to be, sovereign.

The socialist movement that emerged in the early nineteenth

century thus made the humanist ideal of universal emancipation its baseline, imagining communities resting upon principles of equality, soon including sexual equality. Interestingly, as one of the best known of these early socialist thinkers, Charles Fourier, wrote in 1808: 'As a general proposition: *Social changes and changes of historical period are brought about as a result of the progress of women towards liberty; and the decline of social orders is brought about as a result of the diminution of the liberty of women.*'[20] Fourier, like his French compatriots Henri de Saint-Simon and Étienne Cabet, as well as the Welsh Robert Owen, were all socialist visionaries who wanted to see fairness and cooperation between all classes, within self-supporting communities. Their ideals appealed to thousands of men and women in the early decades of the century, promoting programmes to enrich and transform personal and cultural life, hoping through education and example to remodel destructive views and institutions.

Visionaries Versus Revolutionaries

It was Robert Owen who in his late twenties was able to put his vision into practice when he came to manage and then part-own a huge cotton mill in New Lanark, near Glasgow, in 1800. He created a commercially successful model factory, with its own welfare and education programmes, including housing, healthcare and free schooling for all its workers. With states-men and businessmen visiting from around the world, Owen soon became one of the most respected industrial philanthro-pists across Europe.

However, Owen had grander visions, and by 1820 was aiming to relieve human misery overall through the replacement of capitalist enterprises by extensive communities of mutual cooperation and shared possession, where 'wealth and wisdom would be universal', once all 'were treated, trained, educated, employed, and placed, in accordance with the most plain dictates of common sense'.[21]

Seeing existing human character and actions as formed through controlling institutions, such as religion, private property and the patriarchal marriage system, Owen believed that a greater generosity of the human spirit was always possible once people's circumstances were altered. His new communist views were in line with those expressed by other British radicals of the day, including his close friends and supporters William Thomson and Anna Wheeler, as well as William Godwin (to whom Wollstonecraft was briefly married, before her sudden death at forty-two following the birth of her second child, the future Mary Shelley).

Barbara Taylor's *Eve and the New Jerusalem* (1983) provides the most compelling account of the significance of Robert Owen, and those who followed his lead. She assesses the success and failures of the Owenite movement that thrived for several decades, with its call for intensive social education to promote a New Moral World built around classless, cooperative communities, before its collapse in 1845. As Taylor argues, the movement was an early version of socialist feminism, one far broader than the Marxism that very soon replaced it, in encompassing all forms of social oppression, divisions and antagonisms within and alongside institutions of class.

This was evident in the Owenite commitment to egalitarian 'marriages', collectivized family life, greater sexual freedom and communalized housework performed according to rotas, assisted by the very latest technology available. Such practices were designed to enable women's equality and full engagement in society overall, otherwise, as William Thompson wrote, the 'absolute despotism' of family life spread among men 'the contagion of selfishness and the love of domination through all human transactions ... This real obstacle must be removed before any real advance can be made to human happiness'. And this is why it would be Eve who would usher in the New Jerusalem. Illustratively, Taylor records the words of one Owenite feminist in 1839:

> Whatever affects the condition of one sex, must, I conceive, affect the condition of the other. But a woman has been the slave of a slave ... What is the result of [this]? ... To create, by such arrangements, individual interest, till brothers and sisters, husbands and wives, look on each other with jealousy ... to set up one half of the poor people against the other half, to subdue them and make them quiet... But ... I perceive now that through the circulation of truth we are progressing towards the mansion of happiness, which, when gained, will ... give emancipation to every human being from one end of the earth to the other ... my tears flow when I compare this scene of confusion and opposition to that tranquil state of existence.[22]

Owenites, far more than Owen himself, may have firmly promoted the idea that only women's equality could usher in a better world, but spreading that message was difficult in a world that was elsewhere ever more doggedly affirming the bourgeois ideal of two separate spheres: the necessity for a muscular, competitive manhood soothed by the sentimental haven of womanhood. In a paradox that has troubled feminism ever since, Owenites were caught between the need to minimize sexual difference and the desire to reassert it as a civilizing force in women's favour.

The former was a necessity in order to claim equality and social engagement, but the countervailing view, more in line with the sentiments of the day, upheld the opposite, insisting upon women's difference. In fact, the collectivized domestic arrangements in Owenite communities were still performed by women, thereby altering rather than abolishing the domestic division of labour. Additionally, exploring another familiar trajectory today, Taylor notes that although women were welcomed into all the assemblies of the Owenite movement, and were in short bursts often militant and vociferous in raising community grievances, the 'iron hand' of male prejudice alongside women's more habitual diffidence kept men firmly at the centre of its power structure.[23] In the end, despite widespread interest in Owen's achievements as a philanthropic employer, he failed in his grander vision of convincing British politicians of the need for change.

Nevertheless, Owen's followers, many of them skilled tradesmen, formed a national network of cooperative trading and manufacturing associations, affirming his aspirations for a general union of the working classes in the short-lived Grand National Consolidated Trades Union, in 1834. Taylor points out that this was not simply an incredible utopian fantasy, when at the time the capitalist system could perhaps still be seen as a transitory and fragile one: a peaceful transition to a classless society was seen as possible given the 'actual balance of class forces in trades like tailoring, where workers were not yet fully subject to capitalist command, and found in their own skills and self-organization the basis for an alternative economic system'.[24]

However, intensified persecution of these early trade union-ists by both employers and government culminated in the trial and transportation to Australia of six Dorchester workers, the Tolpuddle Martyrs, in 1834, for taking the union oath and refus-ing to work for less than ten shillings a week. That first grand alliance of workers was thus quickly destroyed. It was suc-ceeded by the even more imposing Association of All Classes and All Nations (AACAN), which resulted in a decade of active organizational work, peaking between 1839 and 1842, with the Owenites in AACAN referred to as members of the Rational Society, and later simply as the Socialists.

In 1848 the philosopher John Stuart Mill argued that the Owenites should be gratefully remembered by all future gen-erations for their support of comprehensive equal rights for women, at a time 'when most Britons were hostile or indifferent to women's plight'.[25] Yet, just as accounts of the legacies of the French Revolution did not recall Wollstonecraft's work, so too was the legacy of the Owenites lost. As Taylor notes, it was the feminist aspirations of Owenism that were quickly forgot-ten, not just by academic historians but also in the collective memory of the left itself.[26]

Furthermore, Marxist orthodoxy was soon viewing Owen, Fourier, Saint-Simon and other socialist forerunners as unsci-entific and utopian in their reliance upon the use of skills, education and example in order to change hearts and minds. This was despite Engels, as well as Marx, applauding the 'stu-pendously grand thoughts' of these early socialists. However, without prioritizing the revolutionary role of the proletariat, Engels argued: 'These new social systems were foredoomed as Utopian; the more completely they were worked out in detail, the more they could not avoid drifting off into pure phantasies'.[27]

We might agree with Marx and Engel's assessment in *The Communist Manifesto* (1848) that the early socialist movements were indeed doomed by a strategic failure to make a correct, in their view 'scientific', assessment of the historical balance of class forces. However, it hardly follows that earlier socialists were wrong to oppose women's subordination and all other forms of social hierarchy.

Nor did Marx or Engels offer any compelling argument in defence of their claim that sketching out ideas for better futures in and of itself contributed to earlier failures to overthrow the ever-tightening grip of capitalist modes of production. On the contrary, the disdain of subsequent Marxist and labour movements for outlining any vision of a post-capitalist future seems all the more unwise when both Marx and Engels had mentioned that 'in attacking every principle of existing society', the earlier socialists provided 'the most valuable materials for the enlightenment of the working class'.[28]

Signing off on her reflections, Taylor concludes: 'From the Owenites onward, then, it would seem that what has counted as utopian answers has depended on who has been raising the questions'.[29] There were two reasons for the defeat of women's struggle for independence from patriarchal control. Firstly, for Marxists and non-Marxists alike, once political attention focused exclusively on the overriding contest between capital and labour, it sidelined working women. This was partly because women were rightly seen as a threat to men's status and bargaining power, even if this was precisely because their subordinate status made them – along with children – more exploitable in the rapidly expanding factory system.

The factory system was fast replacing skilled craftsmen by breaking down the labour process, thereby enabling workshops to employ low-skilled or unskilled labourers. Thus, although sympathetic to women, and observing the beatings and frequent inhumanity that husbands inflicted upon spouses (who at the time could still be taken to market and auctioned to the highest bidder), Engels suggested that the wage-earning wife 'unsexes the man and takes from the woman all womanliness', a condition that 'degrades ... Humanity'.[30] Secondly, the definition of womanliness in terms of home-based dependency was itself a product of the cultural triumph of the increasingly hegemonic male middle class. In their outlook, the notion of the domestic space as women's separate sphere was the bedrock of social stability, with any woman fighting for her independence seen as possessing traits that were as unnatural as they were undesirable.[31]

As we have seen, after the 1850s, not only women's dreams of emancipation, but all serious and sustained reflection on the institutions or ethos of any future ideal society were discouraged, not to emerge properly again until the close of the century. While Marx, Engels and working-class movements of the time, including the Chartists in Britain, were seeking political reform, they did so by emphasizing the defects and horrors of capitalism, seeing no need to speculate on what might replace it. Nevertheless, living in the present while looking to the future as a political strategy came back with a vengeance in the later nineteenth century, with the outbreak of the second insurrectionary Paris Commune in 1871.

The commune faced violent state retaliation, with the massive slaughter of communards within the year, but it nevertheless impacted the writings of subsequent radicals and idealists in its wake, whether revolutionary or social democratic.[32] Revisiting the actual words of the communards in her recent book, *Communal Luxury: The Political Imaginary of the Paris Commune* (2015), the American scholar of French culture and literature Kristin Ross demonstrates that much of the elaboration and critique of subsequent visions of emancipatory movements stem from contrasting understandings of the lessons of that second Paris Commune, including the highly contrasting trajectories of anarcho-communism, Marxism-Leninism and social democracy.

As Ross reports, the imaginative vision inspiring this Paris Commune was reducible neither to that of a national middle class nor to that of a state-managed collectivism, since the commune was simultaneously both smaller and more expansive in scope, operating 'on the preferred scale of the local autonomous unit within an international horizon'. In one of many illustrations, she quotes a participant recalling many years later: 'Everywhere the word "commune" was understood in the largest sense, as referring to new humanity, made up of free and equal companions, oblivious to the existence of old boundaries, helping each other in peace from one end of the world to the other'.[33]

On the one hand, it was this vision that inspired the political activity of a new group of utopian thinkers, all appalled by the brutal slaughter of the Paris communards in 1871. This included Peter Kropotkin, William Morris and Edward Carpenter, encouraging their calls for establishing radical communities based upon egalitarian principles which, although they could not survive as isolated entities, might spread to form federations of cooperation and alliance between neighbourhoods, gradually creating a global solidarity. In Kropotkin's words: 'For us, "Commune" no longer means a territorial agglomeration; it is rather a generic name, a synonym for the grouping of equals which knows neither frontiers nor walls'.[34]

On the other hand, the influential Marxist trajectory rejected any such projects or visions as undemocratic, unsustainable and unnecessary, since they denied the freedom of people in the future to decide for themselves. Moreover, speculating on the future was unnecessary, they argued, for when the time came to implement a socialist solution, it would simply emerge from the scientific unfolding of the historical process.[35]

Soon, any such utopic visions or practices would be rejected as inappropriate within the dominant strand of revolutionary Marxism that emerged in the early twentieth century, where the main agenda became (and for many remains) that of building the revolutionary party for the overthrow of capitalism. Imbibing the lessons of Lenin and the building of the Bolshevik Party, the disciplined Marxist revolutionary to this day would approve of the courage of the Bavarian revolutionary communist Eugen Levine announcing before he was shot in 1919: 'We Communists are all dead men on leave'.[36] Such party cadres obviously have neither time nor reason to be planning futures, let alone helping with the childcare.

In contrast, we could argue, and I would agree, that to work for change at all we need to have designs on the future, that is, we need sound reasons to believe that after the collapse of bourgeois society the elements set free really would, as Marx assumed, have altogether different and better outcomes.[37] As the ex-Marxist philosopher, the late Gerry Cohen, remarked tartly in hindsight after the horrors of Stalinism: 'The history of socialist failures shows that socialists do need to write recipes … Unless we write recipes for future kitchens, there's no reason to think we'll get food we like'.[38]

One of Cohen's former students agrees. The British political theorist David Leopold carefully outlines and then rejects all the Marxist arguments against future planning, concluding that even though utopian visions cannot be wholly accurate, and their realization might prove problematic, such aspirations still serve many functions.[39] Importantly, these ideas of the future encourage us in the present to think through goals that make potential change more vivid and worth fighting for, or – as is always necessary – fighting over and with.

Although dystopian scenarios came to dominate as the twentieth century progressed, it began first by contrasting utopian dreams of moving beyond the cruelties and privation of early capitalism, with its inevitable class struggle and imperial rivalry.

In the USA, Edward Bellamy published his bestselling science fiction novel *Looking Backwards: 2000–1887 AD* (1880), in which he imagined the world we now live in, post 2000, as one in which the state had gained full control of the reins of technological growth to become a socialist utopia (although knowing the disparagement of that term in his country, Bellamy substituted the term 'nationalist' for 'socialist'). In this vision, the USA had thus moved in exactly the *opposite* direction to the one it was in fact to pursue.

In the fictional year 2000, the conflict between labour and capitalism had been solved, because the corporations – having expanded to control almost all of the economy – had been nationalized by the state. With the state ownership of industry, it could now make huge improvements in the context and conditions of all workers, insisting that every young adult do their share of necessary labour (after being provided with appropriate jobs), while ensuring that the working day was shortened. There would still be significant divisions of labour based on people's differing skills and capacities, but those doing less pleasant, more menial or dangerous jobs would work the shortest hours. Everyone would retire to pursue their own interests by the age of forty-five. Since production was publicly owned, it could be equally distributed to all citizens, with the provision of public kitchens to ensure food for all as well as numerous other collective spaces, enriched by the latest technology and design. Thus, when Bellamy compared his imagined future to the maladies of the late nineteenth century, he could explain to readers: 'The equal wealth and equal opportunities of culture which all persons now enjoy have simply made us all members of one class, which corresponds to the most fortunate class with you'.[40]

Other forms of scientific technological vision (sometimes directly drawing upon Bellamy) fed into the grander municipal, architectural and social housing projects of the late nineteenth and early twentieth centuries in both the USA and the UK. For instance, Bellamy's novel fuelled the spirit of Ebenezer Howard's creation of the garden cities movement in parts of England, resulting in the design of Letchworth (1903) and Welwyn Garden City (1920), both in Hertfordshire, within easy distance of London and built to encourage people to live in greater harmony with both the city and the countryside.

Liberating Desire

Clearly, Bellamy's utopian vision relied upon the strengthening of state controls over work and environment, as did the diverse types of municipal planning and public housing his vision helped to encourage. On the grandest scale of all, the Bolshevik Revolution in 1917 ushered in complete state, or rather party, control over all planning, resources and welfare, in what would prove to be Lenin's founding delusion of initiating a form of freedom where the state itself would eventually wither away. Thus, in *The State and Revolution* (1917) Lenin justified the revolutionary proletarian party taking full control over the bourgeois state in order to initiate a socialist economic system, one that would eventually allow workers to take direct control over the means of production, instituting the equality of labour and wages.[41]

But even as the role of the state, or the crushing of it, was paramount in one radical tradition, alternative utopian visions moved in quite the opposite direction. The best known and most influential was William Morris's attempt to combine the aesthetics of Romanticism with his journey towards Marxism by using the possibilities of skilled labour in the fashioning of a better world. Morris was as disgusted as Bellamy and the other radicals of his time with the squalor, disease and miseries of late nineteenth-century urban industrialism, but he was also alarmed by the mechanistic work processes presented in Bellamy's instantly popular *Looking Backwards*, which prompted Morris to write his own utopian novel, *News from Nowhere; or, An Epoch of Rest* (1890).

In *News from Nowhere*, its narrator, William Guest, falls asleep and dreams of a society of highly skilled and creative craftsmen who enjoy their labour, since 'happiness without happy daily work is impossible'.[42] In Guest's dream, cities have turned green again, within communities containing numerous public gardens, markets and communal meeting places, and possibilities for facilitating federation between different communities.

Morris published *Nowhere* in instalments in the radical magazine he had founded five years earlier, *Commonweal*, the journal of the Socialist League, committed to principles of

'Revolutionary International Socialism'. The story's episodic appearance highlighted the provisional nature of any such dream, beginning in its first instalment with Guest returning dejectedly from a socialist meeting and, before falling asleep, reflecting on what might be the socialist future: 'If I could but see a day of it ... If I could but see it!' In echo, Morris concludes his final episode with Guest thinking, 'If others can see it as I have seen it, then it may be called a vision rather than a dream'.[43]

It was the maverick Marxist historian E. P. Thompson, however, who did most to put Morris back on left agendas in more recent times. He first published his warm appreciation of Morris while still in the Communist Party in 1955 (he would leave after Russia's invasion of Hungary the next year), and used Morris to vindicate his own plea for a new alliance between socialism and utopianism. In a powerful postscript to the second edition of *William Morris: Romantic to Revolutionary* (1976), Thompson introduced the early work of the then-untranslated French philosopher Miguel Abensour to emphasize the critical and continuing significance of Morris. Abensour argued that Morris's utopianism was deliberately not presenting any concrete blueprint for the future. It was Abensour who coined the memorable phrase 'the education of desire' to suggest instead that what Morris offered was to liberate desire to question all existing values.

In Thompson's translation of Abensour, Morris aspired to 'teach desire to desire, to desire better, to desire more, and above all to desire in a different way'.[44] Thompson repeated Morris's warning that if workers were educated only to heed the contradictions and destructiveness of capitalism, then, apart from their engagement in 'the bitter praxis of class struggle', they were always likely to fall back on the ruling ideas of the moment. It is the lack of any interest in discussing the future in the later Marxist tradition, Thompson argued persuasively, that resulted in the significant failings of the Marxist imagination itself:

> Its lack of a moral self-consciousness or even a vocabulary of desire, its inability to project any images of the future, or even its tendency to fall back in lieu of these upon the Utilitarian's earthly paradise – the maximization of economic growth.[45]

Yet Morris was far from alone in trying to broaden socialist visions of the future as the twentieth century dawned. This was also the time when sexual radicals such as Magnus Hirschfeld in Germany and Havelock Ellis in London were battling with the increasing sexual puritanism of their day. As we have seen, Edward Carpenter, in particular, who would later be known as the 'sexy sage of Sheffield', was tirelessly promoting his vision of an alternative culture and way of life. Carpenter's dream of a more egalitarian world, where people lived simply and closer to nature and other animals, was bonded securely to ideas of enlarging the sphere of love, sexual freedom and women's emancipation, as he put into practice in his own open and welcoming living arrangements at Millthorpe, and as were evident in his extensive friendships, lectures and writing.

Thus, in *Love's Coming of* Age (1906), Carpenter emphasized the significance of sex education, sexual tolerance and women's rights, alongside the need for a communist society to liberate all from daily drudgery.[46] In his long and vivid autobiography, *My Days and Dreams* (begun in 1890, but not published until 1916), Carpenter outlined his thoughts and actions regarding the alternative, inclusive culture he cherished, while detailing all that he loathed in the expanding commercialism and ugliness of his day. He denounced the widespread contempt for manual labour, the hypocrisies of religion, the near ubiquitous disdain for the pleasures of the body, and the cruel constraints imposed on women. In his view, changing any one of these conditions, if 'worked out practically', would have significant consequences on existing institutions, beginning a revolution in human life deeper and more far-reaching than any which we know of belonging to historical times.[47]

As Sheila Rowbotham notes, Carpenter's emphasis on the life of desire angered many of his male socialist contemporaries. The radical designer and craftsman Charles Ashbee declared such interests a 'red-herring trailed in the path of democracy', and George Orwell, in thrall to his ideal of working-class virility, disdained Carpenter and all who followed in his radically humanitarian footsteps.[48] Rowbotham's conclusion, in 2008, was not unlike Thompson's on Morris a generation earlier:

Carpenter's tussles over how to create a new culture within the old without falling into prescription, how to establish collectivities which allow space for the personal and the spiritual aspirations of individuals are of contemporary not just historical interest ... Carpenter lived long enough to observe how hard it was to ensure that grassroots pressure remained linked with the new institutional structures of labour or indeed of humanitarian internationalism. He developed a pragmatic approach to strategies for change, proposing that accepting there could be differing ways of journeying to a broadly similar destination would save a great deal of fruitless argument about *how* to bring about the change.[49]

Feminist Dreamers

It was also Rowbotham, influenced as a student by dissident Marxists of the 1960s and especially by her older friend E. P. Thompson, who most assiduously sought out the feminist visionaries of Morris's and Carpenter's day, those diverse women whose footprints were so easily erased. Continuing what the lost voices of Wollstonecraft and Owenite feminists had begun, in her book *Dreamers of a New Day* Rowbotham resurrects women who, from the 1880s up to the First World War, challenged all existing assumptions around sex and gender. This was the era of first-wave feminism, with its renowned struggle for female enfranchisement. It was headed in the UK by the Pankhurst family, and is still recalled mainly through the heroism of its affluent spokeswomen, such as Lady Emmeline Pethick-Lawrence, who had started the publication *Votes for Women* with her husband in 1907, and remained an active feminist and prominent peace activist throughout her life.

However, the women's suffrage movement stirred all classes of women, globally, during a period of rapid economic change that generated workplace miseries and rising poverty. Some women entered the Fabian movement (later part of the Labour Party, seeking reform by peaceful means), such as the former anarchist Charlotte Wilson or the very respectable Beatrice Webb. Others were militant trade union feminists, including the Lancashire-based labour activists Ada Neil Chew and Selina Cooper. In 1894, at a time of workers campaigning for the eight-hour day, Chew wrote to her local paper to proclaim that factory women needed time to read and enjoy nature: 'We cannot be said to "live" – we merely exist ... A living wage! Ours is a lingering dying wage.'[50]

The working-class activists who made their mark on trade union battles in the mills and elsewhere left fewer traces than their more affluent socialist feminist sisters, including Olive Schreiner, Edith Ellis (married to Havelock Ellis), Hannah Mitchell and Eleanor Marx. Edith Ellis would later recall the intense excitement she and her friends felt viewing Ibsen's play *A Doll's House* in 1889, announcing that they had all become 'breathless with excitement' while thinking optimistically about what the new century might bring: 'We were restive and impetuous and almost savage in our arguments. This was either the end of the world or the beginning of a new world for women.'[51]

If, however, the twentieth century brought neither the end of the world nor a completely new day for women, Rowbotham is able to show that women over a century ago were – for a while – able to broaden their vision of women's emancipation from the struggle for the vote into dreams of comprehensive social transformations in both the political and the economic sphere, as well as in their domestic and sexual lives. It is perhaps why Leon Trotsky would conclude, in 1924, 'In order to change the conditions of life we must learn to see through the eyes of women', though there was scant sign of this in most of the Leninist practice of his day or after, including his own.[52]

Rowbotham introduces us to the Scottish journalist and activist Jane Hume Clapperton, whose thoughts, in *Visions of the Future* (1904), on collectivist housing were linked to plans for the expansion of municipal socialism. In the communal buildings of her design, one wing could provide shared kitchens, nurseries and teaching facilities, another area was for music and other aesthetic pleasures, while elsewhere there would be space for private living quarters. Clapperton knew that conflicts might arise, but remained optimistic that such arrangements would help eliminate family squabbles, believing that both men's and women's 'spontaneous impulses are towards an essentially social life'.[53]

However, others such as the former militant suffragette and anarcho-feminist Dora Marsden decided that any new world for women would need to provide them with their own alternative space. In this spirit, together with Mary Gawthorpe, she established the relatively short-lived feminist journal *The Freewoman* in 1911. Over half a century before women would return to the topic, and expressing the views of other keen sex radicals and birth control campaigners of the day, such as Stella Browne, *The Freewoman* deplored the absence of even a language to encompass women's desire and sexual experiences, apart from one of 'comfort and protection'. Though seen as notorious by other feminists at the time, including the suffragist Millicent Fawcett, *The Freewoman* would open a space for advocating notions of free love, and discussing lesbianism and male homosexuality, alongside criticisms of marriage and alternative approaches to childcare, with Ada Neil Chew, Rebecca West, H. G. Wells and Carpenter, among others, contributing articles.[54]

These ideas on women's personal lives and sexuality circulated alongside those of more mainstream political reformers, including Margaret McMillan and Eleanor Rathbone, who campaigned around education policy and women's formal rights overall. Rathbone argued for a system of family allowances to be paid directly to women from 1918 onwards. It was a campaign that would only re-emerge and meet with full success, with benefits being paid directly to mothers, during the early years of second-wave feminism, almost sixty years later – a victory now under threat.

Meanwhile, ideas were exchanged between women across the Atlantic. Despite very limited means for travel, even militant working-class activists in Britain became aware of the activities of their American sisters. These included the struggles against racial prejudice launched by early black civil rights and suffragist activists, such as the black activists Maggie Lena Walker or the writer Anna Julia Cooper, who published *A View from the South* in 1892 about the penniless, 'pinched, and down-trodden' lives of black women. Race issues also dominated the powerful oratory of Ida B. Wells, campaigning against lynching and visiting Britain for a lecture tour in 1893.[55]

As in the UK, it was a time of fierce labour battles in the USA, producing working-class rebels such as Lizzie Holmes (often, as she had been, uprooted from rural homes) who joined and soon helped organize destitute garment workers in Chicago in 1886. When the women took to the streets to demand an eight-hour day, *The Chicago Tribune* reported that, despite their 'worn faces and threadbare clothing', they 'shouted and sang and laughed in a whirlwind of exuberance'.[56] After a later rally, however, with hundreds of workers injured or killed by brutal police violence, Lizzie Holmes became a life-long anarchist, along with other influential women militants, most prominently the passionate Russian Jewish émigrée Emma Goldman, who became, and remains, one of the key voices of anarchist philosophy and activism as well as feminism.[57] Goldman would soon add calls for birth control and women's suffrage to her public speeches in support of workers' and immigrant rights.[58]

The distinct character of women's defiance remained; a subsequent three-month strike for higher wages and decent working conditions occurred in the Lawrence Textile Factory in Massachusetts in 1912. That strike became iconic for the banners carried by what is thought to be its largely immigrant female activists: 'We want bread, but we want roses, too!' Although those banners were apocryphal, this has rightly done nothing to undermine their metaphorical existence and lasting resonance for feminists ever since.

Another lingering utopian echo from those years is the phrase attributed to Emma Goldman: 'If there is no dancing at the revolution, I'm not coming.' In the same way, these precise words were not uttered by Goldman, although we can trace their source, which is certainly worth revisiting in the context of still-ongoing disputes between goal-oriented revolutionaries and utopians determined to live their desired futures in the present, whatever the obstacles. In her autobiography, *Living My Life* (1931), Goldman angrily rejected the criticism she reported receiving from a comrade who thought her energetic dancing both frivolous and harmful to 'the Cause', by responding: 'I did not believe that a Cause which stood for a beautiful ideal, for anarchism, for release and freedom from convention and prejudice, should demand the denial of life and joy ... I want freedom, the right to self-expression, everybody's right to beautiful, radiant things ... I would live it in spite of the whole world – prisons, persecution, everything ... I would live my beautiful ideal'.[59]

From the American middle class, and similarly utopian in spirit, the pioneering feminist Charlotte Perkins Gilman for a while gained a significant international audience for her powerful short story, *The Yellow Wallpaper* (1892), portraying a wife's isolation and mental collapse after childbearing. Gilman had drawn upon her own breakdown and the coercive 'rest cure' she endured following the birth of her daughter. Although most of Gilman's writing went out of print following her death in 1935, this text became a bestseller when reissued by the Feminist Press in 1973.[60] However, in her lifetime Gilman wrote and lectured widely on a whole range of political issues, including race relations, birth control and the need for economic reform.[61] Inspired by Bellamy's condemnation of market capitalism, Gilman published her own utopic fiction *Herland* (1915), illustrating a world of women, in which they would be able to combine independent living with the joys of motherhood.[62] Gilman worked with many other radical women, including her friends Helen Campbell and Jane Addams, developing what they called 'household science' or 'home-industry', calling for public provision for housing that would enable forms of cooperative living and home-craft, in the form of large apartments with swimming pools, tennis courts and dance halls. These women admired the free-flowing dress and elegant movements associated with the avant-garde American dancer Isadora Duncan, ideas discussed in Gilman's feminist magazine *The Forerunner*, started in 1909, with an emphasis on women and the economy.[63]

Those earlier dreamers, men but above all women, may themselves have died frustrated and forgotten, their differing utopian yearnings submerged by the Depression of the 1930s, yet it was their legacies that eventually helped turn the utopic yearnings of one day into the routine provisions of another. This would include the subsequent welfare provisions, maternity and birth control centres, the opening of nurseries, as well as the building of garden cities, council houses and provisions for the homeless – not to mention the advances brought, too, by indoor lighting, bathrooms, toilets and heating. Of course, once rendered ordinary, these changes lose much of their radical edge, or even value, as many of these critical collective gains are now under serious threat.

Indeed, ironically, with the triumph of consumer capitalism from the 1960s, all the passionate debates about collective
facilities lessening household chores, and the differing ideas for
improving women's lot, were not only forgotten but turned
upside down. The hidden persuaders of advertising targeted
women, as housewives, as solely responsible for creating
picture-perfect homes and cosseted, cheerful children. Beneath
this iconography was the submerged reality of the unhappy,
resentful housewife, despite and also because of all her domestic acquisitions, which Betty Friedan exposed in *The Feminine
Mystique* (1963). Many have since described that book as the
fuse that relit (the second wave of) feminism at the close of
the '60s. It refreshed many of those utopian yearnings of yesterday, once more puzzling over the ties between the personal
and the political, private and public life, home and work, submission and domination, while also addressing issues of class,
race, sexuality, citizenship, consumption, the environment and
much more.

What is certain is that it would be hard to dispute
Rowbotham's observations, concluding *Dreamers of a New Day*,
that in women's earlier and still ongoing battles to translate
their private experiences and desires into the public sphere of
politics, 'there is no automatic accretion of improvement', but
the need to reinvent utopia in every era.[64]

7

Living Differently

It is sometimes said that the twentieth century began with utopian dreaming and ended with nostalgia, as those alternative futures once envisioned seemed by then almost entirely discredited. However, it was never quite so straightforward. The challenge to envisage how to live differently, in ways that seem better than the present, never entirely disappears.

The most prominent American utopian studies scholar, Lyman Tower Sargent, notes that dystopian scenarios increasingly dominated the speculative literary form as the twentieth century progressed. In the UK, the equally eminent utopian studies scholar Ruth Levitas concurs, pointing out, for instance, that as sociology became institutionalized in the academy, it became 'consistently hostile' to any utopian content.[1]

Utopia Scorned and Recuperated

What stands out in speculative fantasies of the future arising towards the end of the twentieth century are their darkly dystopic leanings, whether in books, cinema, comics or elsewhere. The best known would include the mass surveillance depicted in the Russian author Yevgeny Zamyatin's satirical novel *We* (1921).

Set in the future, it describes a scientifically managed totalitarian state, known as One State, governed by logic and reason, where people live in glass buildings, march in step, and are known by their numbers.[2] England's Aldous Huxley called his dystopic science fiction *Brave New World* (1932), where again all individuality has been conditioned out in the pursuit of happiness. Bleaker still was George Orwell's terrifyingly totalitarian *1984* (1945): 'If you want a picture of the future,' Orwell wrote in 1984, 'imagine a boot stamping on a human face – forever.'[3]

These imaginings serve primarily as warnings against futures that are often read, as with Zamyatin and Orwell, as condemnations of Soviet society. The happiness expressed in Huxley's 'utopic' universe depicts a deformed or sinister version of the route where all utopias end up, as totalitarian regimes, in which free will is crushed. As the Marxist political scientist Bertell Ollman later noted: 'From a means of winning people over to the ideal of socialism, the utopian novel had become one of the most effective means of frightening people off it.'[4]

Post-1945, public intellectuals for the most part broadcast the view that democracy and utopic thinking were opposed, the latter declared both impossible and dangerous. The influential émigré and British philosopher of science Karl Popper argued in his classic essay 'Utopia and Violence' (1947) that while 'Utopia' may look desirable, all too desirable, it was in practice a 'dangerous and pernicious' idea, one that is 'self-defeating' and 'leads to violence'. There is no way of deciding rationally between competing utopian ideals, he suggested, since we cannot (contra Marxism) scientifically predict the future, which means our statements are not open to falsification and hence fail his test for any sort of reliability.[5]

Indeed, accusations of 'totalitarian' thinking were the chief weapon of the Cold War, used by Western propaganda to see off any talk of communism. In the USA it was employed to undermine any left or labour movement affiliations, as through the fear and financial ruin inflicted upon hundreds of Americans hauled before Senator McCarthy's House of Un-American Activities Committee in the 1950s – over half of them Jewish Americans.[6]

Nevertheless, suggesting how complicated and volatile moments of renewal can be, this passed into an all-too-brief moment of joyous hope that spanned the sparkling 1960s and, especially among women, continued well into the 1970s, before an even darker mood of imminent catastrophe took over across the political spectrum at the close of the twentieth century. The '60s was the decade in which consumer markets were booming, with profits and wages both rising as social democracies consolidated their welfare systems, in determined repudiation of any need for workers' revolution. The rise in oil prices and subsequent recession, which would pave the way for ideological and economic backlash from the right, determined to overturn social democratic reforms and union power, had yet to occur.

In the meantime, the twenty years of popular protest movements stretched from the rise of the New Left in 1956 to the beginning of the decline of such movements in 1976. This period encompassed student and workers' occupations and confrontations, many of them determined to disrupt the prevailing order of just about everything, with joyful moments of political engagement very much to the fore.

The eyes of the world would be riveted on the three weeks of student and workers' uprisings in France in May 1968. Yet there were other struggles that actually lasted far longer, as in Italy, where the combined labour, student and community struggles in Trento, Turin and Milan continued for eight years, making Italy's unionized workforce the best protected and most democratically organized in Europe.[7] Above all, the spirit of the '60s rejected the authoritarianism, cultural conformity and extreme moderation of the post-war years, including that found within the Old Left, whether communist or social democratic.

The decades of restraint and respectability were replaced by a defiant commitment to direct action and participatory democracy, with the rise of collective resistance. It all fed into the vivid counter-culture of 'free love', music and play, producing its own alternative magazines, fashion, music, clubs, experimental theatre and living spaces, seeking a world dedicated to peace, the elimination of poverty, and all forms of discrimination. The most radical fantasists of May '68 were recycling a slogan coined by the libertarian French Situationists: 'Be realistic – demand the impossible!'[8]

Though less enthralled with demanding the impossible, feminists in the women's liberation movement resonated with another '68 slogan, 'Form Dream Committees', as they began imagining anew how to change every aspect of life, whether rethinking the nature of domestic labour and the distribution of work, challenging all existing presumptions around gender, sexuality, intimacy and desire, or more generally striving to envisage differing cultural and economic structures.

Capturing the opening beat of second-wave feminism in the USA, the American poet Adrienne Rich affirmed optimistically that radical women were now ushering in a renaissance that would prove 'far more extraordinary and influential in shifting perspectives than the earlier European Renaissance from theology to humanism'.[9]

Yet, for quite a while, those of us once more identifying as feminist, myself included, were still ignorant about that earlier 'awakening' of women. It took years for us to excavate the buried diversity of proposals others had presented as the twentieth century kicked off. And, despite the intervening changes over the decades, so many of the dilemmas of the past re-emerged, simply because none of them had been solved. These included all the old impasses around women's sexuality and reproductive rights, how to share caring among men, women and the wider community, how to secure equal training and wages for women, and what to do to end men's violence against women, while at the same time fighting for a transformed democratic economic and social world, one attentive to existing differences and discrimination, where unpaid domestic work would be valued as highly as waged work.

As the British economist Sue Himmelweit suggested in *What Is to Be Done About the Family?* (1983), a book I edited: 'We want ... to take the good aspects that we experience of our private lives and spread them around to invade and transform the public arena, at the same time as getting public recognition of the political nature of personal relations ... Visions of a future society have to ... ensure that the production of things does not have more social importance than the production of people.'[10] Grand hopes!

Intentionally utopian, second-wave feminists were at first seen as, and often claimed to be, 'demanding the moon', yet before too long we had collected many victories in placing women's issues onto government, trade union and left agendas.

These agendas, almost always for the very first time, included demands on reproductive rights, domestic violence, sexual harassment, safety in the street, and much more. Our new awakening, like the old, not only produced an upsurge of activism on all fronts, but women's widespread cultural blooming throughout the 1970s.

We might be singing with ironic delight of women's journey from dusting to dust, in the 'Housewife's Lament', or consuming lesbian delights, reading *Rubyfruit Jungle* – 'Oh, I wouldn't say I was gay. I'd just say I was enchanted.' At other times there was celebration of the distinct difference of women's lives in the energy and wonder of black women's writing and theatre, perhaps listening to Ntozake Shange's words in *For Colored Girls Who Have Considered Suicide when the Rainbow Is Enuf*: 'my spirit is too ancient to understand the separation of soul and gender / my love is too delicate to have thrown back on my face'.[11] Many women were creating their own music, theatre, writings and visual displays, either collectively or individually. They were energized by the movement, as well as by the women's publishing houses, poster workshops, alternative community presses, newspapers and theatre groups emerging around the world.

This accompanied experiments in collective living and the establishment of many other spaces for everyday resistance, including communes for shared child-raising, women's centres, squatting advice centres and numerous other collective community spaces, many of which I participated in.[12] Followers of Foucault would call these ventures 'heterotopias' – the production of shared spaces of 'otherness' through the disruption of the usual conventions.[13] These alternative feminist, left adventures were local, yet through networks and campaigns for exchanging experiences they aimed to shift government policies as well.

If usually more cautiously conceived than earlier utopian fantasy, being far from perfect or conflict-free, there was nonetheless some full-blown feminist utopian writing back then as well, fleshing out visions of alternative futures.

Perhaps the best-known and most successful example is Ursula Le Guin's *The Dispossessed* (1974), which she herself described as an 'ambiguous utopia'. In her complex fiction, the world of Anarres, unlike the others in the text she depicts, maintains itself without coercive institutions or governments, as a type of anarcho-syndicalist society. Yet this seemingly admirable society is not without economic hardship. Le Guin further depicts the dangers of stagnation, incipient hierarchies and centralized bureaucracies always threatening to emerge from within in the absence of the constant effort to maintain its socially based, less individualistic revolutionary ideology.[14]

Similarly, Marge Piercy's *Women on the Edge of Time* (1979) presents two parallel stories. The first describes the abusive situation of an impoverished and suffering Latina woman, Connie, incarcerated in a psychiatric ward in New York of the 1970s, who, along with other inmates, is trying to resist the presiding doctor's scientific experiments. The second story grows out of Connie's hallucinations, transported to a different world in the year 2137, where both race and gender oppression have been superseded and technology serves only to benefit the community – though it is a world still threatened by the encroachment of corporations from the outside. In Piercy's utopic vision, the personal and political are interwoven: new forms of polyamorous intimacy emerge in a society where gender differences are no longer so significant, since malebodied people are able to produce milk and three co-mothers raise each child. Perhaps too faultless in conception, Piercy's idyllic space is created precisely to contrast with the experience of the most injured and helpless women in capitalist society, juxtaposing as well the beneficial and oppressive uses of technology, while offering no necessary happy (or despairing) conclusion.

One point about these and other recent feminist utopias is that their authors were writing about potentially better futures, at the very same time as they were trying in their everyday lives to embody at least some of the aspects of the alternative, caring societies they depicted. This is why contemporary utopian theorists, such as Angelika Bammer and Tom Moylan, describe them as 'partial' or 'critical utopias'. 'They reject utopia as a blueprint while preserving it as a dream', Moylan argues, knowing that trying to live differently will always be contingent and diverse, rather than conforming to any one pattern.[15]

Alas, the initial confidence behind feminist activism inevitably diminished in the harsher political climate of the 1980s, when early gains were being followed by significant and continuing defeats for women overall. Our movement fragmented and shrank, then, along with the rest of the activist left, as the political tide turned against any form of redistributive politics.

The rise and rise of inequality from the close of the 1970s impacted especially hard on the women in low-paid (often caring) jobs, while gradually undermining the public resources that might be called upon for assisting those performing unpaid caring work at home. Thus, though more women now had paid jobs and an independent income, feminist dreams of making employment more compatible with home life were all largely negated – our demands for shorter working days and more social resources for all in need of care, along with democratic

194

involvement in its provision, had all ended in defeat. As the working day continues to lengthen and insecurities on all sides deepen, research has comprehensively shown that it is women, globally, who are disproportionately disadvantaged by what have become continuing government cutbacks. Women's individual struggles to maintain essential care and protection for their families and communities in this context often occur at the expense of their own wellbeing.[16]

As I argued in *Making Trouble*, '70s feminists often hoped to live our whole lives in the shared embrace of an inclusive movement, working in solidarity with others to build a fairer world, while resisting both assertive individualism (long associated with 'masculinity', though hardly confined to men) and the depredations of market forces. Yet, even with hopes of changing the world receding in the last decades of the twentieth century, a less confident dissidence often remained, ready to be ignited or shared with younger generations, if and when opportunities arose. The once-optimistic Adrienne Rich, for instance, was now passionately condemning the inequality she saw accelerating since the 1980s, yet her lyrical protest and fierce yearnings for a better world remained as powerful as ever, expressed here a few years before she died:

> Wherever I turn these days, I'm looking, as from the corner of my eye, for a certain kind of poetry whose balance of dread and beauty is equal to the chaotic negations that pursue us. Amid profiteering language, commoditizing of intimate emotions, and public misery, I want poems that embody ... another principle. A complex, dialogic, coherent poetry to dissolve both complacency and despair.[17]

Apocalyptic Scenarios

Shards of hope lived on in most former activists and vision-aries, along with continued agitation for better times, if more fragmented in form. Nevertheless, by the end of the twenti-eth century, apocalyptic scenarios had reappeared from the left and right alike, peaking in the largely politically stagnant 1990s.

It was Fredric Jameson who in the early 1990s wrote the oft-repeated adage, 'Someone once said that it is easier to imagine the end of the world than it is to imagine the end of capitalism.' It is less often recalled that he then added, even more dra-matically: 'We can now revise that and witness the attempt to imagine capitalism by way of imagining the end of the world.'[18] Vividly depicting 'a situation in which the historical imagina-tion is paralysed and cocooned, as though by a predator's sting', Jameson saw the then-reigning intellectual 'postmodern' nihil-ism as an expression that people could no longer see themselves as part of the making of history, or envisage anything other than an endless repetition of the world we now occupy: 'The problem to be solved is that of breaking out of the windless present of the postmodern back into real historical time, and a history made by human beings.'[19]

In the UK, certainly, much of the 1990s did feel stale and stuck. Governments globally were accepting rather than resisting the corporate conquest of state resources, apparently indifferent to the ballooning inequality. As Jameson noted, academic fashion seemed to mirror the same capitalist conceit that all previous grand narratives of change should be jettisoned, leaving us only to mourn, as many did, the radicalism of former times. Ignoring specific local sites of continued activism, such as the ultimately defeated Liverpool dockers' strike of 1993, or the very significant mobilization of gay communities around HIV/AIDS, the often melancholic mood of the left in the 1990s suggested that all political communities and practices of solidarity had been vacated, with no solid social or political resources remaining for resistance.

The feminist anti-nuclear peace camp at Greenham Common was abandoned in 1991, after ten years of occupation. In the mid 1990s, the impressive feminist political theorist Wendy Brown argued in her book *States of Injury* (1995) that 'our historically and culturally configured fears, anxieties, disorientation, and loss of faith about the future' encourage the formation of 'political identities founded upon a sense of personal injury, and the need for protection, rather than generating any more progressive political vision of the future'.[20]

Whether hatched in Hollywood or popular culture generally, especially coming from North America, the dystopic imagination had become ubiquitous in fantasies of the future in the early twenty-first century. Such visions dominate blockbusters such as *The Hunger Games, Divergent, The Maze Runner* or *Robocop*; appeared in bestselling novels, including Cormac McCarthy's *The Road* (2006), Margaret Atwood's trilogy *MaddAddam* (2003–9), Dave Eggers's *The Circle* (2013), Nathaniel Rich's eerily prescient *Odds Against Tomorrow* (2013), Edan Lepucki's *California: A Novel* (2014), or Chang-rae Lee's *Such a Full Sea* (2014). Indeed, reviewing *Such a Full Sea*, Ursula Le Guin noted that over the last thirty years all literary writers, from whatever genre, were now visiting Dystopia and writing similar, rather dull books: nearly always a place where the privileged few live in total luxury, completely sequestered from the impoverished majority who are seen as wild and primitive. Yet in her view such situations were 'too self-contradictory to serve as warning or satire'.[21]

The American writer Adam Sternbergh, having himself 'dipped into these murky waters' in *Shovel Ready*, says more chillingly that 'the biggest problem with imagining dystopia seems to be coming up with some future world that's worse than what's happening right now', pointing to events such as the routine police shooting of unarmed black men in the USA, the Israeli army's onslaughts on Gaza and the orchestrated brutality of ISIS.[22] Sternbergh hopes that we have reached 'peak dystopia' as he throws out the challenge to his fellow writers: 'If we can all conjure so many worlds gone wrong, it shouldn't be beyond our reach to imagine a single world gone right'.[23]

However, recalling Jameson's words, we can see all too easily why these dystopic images remain ubiquitous: their consistent portrayals of a narrow, endlessly privileged few, who live in highly policed and segregated seclusion from the poor, excluded, disdained and fear-provoking masses on the outside – always trying to break in – can indeed be presented as a mirror of how we live now.

We have only to open our eyes to the horrors facing those currently fleeing their homelands to escape the ravages of war or other types of breakdown, nowadays herded into nightmare camps or willing to board flimsy, overcrowded vessels putting their lives at risk. These are the migrants entering what Frances Stonor Saunders aptly calls 'death zones, portals to the underworld, where explanations of identity are foreclosed', adding in her heart-breaking essay 'Where on Earth Are You?': 'I don't understand the mechanisms by which globalization, with all its hype of mobility and the collapse of distance and terrain, has instead delivered a world of barricades and partition, in which entire populations seem to be living – and dying – in a different history from mine.'[24] Migrants fleeing war zones, seeking asylum or simply a better means of survival in the affluent West are indeed living a different history, in a different world, like those seeking entry to Britain and barely surviving in the wastelands of temporary shelters no sooner established than they are bulldozed down, as experienced by those struggling to survive in the Calais Jungle, including many children, travelling alone.

Sadly, I am not at all sure that we have reached peak dystopia, when the fictional imaginings seem to mirror the cruel realities for so many outside the increasingly fortified enclaves of privilege around the world. Neo-liberalism has had one remarkable success, despite all its own contradictions and disasters.[25] Its extraordinary victory has been ideological: it has convinced so many that its version of predatory, corporate capitalism is inescapable; that political resistance is inevitable. Yet in reality, commercialism and market forces, however hegemonic, are never seamless. However, those spaces where alternative economic and social relations prevail are constantly muted out, making it harder to notice their potential for resistance or hope. Although we regularly hear from left theorists that 'commodification has reached into every nook and cranny of modern life', reshaping our consciousness and 'private life', others have questioned its totalizing grip on the present.[26]

Spaces of Resistance

In Britain, the social scientist Colin Williams, for instance, not only questions such pessimism but reveals that even in the metropolitan heartlands of commodification 'there exist large alternative economic spaces of self-provisioning … where the profit motive is absent'.[27] Such non-commercial, even anti-commercial, practices can have symbolic value as sites of resistance to the assumption of inescapable commercialism.

Similarly, the dissident Marxist feminists Katherine Gibson and the late Julie Graham have indicated that market transactions are never completely hegemonic when the overall economy consists of varying types of transactions. This is what feminists have always highlighted in revealing the variety and extent of unpaid care work. Gibson and Graham also mention other alternative economic practices, from gift giving and volunteering to barter and theft, alongside the occupation of public spaces, both for play and for socializing, as well as for nurturing a politics of defiance.[28]

Certainly, searching for spaces of resistance and ways of keeping hope alive is what most contemporary utopian scholars say they are doing. They reject classical understandings of utopia offering blueprints for engineering human happiness, while applauding universal desires for a better way of living, closer to those of Morris or Carpenter. Thus, almost all the contemporary utopian theorists I have mentioned, especially Sargent and Levitas, align the concept of utopia *not* with final goals or end-points, but rather with desire: the collective longing for 'the improvement of the human condition', as well as the opening up of spaces 'for public debate and democratic decision – insisting always on the provisionality, reflexivity and contingency of what we are able to imagine'.[29] As Fredric Jameson also spells out, what they reject are any 'single-shot solution to all our ills', wanting instead 'reflections on multiple fictional futures' that just might 'serve the quite different function of transforming our own present into the determinate past of something yet to come'.[30]

Like most scholars reflecting on the present, such diverse theorists as Henri Lefebvre, Fredric Jameson or Russell Jacoby have drawn inspiration from the Jewish refugee and renegade Marxist Ernst Bloch and his three-volume *The Principle of Hope* (1954–59), affirming the significance of any form of expectant consciousness for imagining different futures. Written from his exile in the USA as he observed Nazi atrocities and the killing fields in Europe in the 1940s, he clung to threads of fantasy for conceiving of a different Europe, whether in children's play or cultural productions of every kind, insisting that historical change lay in 'the working, creating, human being who reshapes and overhauls the given facts'.[31]

Similarly, in his equally prodigious prose, the heretical French Marxist Henri Lefebvre spent his long life, spanning most of the twentieth century, searching for antidotes to both left party dogmas and bourgeois ideology, exploring the cultural practices of 'everyday life': 'The most extraordinary things are also the most everyday, the strangest things are often the most trivial', he wrote in the opening volume of *The Critique of Everyday Life* (1961).[32] Soon Lefebvre was both providing inspiration for, and rejoicing in, the writings of the French Situationists (such as Guy Debord's 'society of the spectacle' or the Belgian writer Raoul Vaneigem's 'revolution of everyday life').

Lefebvre also welcomed those students and workers who took to the streets in May '68.[33] His interest was to celebrate not only the collective joy and excitement of those days of revolution, but all attempts to 'take back the city' or decommodify urban spaces, as in the white bicycle practices of the anarchists of Amsterdam, the 'Provos'. In such situations, space is not just a background canvas, but becomes constitutive of the utopian.

Thus, even as neo-liberalism promotes its very own 'utopian' fantasy that everyone can succeed in life, despite grossly unequal beginnings, social movements arise determined to reclaim radical public spaces and overcome the personal isolation and misery neo-liberalism spreads in its wake.[34] In our current ominous times, the question remains, to borrow the words of Raymond Williams: how are we to succeed 'in making hope practical, rather than despair convincing'?[35] The need is certain, as expressed by the North American cultural critic Henry Giroux, when he writes: 'The growing lack of justice and equity in American society rises proportionately to the lack of political imagination and collective hope'.[36] Clearly, nurturing hope requires paying attention to any and all sites of resistance and alternative practices whenever they arise, while always trying to broaden the space for political education that encourages democratic participation in political life.

Yet for more than two decades we have seen gusts of radical energy regularly breaking into 'the windless present', with their joyful moments of collective optimism, elation and sense of agency. Such coordinated resistance in Western democracies is often traced back to the international anti-corporate globalization movement, the World Social Forum (WSF), which emerged in Seattle in December 1999 out of the protests against the World Trade Organization's (WTO) latest negotiations. Also known as the Global Justice Movement, the WSF has met annually since its first formal meeting in Porto Alegre in Brazil in 2001, meetings attended by civil society organizations and participants from movements around the world, both formal and informal. Its founding principles, articulated in Porto Alegre, firmly declared that 'Another World Is Possible', stating as its enduring goal to seek out and build alternatives to the current corporate globalization practices of neo-liberalism.[37]

One well-known catalyst in the occupation of urban spaces that followed came from the massive street protests in Athens against the harsh effects of austerity in 2008 – imposed due to Greece's inability to repay or refinance the government debt amassed within the common currency agreement of the European Union (EU). Following police violence and the death of a young student, widespread rioting spread quickly to other Greek cities. It lasted for several weeks, helping to generate solidarity protests across Europe. These protests were supported by and served to sustain what would eventually become the electoral success of Syriza, headed by Alexis Tsipras, which was founded in 2004 as a radical left party hoping to unite left groups and movement politics in one broad electoral coalition.[38]

Nevertheless, it was the protests in 2010–11 that really became part of a worldwide surge in global resistance, as Paul Mason captures vividly in his book, *Why It's Kicking Off Everywhere: The New Global Revolutions* (2012).[39] Least expected, and therefore of the greatest impact globally, were the spectacular uprisings that became known as the Arab Spring, which began in Tunisia in December 2010, before spreading to Oman, Yemen, Egypt, Syria, Morocco and continuing through the region over the next months. The most dramatic of these popular uprisings was the one that brought millions onto the streets in Egypt in January 2011, where they stayed until they overthrew their own Western-supported authoritarian ruler, Hosni Mubarak.[40]

In Spain, the Indignados, as they became known, occupied Spanish squares in their millions in the summer of 2011. Before long some were to put their energies into political formations capable of contesting elections, and in particular into the left populist party Podemos, headed up by their popular figurehead Pablo Iglesias. Similarly, in cities across Portugal hundreds of thousands of protesters took to the streets, some of them affiliated with the broad radical party Left Bloc, which was, like Syriza and Podemos, a party more open to movement politics.

In the Middle East, tragically, a series of political manoeuvres would finally result in the head of the military, Abdel Fatah al-Sisi, gaining control of Egypt and re-instating a rather familiar form of repressive subjugation. In what some have referred to as the 'Arab Winter', the wave of initial revolutions and protests fighting for democratic reform faded the following year, as demonstrations were met with violent responses from authorities. The subsequent power struggles within the Arab world and the spread of fundamentalist Islamic militias, still murderously ongoing in Syria, has meant that only the uprising in Tunisia resulted in any sort of transition to constitutional democratic governance.[41]

Nevertheless, it was the Arab Spring in particular that provided the greatest source of inspiration for the sudden appearance of other occupations around the globe, including the Occupy Wall Street protest in Zuccotti Park, which lasted for two months from September 2011. Occupations mushroomed around the globe, even outside St Paul's Cathedral in London: 'What would Jesus do?' the squatters penned provocatively, knowing that Christianity's founding Jewish rebel and prophet was no friend to money lenders and cared deeply about the poor, the sick, the discarded and destitute. It was the harsh austerity regimes imposed by the governments of Western democracies in order to refinance the banks that so angered these new activists, witnessing ever-deepening inequality while knowing that wealth kept right on flowing upwards into the pockets of the 1 per cent. 'We are the 99 per cent', was the popular chant of the Occupiers.

Whether all too briefly on the streets fighting tyranny and corruption in the Middle East, or denouncing the devastating effects of the financial crisis in the West, these protests all seemed potentially world shattering for those participating in them. Yet we know today that none of these disparate upsurges of resistance have achieved their goals, however forcefully they broadcast their message about the inequities and injustices of the present. Nevertheless, in Spain and Portugal the movements have found some level of representation at state and municipal levels (via Podemos and Left Bloc), or even, as in Greece, helping to elect Syriza to parliamentary victory.

Syriza came to power, as Tsipras hoped, with the assistance of the radical protest movement, its party colours standing for left, Green and movement politics. However, despite a national referendum rejecting capitulation to continuing austerity in 2015, the majority in Syriza have seen no alternative to remaining within the single currency, while so far failing to secure any significant debt relief from the EU's banking institutions or to prevent imposition of the harshest austerity and forced sale of national assets.[42]

A revolutionary multitude can indeed make an impact around the world and, at certain moments in history, overthrow dictators, but they cannot install progressive governments without the most strenuous coalition building in order to establish or connect with a political party that will implement their demands. Even then, as we see in Greece, nothing is guaranteed, at least not without powerful regional or other coalitions that might assist indebted nations to survive the imposition of punitive fiscal and market forces.

Still, there have been other small but significant victories coming from these movements of resistance. These include the number of women moving from lifetimes of radical activism into positions of significant authority, such as Manuela Carmena who was elected mayor of Madrid at seventy-one, in coalition with the anti-austerity party Podemos, in 2015. That same year, another movement radical Ada Calau, who had campaigned to protect householders in mortgage arrears, was elected mayor of Barcelona, representing a new 'citizens' movement' backed by these new left parties.[43]

But what matters most for those stressing the significance of a politics of hope over one of resignation or despair is primarily the consciousness acquired through the exhilarating joy of resistance itself, the sense of shared agency expressed in helping to build any alternative, autonomous spaces, for as long as they might last.

It is important, too, to record the impact of these new movements upon older radicals who visited sites of protest and unexpectedly found their former faith restored. Thus, one of the earliest New York women's liberationists, the late Roz Baxandall, who ventured into Zuccotti Park just five years before she died, found something to delight her: 'The Occupiers have dreams and a vision, too: of a just, peaceful, diverse, democratic world, where democracy serves more than global capitalism and the greedy one percent.'[44] Similarly, Michael Taussig, an Australian anthropologist now living in New York, was busy taking notes during the months in which thousands of people occupied the park, describing his visits there as like going to a street fair: 'There were so many smiling people, radiant with happiness, mixed with a few grim, concentrated ones ... This is not only a struggle about income disparity and corporate control of democracy. It is about corporate control of art, too, including the art of being alive.'[45]

Another anthropologist, the anarchist David Graeber, having been involved in protest networks for decades, remains even more certain that participation in moments of direct action and horizontal decision-making bring to life a new and enduring conception of politics, while providing shared hope and meaning in life, even if their critics see in the outcomes of these movements only defeat:

> What they don't understand is that once people's political horizons have been broadened, the change is permanent. Hundreds of thousands of Americans (and not only Americans, but Greeks, Spaniards and Tunisians) now have direct experience of self-organization, collective action and human solidarity. This makes it almost impossible to go back to one's previous life and see things the same way. While the world's financial and political elite skate blindly towards the next 2008-scale crisis, we're continuing to carry out occupations of buildings, farms, foreclosed homes and workplaces, organizing rent strikes, seminars and debtor's assemblies, and in doing so laying the groundwork for a genuinely democratic culture ... With it has come a revival of the revolutionary imagination that conventional wisdom has long since declared dead.[46]

Discussing what he calls 'The Democracy Project', Graeber celebrates forms of political resistance that in his view move well beyond calls for policy reforms, creating instead permanent spaces of opposition to all existing frameworks. For

Graeber, one fundamental ground for optimism is that the future is unknowable, and one can live dissident politics in the present, or try to.[47] This is both despite, and also because of, the insistent neo-liberal boast that there can be no alternative to its own historical trajectory: which has become a linear project of endless growth and the amassing of wealth by the few, toil and the struggle for precarious survival for so many.

Furthermore, Graeber points out that historically, although few revolutionaries actually succeeded in taking power themselves, the effects of their actions were often experienced far outside their immediate geographical location. In a similar reflection on unintended consequences, Terry Eagleton suggests that even with the gloomiest of estimates in mind, many aspects of utopic thinking may be not only possible but well-nigh inevitable:

> Perhaps it is only when we run out of oil altogether, or when the world system crashes for other reasons, or when ecological catastrophe finally overtakes us, that we will be forced into some kind of co-operative commonwealth of the kind William Morris might have admired.[48]

Even catastrophism, one might say, has its potentials.

It is the ongoing catastrophe of racism in the USA, so regularly resulting in police shootings of black men, which produced the vibrant radical movement Black Lives Matter in 2013, following the acquittal of the white vigilante George Zimmerman for his arbitrary murder of seventeen-year-old Trayvon Martin in Florida. The movement was initiated by a Facebook post written by activist Alicia Garza, which she calls 'a love letter to black people', in which she wrote 'I continue to be surprised at how little black lives matter', closing with the words 'Black people. I love you. I love us. Our lives matter, black lives matter.'[49] Black activists quickly began spreading this message against police brutality and widespread virulent racism on social media, eventually resulting in mobilizations and dozens of groups forming across the USA. In recent years, the movement has regularly organized mass protests in cities across the country against the assault on black lives, which have had an international impact, while remaining a decentralized, non-hierarchical network.[50]

Whether primarily defensive in nature, or determinedly alternative in the spaces they establish, I welcome those diverse campaigners who insist 'another world is possible', whatever the ups and downs of resistance.[51] More people nowadays are aware of the enduring struggle of eco-warriors, especially via the moving words of writers such as Rebecca Solnit, surveying the overlooked resilience of activists around the world, often modelled on the Zapatistas in Mexico. Just as stirring are the books and lecture tours issuing from other environmental activists, such as Naomi Klein, with her increasingly influential insistence that we must shatter the deep denial around the imminent threat of climate change.[52] The recent rise in support for Green Party politics, ecofeminism and other environmental movements all illustrate a significant resistance to the corporate agenda of endless growth, not only highlighting mounting environmental degradation, but conveying the possible pleasures of new patterns of ethical consumption.

In Britain, the philosopher Kate Soper has been at the forefront of arguments for an 'alternative hedonism', suggesting that the promotion of sustainable consumption is also a call for a more pleasant lifestyle. Resisting ubiquitous commercial promotion by moderating our patterns of consumption, Soper suggests, could enhance our more immediate 'sensory pleasures through the enjoyment of better health, more free time, and a slower pace of living'.[53] In this sense, those involved in the politics of consumption can be critical voices for rethinking the nature of happiness and wellbeing.

More generally, it is easy to applaud the open and egalitarian attempts to create what some now call 'everyday utopias', as explored recently by Davina Cooper in her survey of alternative spaces in the UK, spaces set up to enable people in the present to practise 'the change they wish to encounter'. They may not always succeed, and Cooper details for instance the difficulties encountered in setting up a Local Alternative Trading Scheme first established up in the East Midlands. Here skills rather than money were exchanged for products and services, but tensions emerged due to the differing amounts of time people were willing or able to commit.[54] Cooper's point about utopian practices is that they are not trying to offer totally transformed spaces, since they are too connected to the world as it is now. Nevertheless they reflect transformations of thinking with some evidence that alternative practices are always possible, and often worth attempting.

Further afield, one finds other anti-consumer collectives, such as the 'free shop' Skoris in the neighbourhood of Exarcheia in Athens. The free shop was opened in 2009, a time when many people were finding it ever harder to survive the harsh deprivations of the global recession, in the hope of transforming certain patterns of private consumption into collective practices of exchange, while fostering 'a sense of community and identity, which in turn paves the way for collective action'.[55] Those who founded Skoris had earlier been involved in other forms of alternative producer and consumer cooperatives and exchange practices, including solidarity trading with the Zapatistas and other radical producers, as well as supporting the ongoing squats of private and public spaces in the years after 2008 as 'ruptures and cracks' began appearing across Greece. These were the years in which the autonomous Greek left confronted the ever-mounting economic and political crisis via 'forms of utopian praxis from below rather than parliamentary (Syriza-style) politics'.[56]

Yet, while welcoming the significance of subversive utopian practices in revealing possibilities for change, at least for some, however little or large and however uncertain their futures, I remain more cautious about their political impact.[57] I am always looking out for ways of linking any particular radical demands or practices with the solidarity and alliance necessary to build even stronger bases of resistance, one capable of pressuring governments and international bodies to fight against corporate capitalist interests for genuinely redistributive policies. Celebrating the participatory democracy on display in Zuccotti Park, for instance, David Harvey touches on some of these issues in *Rebel Cities*, when he writes: 'Principles are frequently advanced – such as "horizontality" and "non-hierarchy"– or visions of radical democracy and the governance of the commons, that can work for small groups but are impossible to operationalize at the scale of a metropolitan region, let alone for the 7 billion people who now inhabit planet earth.'[58]

It is always obviously daunting to envisage moving on from the urgent particular to elaborate any broader, let alone global, perspective. Moreover, as many experienced feminists know so well, even within a single movement, conflicts and tensions around disclosing the many divisions between us can hasten the end of any notion of a movement's unity – intersected as they are by hierarchies of race, class, sexuality, religious affiliation, age, physical capacity and more. From the input of women of colour, queer women and all those organizing around their distinct struggles, sometimes with other women, we found this out before academic feminists applied deconstructive tools to interrogate all identity formations and to question who is excluded in the maintenance of any collective belongings.

It was also clear that the absence of formal leadership never entirely eliminates the problems of hierarchy, however informal, that arise with differing levels of confidence, eloquence or defensiveness within a community. The result tends to be that some people rather than others participate more easily and gain greater respect and influence, excluding others who more often than not are traditionally more disadvantaged.[59] This can lead to the emergence of conflicts and sectarian divisions, making any form of consensus building impossible. As the American Jo Freeman complained in her influential essay, 'the tyranny of structurelessness' is a constant threat.[60] We need to be aware that genuine democracy is itself a utopian ideal, which does not undermine its significance. Having for decades surveyed women's role globally in leading grass-roots struggles of resistance, demanding basic 'democratic rights' for food, shelter and healthcare, or resisting tyranny and violence, the impressive American feminist scholar Temma Kaplan writes:

> Despite democracy's many failures, it remains a stirring dream, a fantasy, an ideal that has taken various institutional forms over time and generated hopes for creating equitable social, economic, and political arrangements now and in the future.[61]

Whatever the strengths and shortcomings of direct democracy and decision-making by consensus, it will always be necessary to keep listening out for silenced voices, always important to work to extend and refresh forms of democratic engagement. Thus, we need to keep seeking alliance and solidarity, wherever we can find them – however outrageous, strange or quirky. This is because people are drawn into collective resistance in a multitude of unpredictable ways, usually fighting for shared personal issues rather than energized by formal political parties, whether mainstream or radical. We saw this in the sudden appearance of SlutWalks, protests arising to counter the policing of women's dress and behaviour, denouncing violence against women and the continuing ubiquity of rape-cultures. These walks caught on in city after city around the globe, and emerged as one of the most successful and creative forms of feminist action of the past twenty years. New forms of resistance are also evident in the vibrant organizing of trans activists against the repressive gender norms that have stifled them and triggered the violence they have routinely suffered. This has been expressed in the creation of safe queer or trans spaces in recent years, alongside the words to speak of the complexities of non-gendered positions and small legal and other victories conferring greater social recognition.

Equally, however, we need to maintain support for the most progressive party formations, whether through membership or looser alliances, even knowing the compromises necessary in the treacherous terrain of seeking and maintaining electoral success. Both national and transnational progressive alliances, at government levels, will surely be necessary if we are ever going to see a fairer distribution of the world's resources, and less environmentally polluting uses of them.[62]

This thought is clearly why the two ageing socialist politicians, Bernie Sanders and Jeremy Corbyn, unexpectedly proved lightning rods for left radicals, old and, especially, young. Corbyn's winning the leadership of the Labour Party so decisively in September 2015 was such a joyful victory for many on the radical left, with his jubilant acceptance speech: 'We don't have to be unequal, it doesn't have to be unfair, poverty isn't inevitable', before racing off to Parliament Square to address a pro-refugee rally.

Corbyn managed to attract a membership that turned Labour into the largest social democratic party in Europe. However, his history of left militancy, combined with his lack of experience in party leadership and unfamiliarity with the cunning diplomatic skills for maintaining unity, meant Corbyn from the beginning faced unrelenting attacks from across the media, determined to delegitimize him, as well as from many of his own MPs. It all highlights again, for me, the urgency of building coalition politics with all progressive forces.

It should come as no surprise that most of the goals we dream of will usually elude us, at least partially. However, to confront rather than accept the evils of the present, some utopian spirit is always necessary to embrace the complexity of working, against all odds, to create better futures. A wilful optimism is needed, despite and because of our inevitable blind-spots and inadequacies, both personal and collective.

For many of us, it means trying to live differently in the here and now, knowing that the future will never be a complete break with the present or the past, but hopefully something that may develop out of our most supportive engagements with others. To think otherwise inhibits resistance and confirms the dominant conceit that there is no alternative to the present. Thus, I want to close this chapter repeating the words of the late Latin American writer, Eduardo Galeano, which seem to have been translated into almost every language on earth, though I cannot track down their source:

> Utopia is on the horizon. I move two steps closer; it moves two steps further away. I walk another ten steps and the horizon runs ten steps further away. As much as I may walk, I'll never reach it. So what's the point of utopia? The point is this: to keep moving forward.

Our political dreams can end in disappointment, but are likely, nevertheless, to make us feel more alive, and hence happier, along the way, at least when they help to connect us to and express concern for those around us. Happiness (as *eudaimonia*) demands nothing less.

8

The States We're In

Everyone now agrees, often reproachfully, that it is my generation, born into or just after the Second World War, which was the 'lucky' generation, growing up and entering adulthood in the best of times. It is because of this that 'Baby Boomers', as we have been labelled, are often condemned for our privileges – many of us having been upwardly mobile, benefiting from the expanding post-war welfare state which more often met our needs and aspirations for free, providing funding for our university degrees and thereby assisting some of us into professional jobs. The consensus during what is now seen as this golden age of capitalism was that the interventionist state was necessary to ensure a good life for all, 'from cradle to grave', as William Beveridge had promised in his historic 1942 Report 'Social Insurance and Allied Services'. The report stressed the benefits of improved welfare services, whether for paid workers or housewives and, just as importantly for him, to the benefit of business as well.[1]

Forging the Welfare State

Beveridge was influenced by the Keynesian economics elaborated in the years leading up to the Great Depression. In the 1920s, John Maynard Keynes had predicted that the market could not be relied upon to regulate itself, since private and social interests rarely coincide.[2] Following the 1929 Crash, he was critical of the austerity measures of the British government, instead urging state intervention to ensure full employment and forestall what he rightly saw as the looming economic recession of the 1930s, following the slow economic recovery after 1918 – the cycle later known as 'boom and bust'.[3] It was this reformist thinking of Keynes and Beveridge that informed Clement Attlee's Labour Party's post-war reconstruction policies. These policies assumed that it was indeed the state's job to help create better lives through publicly funded social services, by investing in the future not only via free healthcare, education, the planning of municipalities and a vast public housing programme, but also to take responsibility for insuring people against the unpredictability of human affairs through unemployment, sickness and other benefits. Alongside massively extending and improving social services and the public sector in post-war Britain, Attlee's government kept its election promise of nationalizing major industries and public utilities, including the Bank of England, civil aviation, coal mining, the railways, road haulage, cable and wireless, gas and electricity, and finally the steel industry. By 1951, 20 per cent of the British economy was publicly owned.

Ironically and in stark contrast with the Austerity Britain of today that calls for a shrinkage of government, this post-war era, *also* known as the 'Age of Austerity', was a period of government expansion at a time when the Treasury was near bankrupt as a result of the war. In order to allow this growth to occur, the government needed to borrow billions of pounds from the USA to implement its social investment policies. At the same time, rationing was imposed across the board with the unexpected result of an improved diet for some of the poorest.[4]

Significantly, this era of state intervention also involved the public commissioning of artworks and the expansion of publicly financed parks and recreational spaces, as in the 1949 Act of Parliament establishing national parks and providing recreational opportunities for all. Similar forms of state planning, renewal and welfare facilitation were emerging across France, West Germany, Austria, the Netherlands, and even in politically fractious Italy.

The US never developed the same levels of welfare benefits and protection that were achieved in European post-war social democracies. Nevertheless, Franklin Roosevelt's pre-war New Deal back in the 1930s had responded to the intense devastation of the Depression by creating a public works programme to provide jobs for unemployed people, subsidize artists and introduce certain welfare reforms. Later, President Truman's 1940s Fair Deal programme increased the minimum wage, doubled social security benefits and helped lessen poverty, especially after the passing of the G.I. Bill in 1944, which provided funds for all returning veterans to attend college and helped with their housing and other social needs.[5] It was these early reforms – and their subsequent reversals over the last thirty years – which led historian Tony Judt to mourn those post-war years as 'the world we have lost'. In that brief period, he continues, there was near-consensus across the political spectrum: everyone believed in the altruism and benevolence of the state, with conservative politicians offering 'little objection to state control of the "commanding heights" of the economy; along with steeply progressive taxation'.[6]

This may, however, be an exaggeration. The political philosopher David Selbourne, for instance, argues that there was always some hostility among working people in Britain towards those perceived as dependent on public provision. This was an animus which a few decades later was mobilized so efficiently by the right, as those in the most need were disparaged as 'shirkers' and the 'undeserving poor'.[7] The historian of post-war Britain Ben Pimlott also disputes the degree of consensus, suggesting that some Conservatives began questioning the costs of welfare as early as the 1950s.[8] However, this interest in social policy saw the rise and widespread popularity of the social sciences as the forum for the discussions on what was to be done. Indeed, the Cambridge scholar Stefan Collini writes: 'It may now be difficult to recapture the excitement generated in the 1950s and 1960s by the encounter between social science, then enjoying its heyday, and the fast expanding network of services that was known as "the welfare state"'.[9] The maverick academic Richard Titmuss, sometimes called 'the high priest of the welfare state', was a key figure in the shaping and exporting of the sense of consensus, and was also the founder of 'social policy' as a university discipline.[10]

Titmuss was determined to use his research skills to create a better world. In particular, he supported the idea of universal benefits, seen as entitlements, whether for dependent wives involved in childcare or retirement pensions for the elderly, so that all citizens would have an equal interest in and attachment to the state. Above all, Titmuss wanted to reduce the stigma of receiving social security benefits. His daughter, Ann Oakley, later explained that early on in her childhood she was made to understand the overriding significance of 'supporting public sector institutions' and to see gross inequalities of income, resources or chances in life as both 'morally wrong and corrosive of a healthy society'.[11] In these years, taxes remained high in Western democracies generally, with overall living standards and social expectations rising along with improved health and life expectancy.[12]

It was only a generation later that Titmuss's views, and those of all who agreed with him, would start to be routinely derided for ignoring the dangers of 'cheating' and 'malingering', 'shirking' and 'skiving'.[13] The election of Margaret Thatcher heralded the turn that today still dominates our popular media in their fixation on the hordes of the undeserving, whose 'laziness' is subsidized by the hard work of law-abiding men and women.[14] Moreover, for all the emphasis on equality and public service in those relatively prosperous post-war decades, later writers often noted that moderation in social policies and public life overall failed, for the most part, to undermine familiar class hierarchies or other social divisions. On the one hand, the level of benefits, whether for the unemployed or others in need, was never high; on the other, there were also subsidies for those better off, too, through various tax exemptions to help fund private ownership of housing and other tax immunities benefiting those with private means.

The Limits of Post-War Welfare

Looking back, it's clear that all the state-supported post-war structures still managed to maintain traditional class, racial, gender and other hierarchies of power. For instance, unlike in many other European social democracies, in Britain nothing was done to dismantle the role of private education. As Brian Simon reported, private education remained a major force in maintaining the class system.[15] Only a private education at the exclusive 'public schools' was seen as providing the training in 'character' and 'leadership' necessary for running a state and its institutions, as leading social historian Patrick Joyce documents in his book *The State of Freedom*: 'In the 1980s the gentleman's club life of the Whitehall "village" was still almost as strong as half a century before'. Today, as yesterday, although only around 7 per cent of the British population are privately educated, they dominate all the top professions, whether government, civil service, judiciary, military or media.[16] The general benefits accruing from the expansion of the 'welfare' state thus maintained a fairly traditional status quo, even while allowing for some degree of social mobility and the smooth incorporation of change, including the recent changes in the gender, racial and ethnic balance.[17]

Because welfare expansion did not, then, greatly change the personnel, or the outlook of those in control of state resources, many relying on welfare provision disliked or distrusted their contact with the state, which they experienced as inflexible, authoritarian and bureaucratic. In her book *Landscape for a Good Woman*, for instance, Carolyn Steedman recalls, shortly after her younger sister's birth, her mother's shame and bitter tears after being told by a visiting health worker, 'This house isn't fit for a baby.' Still bitter, recalling her working-class childhood over three decades later, Steedman vows: 'And I? I will do everything and anything until the end of my days to stop anyone ever talking to me like that woman talked to my mother.'[18] Nevertheless, Steedman is also aware of her own debt to that moment of heightened welfare, leading her to write eloquently of the confidence she gained from its ministrations: 'I think I would be a different person now if orange juice and milk and dinners at school hadn't told me, in a covert way, that I had a right to exist, was worth something … its central benefit being that, unlike my mother, the state asked for nothing in return.'[19]

However, protection from the state at that time felt more distant if you were both poor and black, as the feminist scholar Gail Lewis notes, recalling her more challenging trajectory of upward mobility, starting out from a bedsit tenement in Kilburn. Outside home, the deep racism of the white working class around her meant she had to remain permanently vigilant, knowing that danger always lurked around the corner in the form of local white gangs determined to keep 'their territory' free of blacks. Inside her home, she faced the inevitable tensions of a 'mixed marriage' in the '50s, the noxious, often violent, dynamics of her father driven to assert his authority over the white woman, his wife, in a tenement block where she was the only white resident.

As one of the many young Jamaicans who had embarked so hopefully for the 'mother country' as a teenager, this father encountered the vicious racism of the day: 'They came looking for the rainbow and got abuse, subjugation and disillusionment instead'. Indeed, at the height of racial tensions in 1958, a firebomb was lobbed into their home. Yet Lewis too recalls the 'wonderful orange' juice and free milk she enjoyed, not even minding her daily dose of cod-liver oil. When domestic tension mounted, she would be sent off to the relative luxury of her grandmother's house on one of the new housing estates built in Harrow. Finally, however, Lewis feels she owes her own significant upward mobility into the heights of academia not to her experience of a more benevolent state, but rather to the Black Power politics she absorbed in the early 1970s, joining the Angela Davis Defence campaign, and coming out as a black lesbian in the early years of women's liberation.[20]

Editing a collection of second-wave feminists recalling their very diverse post-war childhoods, which included those of both Steedman and Lewis, alongside her own memories of being raised in working-class Glasgow in the '50s, Liz Heron echoes Steedman's conclusions. Heron suggests that while so many of the women born into the 'fever of optimism' around 1945 expressed a certain sense of displacement or unease as they entered adulthood, they nonetheless benefited from the educational opportunities, subsidies for house building and municipal housing, alongside the other welfare provision unavailable to their parents. This, in turn, emboldened them to grab the future: 'Along with the orange juice and the cod-liver oil, the malt supplement and the free school milk, we may also have absorbed a certain sense of our own worth and the sense of a future that would get better and better, as if history were on our side.'[21]

History was on their side, although this more upwardly mobile generation never forgot the indignities of their working-class childhood. Coming from a different form of poverty and exclusion, yet another child who would climb upwards to enjoy a stellar academic and publishing career is the literary critic, my friend Alan Sinfield. Not only was he born into a working-class family mid war, but when he was only two his father was killed in that war, leaving behind a pregnant wife, Lucy, in her early thirties, who was very soon disabled by Parkinson's disease: 'We were poor, and could never forget it.'

This absent father may have died heroically fighting for his country, yet as Sinfield recalls of his mother's hardship and isolation: 'The disability of not having a husband, combined with her disease, moved Lucy, decisively, to the bottom of the pile … Her social life shrank almost to nothing'. The 1950s was not a good time to be a lone mother: 'My sense of anger at the injustice in the world is undoubtedly linked with distresses of Lucy's life'. It was the indignities and impoverishment of that life, Sinfield later reflected, which created his own life-long commitment to all who are similarly disadvantaged: 'the elderly, infirm, unemployed, black, queer, lone parents, and more'.[22] However, as a fatherless child with a disabled mother, Sinfield was sent off to a charity-run boarding school for orphans and other children in need, thereby beginning his rapid climb out of poverty and the life he had known. As he later noted sadly, every step of his advance took him further away from the small world his mother occupied.

Another '50s memoirist, Valerie Walkerdine also narrates the ambivalent experience of scrambling out of the provincial safety of Northern working-class life via the new openings for educational achievement: 'They held out a dream … They didn't tell me, however, that for years I would no longer feel any sense of belonging, nor any sense of safety … Leaving one's class was to be both admired and scorned.' Later, however, she elaborated on the consequences of such social policies: 'You should never have educated us, the ordinary girls of the fifties, for we are dangerous … We are beginning to speak of our histories, and as we do it will be able to reveal the burden and pain and desire that formed us'.[23] Perhaps the most telling success of the welfare state, however brusquely offered, and however confusing the transition, was the resulting collective confidence needed to bite the hand that had fed its beneficiaries so well, enabling them to object to the paternalism it appeared from. Few guessed how quickly it could vanish, mere decades later.

It was not only those upwardly mobile working-class children, but also feminists in general who always had a conspicuously conflicted, yet resolute, relationship to the state. We were comprehensively fighting the paternalism that had enshrined women's dependence on men in the '50s welfare consensus, while also insisting that the state should provide the type of social provision and community resources essential to help this transformation. Writing about Titmuss's and his male colleagues' academic authority in the 1950s, for instance, his daughter Ann Oakley is utterly scathing in her descriptions of the patriarchal nature of the intellectual networks at the heart of the new social policy establishment. None of the female experts could find an equal place within these discussions, just as the wives at home were expected to subordinate themselves to their husbands' interests and career.[24]

Confronting this situation two decades later, some of the leading feminist sociologists in the 1970s, including Elizabeth Wilson and Mary McIntosh, emphasized the potential for and significance of women helping to transform the state in their own interests. Indeed, they saw women's dependence on state provision as less oppressive than their traditional dependence on men in the family: 'The state "intervenes" less conspicuously in the lives of women than of men, and when it does so it appears to be done more benevolently'.[25]

Other feminists, however, quickly responded that the state relates differently to women depending upon their race, class and circumstances, being far more repressive in the lives of some women than others and making it much harder for certain women to access its resources, especially black women in Britain.[26] Unsurprisingly, then, even as the welfare system expanded, there were always significant inconsistencies in its delivery. There was a rigid bureaucracy. And in addition, middle classes benefited disproportionately from its resources, assisted by their greater cultural confidence and sense of entitlement, whereas the working class was less successfully assertive in its demands on the state.[27]

Furthermore, by the 1960s, despite the government's commitment to welfare, there remained large pockets of poverty, homelessness, hardship and misery in Britain, as in other Western economies. It was this knowledge that led to the formation of new campaigning institutions in public life, such as the Child Poverty Action Group (CPAG) founded in 1965, and Shelter founded the following year. The aim of these charities was to put a final end to social blight through pressure on the state to increase their welfare budgets and provide more community resources to overcome the remaining forms of social exclusion, regardless of their origins.

It was all of these contradictions and dilemmas that led various feminists, left economists and public sector employees (sometimes all three at once) to develop strategies for working 'In and Against the State'.[28] Many were seeking to ride the contradictions of being full-time state employees (perhaps as teachers, social workers, health visitors, whatever), while also seeking radical change. There is obviously a certain strength in collectivities that can make clear demands on the state, especially as employees. Yet there were other pressures coming from the right, who believed the welfare state was providing far too many services.

It is now almost twenty years since I suggested that the

continuing offensive against welfare was probably 'the single most general threat to Western women's interests at present – at least for those many women who are not wealthy, and who still take the major responsibility for caring work in the home'.[29] There is little doubt now that I was right, in particular in relation to the wellbeing of women and children overall. These cuts in the welfare state have all hit women hardest because of their still distinct role in the provision of care. From his exhaustive research into the effects of austerity, the political geographer Danny Dorling summarizes the situation in Britain today: 'Some 85 per cent of cuts to benefits have already been taken from women ... Almost the entire UK government deficit is to be repaid through sacrifices made by women'.[30]

Our need for help from the state varies across our lifetimes, especially for women. As John Hills notes in his book *Good Times, Bad Times* (2014), the benefits of income do not endure across a lifetime. Thus, one major aim of welfare provision was precisely to smooth out these variations. Moreover, Hills notes that over their lifetime, the majority of people contribute less to the state than they get back from it, as they move through life from receiving as children and adolescents, to contributing, and back again to receiving in late life.[31] Tragically, it is just this security of provision when they need it that has been disappearing in recent decades.

Nearly all other European countries now spend more on health than we do in the UK, and we tolerate a far higher degree of economic inequality.[32] Though hit hardest, women are not the only ones who are suffering; the struggle to end austerity and rebuild public life remains essential for anyone seriously interested in questions of happiness and social wellbeing. On the same day that the United Kingdom voted to leave the EU in

June 2016, Dorling notes, a report on the huge rise in UK death rates was released; indeed, there have been continuous rises following the austerity policies enacted since a Tory (coalition) government came to office in 2010. Self-reported health indices were a central component of Cameron's wellbeing index, yet they declined every year while he was in office, most rapidly towards the end, and these indices are showing no sign of abating under Theresa May. Again, as Dorling, among others, has been arguing for many years, we cannot be collectively happier and healthier as individuals without a government genuinely committed to making all our lives happier. Since for good or ill our lives are entwined with and affected by those of our fellow citizens, 'we cannot be truly happy if those around us are not happy'.[33]

Retailing State Resources

Not so long ago, many would have seen Dorling's argument as a truism. In the 1970s, for instance, the majority of government employees, then including most workers in professional jobs, remained receptive to the more collective sentiments 'of altruism, reciprocity and social duty' that Titmuss had exemplified in his classic *The Gift Relationship*. Here, for instance, Titmuss showed that more people were prepared to give blood for medical transfusions driven by selflessness and a sense of shared investment in the future than they were to cash payment as an inducement.[34] Yet today the idea that our personal happiness has something to do with collective happiness is largely dismissed. Much ideological work has gone into this shift, which takes us to the story of neo-liberalism.

Neo-liberalism began as an economic theory in 1930s Austria and soon became associated with the anti-collectivist thinking and control over money supply promoted by Friedrich Hayek, who was equally suspicious of fascism and communism, seeing both as an assault on individual freedom. In the post-war period, the theory was kept alive in the Chicago School of Economics, in the writing of Milton Friedman and a few others. However, during this welfare era it appeared to have little impact on Western democracies as Keynesianism held much greater sway. Nevertheless, the various financial jolts of the 1970s, including the sudden increase in oil prices, meant that welfare states soon faced mounting debt as well as industrial slow-down and rising inflation. This allowed neo-liberal ideas traction, with both the Democratic Jimmy Carter in the US and Callaghan's Labour government in the UK instituting cutbacks. Notably, however, these partial curbs on state spending had none of the ideological fervour that the next set of leaders, Reagan and Thatcher, brought to their promotion of unfettered markets and an all-out assault on state resources, welfare and trade union militancy in the 1980s.[35]

Margaret Thatcher had a clear and resolute agenda, rigorously sketched in the speech she delivered two months after her election in 1979, constructing – though never naming – the neo-liberal mentality that was soon to dominate the airwaves. A key function of the state, she spelt out, should be to ensure the success of market forces, which could only be done by reviving competitiveness and the entrepreneurial spirit, and assisted through the lowering of taxes on high incomes. Saluting entrepreneurial individualism, she insisted that riches would always accrue to the talented and hard-working: 'Nations depend for their health, economically, culturally and psychologically', she announced, 'upon the achievement of a comparatively small number of talented and determined people'.[36] This was the ideological underpinning justifying all the practical policies she, alongside Reagan in the USA, implemented to favour business, 'free trade' and financial speculation. They had dedicated backers all spreading the neo-liberal narrative and mindset, enabling the austerity programmes that governments have imposed in the three decades since that have impoverished so many, while enriching a tiny minority of the extremely wealthy.[37]

It is easy to trace the shift. When Margaret Thatcher came to power in 1979, much of Britain's economy and almost all its basic infrastructure were owned by the state, including the gas, electricity, water, coal and steel industries, while British Telecom, British Airways, BP, the postal and health services, most schools, a third of the housing stock and much more, were state-owned. Indeed, at the end of the 1970s almost half of the British population lived in council housing, and the gap between the richest and poorest in Britain had never been narrower than in 1979.[38] Today, that situation has completely reversed, with what remains of British industry, services, housing and resources largely sold off, cheaply, into various forms of 'private' ownership.[39] Moreover, the termination of public funding for industry, housing and job creation, combined with contractions in welfare were just one side of the fiscal strategy. Its goal was the comprehensive commercialization of public resources, deregulation of the monetary supply, removal of restrictions on borrowing, alongside cuts in taxes on business and wealth accumulation (replaced by increases in regressive flat-rate tax, such as raising VAT even on the most necessary of items or transactions).

Meanwhile, with economic insecurity soaring and government debt failing to fall, we all remain at the mercy of the form of financial capitalism that has developed since the 1980s, replacing traditional industrial and agricultural economies as sources of income and generating a host of speculative practices, such as the trading in 'derivatives' – whose value is based on the expected *future* price of underlying assets, hence always open to forthcoming collapse.[40]

It is the idea that markets can self-regulate, an idea pursued with a vengeance in neo-liberal economics, that was the fundamental fallacy generating the banking collapse of 2008. The majority of us are still paying for that delusion through falling living standards, even as the state stepped in to bail out the banks and the wealth of the richest has continued to soar.[41] Thus, profits remain strictly private and only lightly taxed (if taxed at all) in this new financial regime, while losses are shared. In contradiction to its founding principles against state intervention, the more the neo-liberal experiment fails, the more governments have stepped in to save it. Moreover, the whole notion that there can be a real separation of the state and the market is a myth, as the economic historian Karl Polanyi argued back in the 1940s: capitalism itself and the whole notion of the free market have always been dependent upon and strongly shaped by 'continuous, centrally organized and controlled interventionism' from the beginning.[42]

These, then, are the maddening deceptions we live with, as local governments are also forced by draconian cuts in national funding to sell off housing stock and children's playgrounds, close down libraries and sell off leisure centres and other essential resources for maintaining community welfare, outsource caring responsibilities and much else. Even state schools are now being handed over to the private sphere via the creation of academies, where the government still pays for the tuition of students but all curriculum, facilities and planning responsibilities are increasingly entrusted to profit-making private companies and their investors.

This is the policy of austerity and privatization in favour of enterprise that has fuelled the desperate housing crisis, especially in cities like London, where very few can now afford to buy, rents soar and people face the distress of homelessness or crippling debt. There would have to be a full revival of state investment in the housing sector to end this social misery, yet what we are currently witnessing is exactly the opposite: the abolition of secure tenure in public housing and the accelerated sale of what remains of it.

It is all part of the highly successful marketing of so many of the institutions built to house or control the poor and needy, whether council estates, mental hospitals or prisons. As the astute cultural critic Owen Hatherley notes, the terrible irony of all this is that today in Britain there is a nostalgia for the solidity and aesthetics of a century ago, yet a rejection of the politics that inspired it. We face a massive housing problem for which we once had a solution in public funding for the construction of well-planned and designed modernist buildings, but instead we turn the surviving fragments of that solution into the problem: 'We are living through exactly the kind of housing crisis for which council housing was invented in the first place, at exactly the same time as we're alternatively fetishizing and privatising its remnants ... social housing becomes the new front line of gentrification, and the architect-designed modernist flat the new loft conversion'.[43]

Meanwhile, the imposition of these destructive or, at the very least, dangerously experimental strategies makes little commercial sense, despite government decrees that such measures promote 'business efficiency'. Indeed, even the people working in the state sector are being driven out by its failings and excessive bureaucracy, with several polls revealing that many choose to leave it as early as they possibly can.[44]

Given the levels of anger over rising inequality globally and declining living standards, it is not as surprising as it might otherwise seem that when, in 2014, the French economist Thomas Piketty published his *Capital in the Twenty-First Century*, it quickly became a bestseller – despite its 685 pages, filled with difficult equations and obscure graphs. Piketty's success came from his authority as a hitherto mainstream economist, yet one who was now demolishing the classic economics that neoliberal evangelists relied upon to promote their narratives of economic efficiency.

Piketty showed, firstly, that the huge resurgence of inequality since 1980 was due primarily to the 'political shifts' of recent decades, especially in relation to taxation and finance; secondly, that 'there is no natural, spontaneous process to prevent destabilizing, inegalitarian forces from prevailing permanently in a capitalist economy'.[45] It is rather the norm (intensified in today's expansion of the financial sector) for wealth to increase faster than income. This means not only that hard work does *not* bring riches, but that wealth at the top of society will always become ever more concentrated, with little or no relation to the labour of those who have it but usually deriving from what they have inherited.[46] This is why today the top 1 per cent of the wealthy are almost 2,000 times richer than the bottom 50 per cent of the world population, and there is a steep gradient of wealth even within that top percentile. It is also why wealth nowadays overwhelmingly arises not from any form of production, but from 'rentier' capital, that is, from rents or money invested in bonds.[47] Historically, only in short periods, such as in the exceptional circumstances post 1945, have governments intervened to lessen flagrant levels of inequality. Piketty's solution to our present circumstances is to argue for a return to a large tax on wealth, even though he adds that this is the 'utopian' idea.[48]

We know that the enduring justification for both the shrinking of welfare and the privatizing of resources was the insistence that the state was incapable of running its own social infrastructure – let alone managing economic life – efficiently or creatively, while almost any form of state dependency was deemed unhealthy. Were we not kept so ignorant, the absurd nature of this dogma would be obvious to everyone. Indeed, many of those who have, sensibly, raced to buy Britain's once state-owned public resources include not just the global corporations (often resident in tax havens and paying little or no tax to any state) but also corporations sponsored by *other* states. Thus, in practice many of Britain's former assets have been renationalized, only now they rest in the hands of other nations.

This is what James Meek reveals in his scathing overview of the dismal outcome of privatization in his book *Private Island: Why Britain Belongs to Someone Else*. Here we learn that different European state railways at present own a quarter of British rail, while the French state subsidizes the energy company EDF, now one of the UK's main suppliers of energy, whose assets include several nuclear plants which were all once owned by the British state.[49] Meanwhile, the Chinese government has a significant stake in Thames water supplies, leading Meek to mock the extraordinary duplicity of those who hate both communism and state control obliging Londoners 'to pay an annual tax to the world's biggest communist country' every time we turn on a tap.[50] Since we have no choice but to use the essential services recent governments have jettisoned, we are in effect paying taxes every time we use these resources, but taxes the income of which accrue either to individuals or to other states which own, or part own, these 'private' companies. Privatizing state resources enriches neither nation states nor local governments, let alone enables more people to flourish as shareholders, when today fewer people directly own shares than before privatization began.[51] Yet, as Nigel Lawson, one of Thatcher's key policy advisers, later admitted in his memoirs, restocking the Treasury was never the main motive for privatization, but rather it was motivated by 'an ideological belief' in free markets and private ownership.[52]

Adding further weight to calls to rethink the relation between the state, civil society and the economy if we have any genuine concern for overall social prosperity or personal wellbeing, Britain-based economist Mariana Mazzucato also persuasively challenges the conviction that the private sector is more dynamic and inventive than the public one. Thatcher's guru Milton Friedman had insisted that no 'great advances in civilization' had ever 'come from centralized government', a belief, Mazzucato retorts, that 'is as wrong as it is widespread'.[53] In a series of incisive case studies, she illustrates that over the decades it is states themselves that have been the most comprehensive innovators of new technologies, often prepared to take far more risks in their invention than are private firms.

Her examples are numerous; for instance, although Steve Jobs's ambition and skills made him proficient at designing and marketing Apple products, the scientific research on his products had mostly been undertaken and completed by government-backed scientists and engineers across Europe and the USA a few decades earlier. Similarly, though pharmaceutical corporations would have us believe that it is their research that pioneers new cures and treatments, Mazzucato shows that it was public institutions that produced 75 per cent of the molecular entities responsible for major medical breakthroughs between 1993 and 2004. Moreover, she notes, Pfizer moved its pharmaceutical research labs from the UK to the USA in 2011, resulting in thousands of lost jobs here, a move sparked not in search of lower taxes (which Britain likes to offer multinationals) but because of the £32 billion a year the US government invests in bio-medical research at its universities. Worse, the fraudulence of always privileging the private sector has meant that today there is *less* pioneering creative research being undertaken by venture capital, with business even more averse to risks than government researchers. The shrinking mega-corporations nowadays are spending less on R&D, primarily interested as they are in short-term financial investment and financial speculation, even as government funding for research also shrinks.[54]

Most importantly, Mazzucato stresses that nowadays it is imperative that we have far more rather than less state involvement in industry and commerce if we are to have a sustainable environmental future, nationally or globally. The wellbeing of all future generations depends upon states cooperating to ensure a shift towards renewable solar energy, recyclable materials, advanced waste management and far greater regulation across the industrial and financial sectors.[55] The one thing that is certain, however, is that Green growth, rather than the ceaseless production of environmentally destructive commodities, will *not* happen if left to the market sector alone. Thus, whether we are thinking about the sustainability of the planet, the lowering of inequality or the wellbeing of the majority, Mazzucato provides one of the most convincing cases I have seen for the *potential* value in, and competence of, governments doing what the private sector simply will not do: namely, eschew short-term goals in favour of progressive visions for the future.

The morbid symptoms of our times are today confirmed even by the IMF, despite having for decades enthusiastically embraced the slashing of welfare programmes and the cheap sale of government resources, while imposing austerity regimes upon and asset-stripping struggling indebted countries. Without a word of apology for a tactic it has enforced since the 1980s, the IMF has recently started admitting: 'Austerity policies do more harm than good'.[56] No one turns a deafer ear to this message than the Tory governments in Britain, a fact which adds depressing weight to the Oxford philosopher John Gray's comment in 2015: 'Intellectually, neoliberalism has long been thoroughly discredited. Politically, it has rarely been more secure.'[57]

Similarly, the British writer John Lancaster is passionate about the need for change in the wake of the financial crisis, yet sceptical about its possibility, with governments so frightened of scaring off those seen as the 'wealth creators': 'The robber baron's castle glitters so brightly precisely because it devastates the landscape in which it sits'.[58] Ironically, sometimes this truth even beams out from Hollywood. In the last James Bond film, *Spectre*, the villains to be vanquished are no longer evil spies from elsewhere, but Bond's own stepbrother, who is both part of the respectable business world and has criminal and terrorist connections, since crime and legitimate business have intertwined. As that most discerning of film commentators, Liz Heron, notes: 'Bond to the rescue, then, as usual. But this time he has to save the state from itself and its neoliberal faith in a privatised Big Brother'.[59]

The Personal Cost: Overseeing Misery

It is hard to escape from pessimism, when the devastation of recent decades is visible everywhere, on both an individual and a collective level. It is evident especially when we look at the effects of much of the outsourcing of government and municipal services that has occurred over the last three decades. Research commissioned by trade unions as well as by diverse charities has for years been highlighting the drastic deterioration of service provision, not only leading to greater job insecurity and worsening conditions for workers, but inevitably resulting in an altogether more fragmented and poorer quality of care at almost every level for those in most need.[60]

For many years, the British news reporter Alan White has reported on this decline. His findings have been brought together in his powerful new book *Shadow State: Inside the Secret Companies That Run Britain*.[61] Surveying the £82 billion currently spent by our government on outsourced services, White easily reveals that not only can this rarely be seen as cost saving, but that the few giant companies that have overwhelmingly secured state contracts – such as G4S (Group 4 Securicor), Serco, Capita and Atos – have repeatedly been exposed as responsible for major calamities, without incurring either penalties or termination of their contracts. These large corporations finesse well-designed brochures and follow-up service reports, promising efficiency and success, while proving routinely unsatisfactory in the actual delivery of services. In the process, they eliminate smaller competitors unable to hire equivalent experts in self-presentation and instantly sack whistle-blowers, such as Sarah Hubble from G4S, who tried to warn the public of the shortcuts being taken, in this case when vetting security staff for the Olympics.[62]

Thus, the fact that workers for G4S were responsible for the death of the Angolan Jimmy Mubenga while he was being restrained on a deportation flight in 2010 did not stop the corporation from being commissioned to supply security for the Olympics in London in 2012, with exactly the results Hubble had been sacked for fearing would come about. Nor did the subsequent fiasco of their complete failure to supply adequate security for that event hinder their success in securing further contracts, leading to the next episode of several G4S workers being arrested for the abuse and bullying of teenagers at Medway Secure Training Centre in Kent. G4S originated when British Securicor merged with a similar Danish corporation in 2004, and like all the other global corporations has barely been subject to any regulation at all, even as they themselves are responsible for 'policing' around the world.

Serco, too, has been accused of the mistreatment of women at Yarl's Wood Immigration Removal Centre and a host of other failures, including charging for electronic tags used on dead prisoners and 'rogue staff' falsifying records on a £285 million contract to transport prisoners.[63] Meanwhile, like other private company directors pocketing government funds for themselves, the chief executive of the company A4e (Action for Employment), Emma Harrison, paid herself £8.6 million in a year when fewer than four in every hundred unemployed people supposed to be helped into work by the company secured jobs for longer than thirteen weeks; nine of her staff were also charged with fraud relating to these employment schemes.[64]

The chief victims in all this privatization – and Alan White provides a horrifying catalogue – range from disabled welfare claimants and old people in care homes or in need of home help, to young offenders in privatized secure training centres, detained asylum seekers, job seekers sent for retraining and many more. Outsourcing may at times seem to save the state money, but it has been responsible for wages falling across the country, with workers routinely paid far less than a living wage, thus again doing more to harm the British economy. White's conclusion is that scandals in the delivery of services will continue to grow around outsourcing in the UK, given that the state has been hijacked by a small group of companies that provide neither the value nor the care they purport to, and who are not accountable to any constituency, while squeezing out smaller providers who often have greater expertise and local knowledge. With no effective government control over the giant companies it hires, we now live with a 'shadow state' that takes advantage of the actual state, even as it brings anguish to the lives of vulnerable people.[65]

I have referred often in this book to the expanding levels of individual misery, depression, anxiety, loneliness and isolation in our time. According to a recent report from Mind, one in four people in the UK will experience a mental health problem each year, and globally similar figures come from the World Health Organization.[66] Exactly when we need to be improving the quality of the provisioning of care, we are creating the conditions where the levels of support available for most people are at their minimum, and the morale of those on the front line providing it could hardly be lower. This surely helps explain why, on a broader canvas, polls checking the pulse of the nation have been detecting a collective negativity or pessimism around much of the UK.

This despair is especially true in relation to the future of young people, in whom depression has soared over the last twenty-five years, increasing by 70 per cent in the UK alone.[67] Similar rates of mental stress and social pessimism have also been reported in the USA and in other parts of Europe.[68] Drawing on polling and other research data, the British feminist theorist Rebecca Coleman writes of a sense of 'pessimism about the future' as the 'enveloping atmosphere' in which many people now dwell, and in particular women and young people.[69] Unsurprisingly, studies repeatedly show high levels of stress in poorer households with children, with anxiety and conflict between parents passed on to children.[70] Moreover, just as personal and family life is undermined by the tribulations of the present moment, so too have the spirit and atmosphere of entire communities been blighted by prolonged economic insecurity and hardship.

It is not hard to map out geographical patterns of distress, anxiety and depression. These sentiments display a strong hold in places where communities have been torn apart by state policies, or by the lack of them, following the reduction or wholesale destruction of national or regional industrial production in a trend of deindustrialization that is evident in both the USA and the UK. Community life in many parts of Britain has deteriorated with the decline of heavy industry over the last thirty years, most obviously as a result of government decisions to allow the collapse of the once-extensive coal industry, along with steel and other industrial manufacturing.

There is now a growing literature and other cultural production on the effects of the decline of old industrial sites on displaced workers and their families. In the UK, one of the first representations of the personal devastations of economic insecurity was Alan Bleasdale's TV soap broadcast on BBC2 at the start of the 1980s, *Boys from the Blackstuff*. Set in Liverpool, it chronicled Bleasdale's experiences of life in that city of mushrooming unemployment, reflecting the effects of industrial decline soon occurring throughout the North of Britain. In retrospect, however, it is interesting to compare the sympathetic portrayals of the jobless in this TV series from the early '80s with the far more negative portrayals of the 'scroungers' on *Benefits Street*, a documentary series made for Channel 4 over thirty years later.[71]

In scholarly literature, Valerie Walkerdine is just one of many to explore the sense of melancholy and pessimism dominating whole communities with the decline of industrial jobs. She studied one small Welsh town after the closure of the iron and steelworks that had employed most of the local men in the past, arguing that the closure of the steelworks ruptured the community's sense of continuity of being in a catastrophic way that none could escape. Indeed, Walkerdine uses the notion of 'collective trauma', as whole communities continued to grieve following the loss of the stability their industrial labour had once provided. For the men in particular, both old and young, if they could find work at all, they were shunted into precarious, low-paid and, in their view, 'demeaning' service jobs.[72]

In Walkerdine's summary of life in these Welsh villages: 'The next generation of young men has never known the steelworks, which closed in 2002. They long for heavy manual work, but mostly find low-paid service work like stacking super-market shelves, pizza delivery and contract cleaning. Their accounts reveal how much distress is being communicated to them and by them'.[73] The Danish sociologist Kristian Thorup notes that as capital moves effortlessly around the globe, seeking out the cheapest labour, it leaves a trail of 'zombie identities' in its wake, as people search to recover their former status and meaning. Those old identities are rendered useless but live on, creating ghost towns of the disgruntled – a demographic who all too often turn their back upon immigrants or other minorities.[74]

In the USA, a similar picture emerges from interviews with displaced industrial workers and films made about them, all capturing the swelling waves of depression that continue long after plants or mines have closed. The film-maker Michael Moore memorably captured the devastating effects of auto industry closures on his friends' morale in his own hometown of Flint, Michigan, in the film *Roger and Me* (1989). Over twenty-five years later, British journalist Gary Younge would tell a similar story about a place called Muncie, Indiana, where again almost everyone, in this case mainly unemployed white workers, were 'hurting' from decades of industrial closures that killed the economic life of the town and were killing off communities as well. As one informant tells Younge: 'It's just a mess. People addicted to drugs. There's nothing to do. It's a sad situation'.[75] As so many others have observed over recent decades, it's not just the effects of the personal loss of wages and status that hurt, but men, in particular, feel that they have lost not just a job, but a whole identity, since neither they, nor their sons, could find any work they could be proud of doing.[76]

It is also the racial dimension in American cities that is particularly stark, with researchers, such as Thomas Sugrue, in his classic study of post-war Detroit, tracing the devastating impact of post-war deindustrialization on the black community. In Detroit, persistent racial discrimination meant that black people bore the worst effects, it always being easier for white workers to transfer to areas where factories might be relocated: 'As Detroit's population shrank, it also grew poorer and blacker. Increasingly, the city became the home for the dispossessed, those marginalized in the housing market, in greater peril of unemployment, most subject to the vagaries of a troubled economy'.[77]

Introducing their collection of research on deindustrialization, *Beyond the Ruins*, Jefferson Cowie and Joseph Heathcott write of the 'body count' of lives ruined, evident in the evocative words of jobless workers they collected through interviews, expressing a poignant sense of anger, regret, confusion and loss over all that had been taken away.[78] That balance between hardship and hurt, rage and possible resistance takes different forms. However, for many, hardship, hurt and rage became the basis of individual support for populist politics, specifically support for Donald Trump, Nigel Farage and other opportunistic, demagogic far-right nationalist leaders across Europe. A similar, if more appropriately targeted, rage and resistance turn against government policies that have failed to build houses or expand jobs, have curtailed welfare and have done nothing to control vicious inequality. This is evident in many of the movement struggles that have emerged globally in recent decades, around the scandal of homelessness as house prices and rents soar, among students resisting escalating fees and the other flashpoints of occupation and mobilization occurring since the banking meltdown of 2007–2009.

While the relation between the state and civil society is always somewhat troubled in any democracy, today it is civil society that feels itself increasingly threatened.[79] Indeed, Britain recently emerged as the capital of loneliness in Europe according to our government's own happiness index.[80] This is in line with similar findings from the British charity Relate, which was formed at the very birth of the welfare state some seventy years ago and was then known as the National Marriage Guidance Council. Its ongoing research reveals that an astonishing 5 million people in Britain, that is, one in ten, say they have no close friends, with a third of working parents complaining that job demands mean they do not even see or speak to their own children every day. Yet, despite the escalating time spent on work-related matters and people spending overall twice as much of their waking time with their colleagues as with families or partners, almost half of them said that they had no real friends at work. The majority of adults in partnerships, of whatever nature, did feel happy in them, although 62 per cent said financial problems were one of the biggest strains on relationships.[81]

More recently, we have witnessed the success of the 'Leave' or Brexit campaign in the EU referendum vote, showing correlations again between regions of geographical impoverishment and those wanting their old lives and their country 'back again'.[82] This result seemed to echo the worries of a growing restive population in the UK who saw few government policies as working in their interests, with so many of their communities and support structures threatened. This was especially evident in much of the North of England and the Welsh valleys, once old Labour heartlands.[83] The voting figures are complex, with age and employment crucial variables: 73 per cent of those under twenty-five voted to remain, as did the majority of those with jobs, overall expressing a more pluralist, feminist, multicultural outlook; 60 per cent of those over sixty-five and the majority of the unemployed or on pensions voted Leave, overall expressing fear of the effects of immigration on employment and the dangers of globalization.[84] However we look at it, the result shines a glaring light on the lack of trust and the rage and resentment felt by so many against mainstream politicians and remote bureaucrats or bankers in London or Brussels, which is hardly surprising with all we now know of three decades of economic deterioration.[85]

The terrible irony is not only that Brexit has thrown Britain into economic turmoil, simultaneously weakening the left through implosion within the Labour Party and the fanning of xenophobia. It is also that many of those voting Leave came from the very places most economically dependent on assistance from the EU and most likely to be harmed by our leaving it. The nation could hardly be a less happy one at present, nor could the need for a more redistributive state, capable of restoring greater trust and equality, be more urgent. Indeed, David Cameron himself announced that he saw the Brexit vote as part of a 'movement of unhappiness' – not much of a legacy one would think for over six years as Prime Minister, especially one who had in 2010 promised to make happiness his chief Gross Domestic Product.[86]

Reclaiming Public Life

Pessimism may be widespread in public life, and yet, against a backdrop of hyper-individualism and declining social welfare, once we look hard enough we can usually glimpse alternative practices of support, solidarity and struggle on the fringes. These are the spaces of resistance, where collective joy, as well as anger, is as frequent as it is infectious. For decades, such resistance has been visible in both spontaneous events and more organized movements, some of them knowingly referring back to Lefebvre's 'Take Back the City', the slogan jubilantly embraced in that volatile period of civil unrest in France in May '68.[87] Today, this accompanies similar thoughts about reclaiming 'the commons', which as David Harvey writes involves cultivating a radical imaginary for rethinking how emancipatory urban practices can wrest back power 'to reshape the process of urbanization' and demand that state authorities prevent the breaking up, and breaking down, of existing communities.[88] Alternative communities might crop up anywhere, of course, although the call to 'take back the commons' has mostly occurred in urban spaces. It is in cities that empty spaces are most desired by commercial interests, and where the combination of glaring inequality as well as heterogeneity and anonymity can at times facilitate new kinds of alliances and struggle, creating different configurations of public space.[89]

Such struggles over urban space often begin with protests from increasingly disenfranchised youth, who watch the unrelenting commercial take-over of every nook and cranny of their cities, punctuated by the ghostlike sterility of empty buildings in the hands of property speculators. The issue of urban homelessness and overpriced, insecure lodgings lies behind the long history of squatting, which exploded in many Western democracies in the 1970s and 1980s.

One of the most archetypal, extensive and enduring of these squatting movements was the occupation of an abandoned military barracks in the heart of Copenhagen in 1971, known as Freetown Christiania. It quickly developed into a commune of around 850 residents, providing not just housing but its own alternative workshops, bars, cafés, performance venues and even parallel social services, in coordination with the rest of the municipality. In the words of one of its founding members, Jacob Ludvigsen, a well-known journalist and Provo (the name of the autonomous radical Dutch activists), who co-wrote its original mission statement, Christiania's goal is to be a self-sustaining community and 'a self-governing society whereby each and every individual holds themselves responsible over the wellbeing of the entire community'.[90] Indeed, it has its own flag, red with three yellow dots said to be the Os in 'Love, Love, Love'.[91] The production and sale of cannabis led to serious drug-related problems for this quickly notorious alternative community, but differing negotiations with the authorities have meant that Christiania has survived for over forty-five years as a colourful, semi-autonomous community.[92]

In London at the close of the 1960s, a more fleeting Street Commune movement had begun, which squatted several large, empty stately buildings under the slogan, 'We are the Writing on your Walls', most famously the Queen Mother's once-grand ex-residence in 144 Piccadilly, near Hyde Park. Short-lived and notorious as these squats were, they attracted thousands of young people from all over Britain. As its leading initiator, Phil Cohen, then known as 'Dr John', later recalled in his eloquent memoir *Reading Room Only*: 'Our biggest success was to accommodate and feed nearly a thousand souls, and provide them with a reasonably secure and peaceable environment in which to have fun together'. He went on to reflect that in the nightly meetings at these squats it was never clear whether people wanted mainly to change the law so that empty buildings could be used to provide homes for the homeless, or create an altogether different society. However, what did happen was that each nightly meeting provided 'a crash course in the workings of direct democracy ... an instant political education for many young people who had never before been involved in any kind of collective decision making, and whose opinions had rarely been consulted in any matter that concerned their lives'.[93] The beauty of urban existence meant that as media hysteria grew around the infamous squat and Cohen found himself personally attacked and demonized, he could flee to the Reading Room of the British Library, which became his sanctuary, 'my true home from home'.[94]

As the squatting movement spread around the UK, it not only initiated interest in living differently, but was often the backbone for significant community and political engagement, including housing struggles, alongside feminist and anti-racist politics in particular. I described these diverse community engagements in my contribution to *Beyond the Fragments* at the close of the 1970s, which illustrated the extent to which alternative cultural productions and community engagement flowered throughout that decade. Much of the energetic socializing and memorable fun of those times came from all the ways of working together in the alternative newspapers, magazines, presses, resource centres, musical groups, throughout the boisterous, hopeful days of the 1970s, as well as the musical benefits and other entertainments necessary to support their existence. For many of us, including myself, it also meant continuous, confrontational engagement with our borough councils, demanding that they become more accountable and responsive to the multitude of local needs.[95]

On the global stage, there have always been extensive squatter settlements, which have often helped to propel more creative urban design and cooperative ownership. This can be seen throughout much of Latin America, where every large city is ringed by squatter colonies which often end up forcing some accommodation from state authorities.[96] These occupations have sometimes provided the inspiration for exciting urban experiments, in which activist architects have worked with radical politicians and homeless people to construct new forms of cheap and desirable community housing.

One such development occurred when the radical Chilean

architect Alejandro Aravena worked with people in one of the poorest areas of Chile, resulting in the social housing project in Quinta Monroy, completed in 2004. It was built on a site that had been illegally occupied by ninety-seven families for the previous thirty years in the very centre of Iquique in northern Chile. Justin McGuirk's vivid account of cityscapes in his book *Radical Cities* describes the construction of Quinta Monroy and many other forms of innovative planning, including shelters for street children built under an underpass, homes at the top of abandoned skyscrapers, or the cable car transport system in Caracas, many of these projects designed by the US-based, international architects associated with Urban Think Tanks.[97]

However, in the harsher economic climate of recent decades, we know that militant action has not always been successful in achieving its goals, despite the exuberance of struggles along the way. As we've seen, urban protest peaked around the world in 2011, and has been rising and falling with anti-austerity movements ever since. In certain cities, especially in debt-ridden Southern Europe, these movements have persisted for over a decade, as evident in the perennial hum of grass-roots resistance seeking out spaces for alternative initiatives from those most affected by austerity measures.

In Greece, for instance, and especially in Athens, this has involved squatting in empty buildings, support for asylum seekers, initiatives for the free distribution of clothes and food, and even the organized provision of free medicine and health-care. The successful occupation of a local park in the heart of Exarcheia, scheduled to be transformed into a parking lot, has also meant the creation of an alternative site for community gatherings, where a children's playground now operates. Openness, autonomy and flexibility remain at the heart of these ventures based upon mutual aid and the sharing of resources, usually accompanying an anti-consumerism politics.

After 2012, many of these networks were, at least for a while, supported and subsidized by the rising party Syriza, as mentioned before, describing itself as the Coalition of the Radical Left. Along with many other observers, the sociologist Athina Arampatzi sums up these cooperative ventures as providing solidarity structures that create 'spaces where alternative modes of economic conduct and social relations are narrated, imagined and experimented with through everyday practices grounded in neighbourhoods and spanning across the city of Athens and beyond'.[98] More concretely, as one of the people engaged in an anti-consumerist collective in Exarcheia recalled about setting up and running the free shop Skoris: 'It is the joy of collectivity itself that is counter-hegemonic ... our affluence came not from the things we have ... we dressed up, danced, invited people over, ate, partied... People arrived from the neighbourhood, helping them overcome their fear, anger, isolation.'[99] Skoris has been open for over seven years now, with many refugees and asylum seekers regular visitors, as well as others relieving the stresses of unemployment and the anxieties of lives in crisis. I met people from all these groups on visiting Skoris in the summer of 2016.

Importantly, in all these ventures there exist a variety of particular tensions not just over the distinctions that are made and blurred between solidarity and charity, or anti-consumerist politics and costless consumption, but more generally between movement activists and their differing relation to the state. Solidarity initiatives often stress their bottom-up, participatory democratic nature, with some activists seeking full consensus along anarchist lines and eager to bypass or oppose the state, hoping eventually to do away with it. Others involved, though, see a more sustainable future and security of provision only emerging from their attempts to work creatively with some form of state support.[100] There is now a burgeoning literature that explores both the possibilities and the limitations of these events in instituting a democratic politics that can transform everyday life. What is most significant, however, as urban political theorists such as Maria Kaika and Luca Ruggiero illustrate, is that struggles over the economic, social and symbolic role of urban land have historically played a critical role in changing the nature and outcome of urban planning.[101]

Similarly, in many cities across Spain, movement activists have occupied empty buildings, opposed evictions and created liberated spaces for developing their networked approach to politics following the upsurge of the Indignados (or 15 May) movement in 2011. Here, the ties between movement activists and shared aspirations for municipal and state power have developed even more strongly than in Greece, following the formation of the genuinely grass-roots radical coalition party Podemos in 2014, headed by its charismatic, media-savvy young leader Pablo Iglesias. In Madrid and Barcelona, in particular, public engagement in politics has continued, including developing ideas for using digital platforms to encourage people's municipal activism.

As I have mentioned before, the extraordinary fertilization between radical movement and mainstream politics was evident in the recent election of committed activists in municipal elections, including the septuagenarian feminist Manuela Carmena as mayor of Madrid in 2015, backed by Podemos. A year after her victory, Carmena remained adamant in her support for collective resistance and grass-roots engagement in politics, insisting: 'Change always involves continuous confrontation'.[102]

Even more striking was the election of the young, feminist anti-eviction champion Ada Calau to become mayor of Barcelona, that same year. She represented the citizenship platform Barcelona en Comú (BComú) that had emerged directly from movement struggles and which has been able to form a minority government, supported by Podemos and two Catalan independence parties. 'We're living in extraordinary times that demand brave and creative solutions. If we're able to imagine a different city, we'll have the power to transform it', Colau announced.[103]

These two women mayors are both determined to take action against corporate control of their cities, restoring support for the neediest, while fining banks if they leave property empty. They have not sought to blame immigrants for economic problems caused by the financial elite, greedy landlords and the lack of social housing. Instead, they stress the role of community engagement in creating better futures through participatory budgeting and tackling poverty via subsidized energy and transport for the unemployed, alongside campaigns against sexist violence and the feminization of poverty. BComú also plays a leading role internationally in the Global Network of Cities, founded in 2004, which draws together movement politics and progressive municipal networks around the world, aiming for more fluid relations between the new coalitions and political parties, often bypassing central leadership structures.[104] Meanwhile, despite only coming third in the Spanish general elections in 2016, Podemos remains a catalyst for maintaining the hope that the creativity and energies of movement politics can be directed into the mechanisms of both democratically elected municipal and state power.[105]

In the UK, the tensions within public life between movement

politics and state engagement have appeared and receded over the years, ever since Thatcher's privatization and anti-welfare agenda, beginning in 1979. They came to a head exactly two years after Thatcher's victory, when Ken Livingstone, a key figure on the left of the Labour Party, staged an internal coup against the more centrist Andrew McIntosh to become leader of the Greater London Council (GLC) in 1981. He immediately raised hopes for the development of new forms of more democratic and participatory municipal socialism, which had echoes in other municipalities around the UK.

Livingstone was determined to combat Thatcher's key ideological agenda, which she announced in an interview the same year he become mayor: 'What's irritated me about the whole direction of politics in the last thirty years is that it's always been towards the collectivist society.'[106] It was this commitment to commonality that Thatcher was determined to smash in order to change the 'soul' of the nation, and that Livingstone was equally dedicated to maintain, offering assistance to collective movements of every stripe. Feminist, anti-racist, lesbian and gay activists were all invited into positions in County Hall, with support offered for their activities on the outside. This accompanied plans for workers' cooperatives, and support for other collective initiatives, such as the Women's Committee headed by Valerie Wise, all working to create more open and responsive government.

The GLC set up a popular planning unit for investing in older industrial areas as well as for creating new jobs, while sharing some of its resources with other local groups working for change. In its efforts to reach out, the GLC encouraged not just public meetings, debates and discussion, but regularly staged popular festivals and entertainments, drawing tens of thousands of people down to its location on the Thames. One huge concert against unemployment in 1985 attracted a quarter of a million people, while another event that same year provided an evening of jazz and African music at the Royal Albert Hall.[107]

It was Livingstone's radical determination to strengthen the democratic relationship between the state and its citizens that so enraged Thatcher, leading her to abolish the GLC in 1986, at the very height of its popularity as a symbol of collective resistance to her agenda. These experiences left most of the activists working in the GLC in the early 1980s, such as Hilary Wainwright, Jamie Gough and Robin Murray, determined ever since to keep working on the possibilities for refashioning state practices, practices that could rebuild and thicken democracy.[108]

In recent years, for instance, Hilary Wainwright has been immersed in the broad-ranging anti-corporate globalization movement, which kicked off in Porto Alegre in 1999. As the founder of the British movement magazine *Red Pepper*, in 1995, and one of its editors ever since, my friend Hilary has been indefatigable in celebrating the excitement and energy of horizontal or grass-roots resistance whenever and wherever she finds it. She has also kept looking out for ways of fostering left energies for harnessing the powers and resources of the state or, better still, regional state coalitions, as the only means of sustaining an anti-establishment opposition and securing a fairer redistribution of resources, whether locally or, especially, globally. One thing Wainwright has never lacked is the optimism that clearly sustains her own political enthusiasm for democratic engagement.

We see it shine forth in her book *Reclaim the State* (2003), where she concludes: 'Across the world, from Scotland to South Korea, an increasing number of parties are emerging that are in effect the electoral voice of coalitions of social movements. They see many sources of power to challenge capitalism and create in its place an equal, democratic and environmentally sustainable society.'[109] She was not wrong to see a greater openness between some electoral parties and movement activists, citing for instance the idea of participatory budgeting allowing citizens to decide how to allocate part of municipal spending, which was first developed by the Brazilian Workers' Party when it held sway in various Brazilian cities, beginning with Porto Alegre in 1989. This idea spread to many other parts of Latin America, before being tried by some municipalities in Europe, including Seville, Lisbon and Paris.[110] Nevertheless, despite scattered victories, Wainwright has to date been exceedingly over-optimistic in her hopes: sadly, we have yet to see any party in government managing to reverse the steady expansion of capitalist corporations making inroads into state structures and raiding their – and our – public resources.

No matter who is in government, the state will never be the answer to all our hopes for a better world, least of all in the global arena; more often, it is quite the reverse. Yet, so long as we have nation states, they will always be part of public life in a multitude of ways both enabling and repressive, porous and, at times, malleable. Why else would we go marching, marching, in Britain often to Downing Street or Parliament Square, rather than simply battening down the hatches wherever we are? This is what governments usually prefer us to do, although not what the current leader of the Labour Party Jeremy Corbyn would ever desire. More than ever, then, as so many others, especially feminists, often note, we need to make calls upon the state for radical purposes, beginning with prioritizing the struggles to stop the outsourcing of its resources.

Only the privileged, who content themselves with dabbling in abstraction forever, can indulge the romanticism of believing the state irrelevant to the changes we must seek in order to reduce the avoidable misery of so many. Neither Žižek, sneering at the 'bleeding heart' liberals with their respect for 'democracy' and desire for 'decaffeinated revolution', nor Alain Badiou, refusing to partake in elections or anything short of full 'revolutionary rupture', will ever have to line up for free food or see their benefits removed.[111]

In the states we now occupy, many of which have simply chosen, as has the UK, or have been forced, as has Greece, to relinquish much of their control over public resources, it is more useful to argue that it is the desire for 'democracy' itself that must be fought for anew. In the words of the Portuguese scholar Boaventura de Sousa Santos: 'The struggle for democracy is today above all a struggle for the democratization of democracy'.[112] This struggle can be a lively and life-affirming one, whether involving large-scale marches, strike actions or other forms of refusal attempting to force change, or can begin from any number of more local, collective engagements. The latter have often been undertaken to add beauty and comfort to urban life, whether efforts to cover the metal spikes sometimes placed on benches outside luxury buildings with cushions so the homeless can sleep on them, the creation of guerrilla gardens in underused urban spaces, or in other ways occupying or reclaiming such spaces.

As Leo Hollis writes in his enthusiastic overview *Cities Are Good for Us*, at least 640 communal gardens have been created in abandoned spaces in New York alone: 'It struck me that the gardens were not just built by the community, but formed one as well.'[113] His book also highlights the role of successful urban struggles for any genuinely sustainable future, noting in the contrast, for instance, between Stockholm and New York, that 'the more equal and trustful a city is, the more likely it is to be green'.[114] Similarly, he cites other examples where, for instance, changing and improving the transport system to get cars off the road serves equally to enhance community life by producing greater space for pedestrianization, social gathering and community enjoyment.

It is also true that even when campaigns begin as purely defensive ones, whether against the privatization of public resources or opposing harmful spending cuts, they easily transform into spaces of hope, at least for a while.[115] Such struggles always subvert the now ruling rationality to individualize every moment of our existence, simply through the collectivity and mutual support they encourage. This is the vitality that allows us to keep desire alive, as Francesca Polletta describes in her book *Freedom Is an Endless Meeting*, pointing out the lasting gains, and occasional victories, that emerge from involvement in participatory democratic activities.[116]

We all know that there are no guarantees in our efforts to strengthen democracy and force state institutions to act more decisively against the encroachment of the mega-corporations which evade any sort of accountability. Yet, as so many have noticed, it is not so hard to turn the struggles for greater participatory democracy into sites of collective exhilaration, given the creativity, strength and agency we can gain from one another along the way.[117] Exactly the same is true about collective protest against all the other abuses of power, as the millions of women in recent years regularly taking to the streets globally against the continuing menace of men's violence testify: 'Pussies against Patriarchy' are having fun, as are those young women joyfully asserting 'Girls just want FUN-ding' – for reproductive rights, sex education or to counter all the other ways men use their authority to curb women's personal and collective strength and autonomy.

Nothing better exemplifies this collective spirit than the contrast between the isolation felt by those trapped in the home as targets of domestic violence compared with the excitement and pleasure evident among women taking action together against such violence. We saw this when Sisters Uncut simultaneously blocked bridges in four cities across the UK, London, Bristol, Newcastle and Glasgow, against cuts to women's refuges in November 2016.[118] Such joy may be fleeting, but it gives rise to new types of political perceptions and possibilities, perhaps to enable even the most threatened to feel more grounded and alive in the claims they need to be able to make. And sometimes, the strength, confidence and sense of purpose we gain from moments of joyful solidarity lasts a very long time.

Afterword: Happy Endings?

Change is always possible, and can arrive unexpectedly, both personally and on a broader canvas: indeed, social and personal change are often connected. Yet are we finally any clearer about the nature of joy?

I have explained that this is not an easy question to answer, there being something intangible about the notion of joy itself. Since joy is a feeling that lifts us outside the everyday, we cannot easily seek it out, even if we manage to acquire routine ways to escape anxieties or sources of sadness. Contentment is certainly a simpler emotion to grasp, whereas joy can rarely be predicted.

It arrives in some of the most unexpected moments and contexts, as Christine Corton notes reporting the words of the English journalist and travel writer Henry Morton, describing the now largely forgotten opacity of the London fogs a century ago, as eerie and mysterious: 'The stranger in his first fog finds thrills innumerable; the Londoner, hate it as he does, cannot deny that there is a childish joy in the sudden dislocation of routine, the astonishing realisation that the other side of the road is an adventure and a peril.'[1] Perhaps it accounts for the perverse pleasure people find watching horror movies (though

I am not one of them), aroused and excited, knowing they will survive the phantasmatic slaughter.

Of course, one does not have to be a poet or composer to be surprised by joy, whether suddenly finding beauty in nature or as a product of human creation, in whatever form it takes – the bird-watcher exhilarated as the stints swirl by, the walker enchanted, encountering a rare orchid, those Europeans who watched and heard Beethoven conducting his very last symphony (No. 9), after which they all kept clapping, throwing their hats and scarves in the air, long before the *Ode to Joy* became the international anthem of the European Union.

I recall a similar feeling in Sydney, out with school friends, watching Margot Fonteyn and Rudolph Nureyev dancing *Swan Lake*. I wasn't at all familiar with ballet at the time, but we simply knew this was an incredibly exciting occasion, that we were lucky to be there, and then lost ourselves in the moment. I even recall what I wore, or I imagine I do. But whatever the occasion, and however pure or mixed the sense of pleasure, it seems to me that a thing of beauty will not remain a joy forever, except in our shared memories of it.

When we are, indeed, surprised by joy, no longer simply at the mercy of the routine or familiar, what makes it linger is our capacity to convey the response: even if, like Wordsworth expressing his sudden moment of delight, sadness swiftly follows, mourning the little daughter who cannot share his joy.[2] Those of an enduringly solitary bent may choose merely to share joyful moments with their diaries, or to convey what has stirred them in the material world to some presumptively more elevated spirit, or to God.

We are perhaps less surprised by joy when we feel it in care-free or inspiring moments with our friends, or when we are close to our particular loved ones. Being open and receptive to joy is surely the very opposite of having to watch and monitor our behaviour to ensure we are making just the right impression on others, when we are doing that work of self-display before calculating eyes, even if, when we feel we are doing it well, our performance might provide a certain narcissistic gratification.

The more peaceful joy that I find easiest to describe and understand, and therefore what I keep returning to, is when we are most fully absorbed or lost in something clearly bigger than ourselves, free for a while from exactly that self-monitoring that disciplines our daily lives. Anxious self-scrutiny also more easily slips away when we find ourselves caught up with others in public spaces. Yet crowds have often been vilified in Western thought, taking us back to Le Bon's fierce contempt observing events in Paris in the 1890s.

However, as soon as crowds began to be studied more seriously, historians recognized that the negative perception they earned was that usually they represented gatherings of people without institutional power. Even social psychologists, less attuned to providing broader context than those from disciplines that study social behaviour, observed that actual crowd behaviour was almost always rational. Indeed, when it turns confrontational or violent, this is usually precipitated by coercive attempts to disperse it.[3] Moreover, it is in crowds, little and large, that joy has often been detected, creating forms of bonding that are both meaningful and often empowering. The seductive force of collective energies, drawing people together as communities – whether embedded or elective – is hardly new, and most of us will have encountered this shared energy one way or another, whether or not we would describe it as progressive.

Sometimes, the spectacles arousing joy are socially orchestrated. Only a few years ago in Britain, there was an overwhelming outpouring of pleasure across all possible social divisions on the opening ceremonies of the Olympic Games in July 2012. People's joy was captured in tweets throughout the evening: 'I forgot how rare and intoxicating collective joy is. It revives the heart, a bit, doesn't it?' someone tweeted from Dundee. The next day it was all summed in my morning paper: 'Oh, the joy of people! It made me cry', the journalist Miranda Sawyer announced, while the poet Jackie Kay rejoiced in the shared passion as 'breath-taking, bold, brazen … it might be the only gold we get'.[4] Of course, for those of us on the left our pleasure was only enhanced when we learned that some of those among our welfare-cutting Tory MPs had hated the event, complaining that the NHS had been 'shamefully glorified'.[5]

Even more special are those moments of collective joy that we have helped to generate ourselves. For feminists of my generation, joy was encountered anew at every women's liberation conference in its opening years in the early 1970s, primarily at their close, as women's bands took to the stage and we conga danced 'The Women's Army Is Marching'. Despite the internal conflicts evident in some of the debates, it was for the most part a peaceful army, at least when we were still singing and dancing together.

Such celebration was not so far removed from the joyful rituals and festivities that a host of anthropologists and others, from Durkheim through Victor Turner to his wife, Eve Turner, today, have described in their ethnographic observations around the world. There is always some joy in gatherings where people come together to mingle and lose themselves in spectacles or performances (especially when dancing) that bring them closer to each other. This is all the more true when we find ourselves within the very groups to which we want to belong, and when there is no pressure to be there – if, indeed, we are lucky enough to have such groups.

The Guyana-born authority on the calypso, Gordon Rohlehr, who lived and worked mainly in Trinidad, wrote of the great importance of music and festivals in overcoming the degree of ethnic conflict and depression within the Trinidadian society he studied, since they help to maintain the possibilities for warmth and community.[6] More recently, the Australian anthropologist Graham St John, an authority on diverse cultures of dance, has been studying the spread of electronic dance (EDM) music cultures, and he conveys much the same story: 'Worldwide, throughout human history and across cultures, festivals are integral to reproducing socioeconomic, religious and political life, but they are also thresholds of innovation, sources of joy and happiness among participants, and barometers of peace beyond their borders'.[7] Similarly, from the West Bank, Saeed Sulimen describes Palestinian Dabke dancing as a way of reinforcing energy and pride, and hence an 'important weapon in the cultural resistance of Palestinians'.[8]

Hannah Arendt argued that 'no one could be called either happy or free without participating, and having a share, in public power'.[9] For Arendt, it was precisely in the possibility of public engagement that one could consolidate not just political friendships and democratic belonging, but *amor mundi*, love of the world. What Arendt held dear was 'the power that arises out of joint action and deliberation'.[10]

Judith Butler, among many others, calls for much the same thing in her recent writing, stressing the need for public spaces in which to assemble and debate, and to realize democratic belonging and the possibilities for new publics to come into being by means of concerted actions, whether of resistance, celebration or mourning. This would include the spontaneous vigils that took place all around the world following the Orlando shooting in a gay nightclub in June 2016, or across the UK following the murder of the Labour MP Jo Cox for xenophobic reasons a few months later. What Butler suggests is that these forms of assembly 'can be understood as nascent and provisional versions of popular sovereignty ... indispensable reminders of how legitimation functions in democratic theory and practice'.[11] They are not in any way a triumph over the many differing forms of insecurity or precarity people live with, but rather a vital and strengthening opposition to it.

Hundreds of thousands of women from around the world joined massive protests the day after Donald Trump's inauguration as president of the USA, in January 2017. There was surprising joy in the air, with people delighting in the amazing solidarity not just in any one place, but visible all around the globe, against a man whose contempt for women was so obvious throughout his campaign. Indeed, an oddly hopeful spirit of defiance has persisted against each repressive piece of legislation Trump has signed since assuming office. Thus, for weeks following his initial blanket ban on travellers from seven Muslim-majority countries, impressively organized groups of activists gathered at airports across the country, holding up welcome signs, distributing gifts and supporting lawyers ready to offer legal help whenever it might be needed. There is now a comprehensive list of resources for resisting Trump being continually updated as new initiatives appear, assembled by the vast array of movement activists whose energy, to date, has been growing week by week.[12]

More generally, looking back at the subversive and utopian spirit I covered earlier in this book, it remains clear to me that we often renew our attachments to life by embracing the sorrows as well as the joys that are far larger than our own. Some people will always manage to remain more optimistic than others, and thereby persist in helping to keep open spaces of hope and possibility for others to enter.

Sometimes, a certain amount of naïveté is necessary for engaging in the world, putting to one side the statistical likelihood of failure for any specific instance, as another New York feminist who has always inspired me, Ann Snitow, wrote recently. Despite the obstacles we will always face, the potential joy of solidarity still remains along the way: 'Happy endings', Snitow writes, 'require that one set sail toward a near enough horizon and keep one's eyes off the inevitable: failure, confusion, and the falling out of comrades.'[13] Meanwhile, one way or another, simply being together strengthens us, though such assemblies will need to be endlessly repeated, whether in the face of rampant oppression, or confronting the more routine conformity that stifles creativity.

Another American feminist, Lauren Berlant, argues optimistically that 'the political' is 'that which magnetises a desire for intimacy, sociality, affective solidarity, and happiness'.[14] The black radical leader, Angela Davis, has spent her life affirming that freedom is a constant struggle. Yet happy endings arrive now and then, when we are able to take joy in the flourishing of others, especially when it happens after shared struggle. The late Australian ecological feminist Val Plumwood urges us to acknowledge kinship with all those we are close to, even as we grow strong in respecting difference: 'If we are to survive into a liveable future, we must take into our own hands the power to create, restore and explore different stories, with new main characters, better plots, and at least the possibility of some happy endings'.[15]

The point is that even trying to envisage how we might help to create a more equitable, peaceful and fairer world brings a certain audacity and energy to life, at least in the process of sharing such imaginings. As Brecht asked and answered,

> In dark times
> Will there also be singing?
> Yes, there will also be singing
> About the dark times.[16]

Even in such times, we sometimes manage to kiss 'joy as it flies', though I certainly have no sense of 'eternity's sunrise'. Happy endings can be joyfully pursued when we feel empowered together with others, although as we surely should know by now, such endings can never be said to have finally arrived.

Acknowledgements

I am grateful to all those who have given me confidence to write about the perplexing terrain of happiness and the disappearing language of joy in these markedly gloomy and pessimistic times. This includes new friends and old who have encouraged me every step of the way. In the former category, I am especially grateful to Andreas Chatzidakis and Catherine Rottenberg who read many of my chapters, offering useful critical commentary and above all their wonderful warmth, generosity and companionship, along with Neve Gordon and Joe Hearty. It is harder to list all my old friends who have cheered and supported me over the last few years. The thoughtful commentary and friendship of Catherine Hall, Barbara Taylor, Sally Alexander and Cora Kaplan, who are in my writing group, have assisted me for over twenty years now. Many others keep me cheerful and comforted by their precious friendship, including Éamonn McKeown, Amber Jacobs, Paddy Maynes, Sheila Rowbotham, Kjetil Berge, Nick Davidson, Rachel Moore, Tariq Saleem, Mehmet-Ali Dikerdem, Anke Hennig, Maria Brock, Sarah Benton, Daniel Monk, Matt Cook, Mirjam Hadar, Uri Hadar, Chris Whitbread, Steve Skaith, João Manuel de Oliveira and Marina Warner, to name only a few whom I saw or spoke with

RADICAL HAPPINESS

most often in recent years. In working on this book, I was particularly indebted to my invariably encouraging, enthusiastic and dedicated editor at Verso, Leo Hollis, and I would also like to thank my agent, David Godwin, and the painstaking copyediting of Angelica Sgouros and Mark Martin. Finally, I am lucky to have Graeme, Barbara and Zimri Segal in my life, as well as my partner, Agnes Bolsø, along with all the Bolsø clan.

270

Notes

Preface

1 Lynne Segal, *Straight Sex: The Politics of Pleasure*, London, Virago, 1994; Verso, 2014.

2 Mervyn Rothstein, 'Remembering Tennessee Williams as a Gentle Genius of Empathy', *New York Times*, 30 May 1990, nytimes.com.

3 Office for National Statistics, *Measuring National Well-being: Life in the UK, 2015*, 25 March 2015, ons.gov.uk. In more detail, the report noted that around a quarter (26.8 per cent) of people aged sixteen and over in the UK rated their life satisfaction at the highest levels, compared to 5.6 per cent at the lowest. Similarly, just under a third (32.6 per cent) rated their happiness at the highest levels, while 9.7 per cent rated their happiness at the lowest levels. A higher proportion (39.4 per cent) rated their anxiety at the lowest levels and 20.0 per cent rated it at the highest levels.

4 Josh Hrala, 'The World Happiness Index 2016 Just Ranked the Happiest Countries on Earth: How Does Your Home Rate?', *Science Alert*, 17 March 2016, sciencealert.com.

5 Terry Eagleton, *The Meaning of Life: A Very Short Introduction*, Oxford, Oxford University Press, 2007, pp. 82–3.

6 Barbara Ehrenreich, *Dancing in the Streets: A History of Collective Joy*, London, Granta, 2008.

7 David Graeber, 'On the Phenomenon of Bullshit Jobs', *Strike!*, Summer 2013; Thomas Frank, 'Bullshit Jobs, the Caring Classes, and the Future of Labor: An Interview with David Graeber', *Labor Issues*, 3 June 2014; Joyce Canaan, 'Bullshit Jobs: A Critical Pedagogy Provocation', *Concept*, Vol. 6, No. 1, Spring 2015, concept.lib.ed.ac.uk; 'Absurdes et vides de sens: ces jobs d'enfer', *Le Monde*, 22 April 2016.

8 '"Bullshit Jobs": 35% of Brits Think Their Job Is Pointless, Survey Finds', *RT*, 13 August 2015, rt.com.

9 Zygmunt Bauman, *Liquid Modernity*, Cambridge, Polity Press, 2000.

10 Judith Levine, 'The Passion of Ellen Willis', *Boston Review*, 8 September 2015, http://bostonreview.net.

11 Russell Jacoby, *Picture Imperfect: Utopian Thought for an Anti-Utopian Age*, New York, Columbia University Press, 2005; Fredric Jameson, *Archaeologies of the Future: The Desire Called Utopia and Other Science Fictions*, London, Verso, 2005.

1. What's Wrong with Happiness?

1 Jeanette Winterson, *Why Be Happy When You Could Be Normal?*, London, Vintage, 2012, p. 114.

2 W. H. Auden, 'New Year Letter', *Letters* (1941), in *Collected Longer Poems of W.H. Auden*, New York, Random House, 1965, p. 79.

3 Paul Dolan, *Happiness by Design: Finding Pleasure and Purpose in Everyday Life*, London, Allen Lane, pp. 3, 4.

4 Edward Luttwak, *Turbo-Capitalism: Winners and Losers in the Global Economy*, New York, Harper Perennial, 2000.

5 Richard Easterlin, 'Does Economic Growth Improve the Human Lot? Some Empirical Evidence' (1974), in *Nations and Households in Economic Growth: Essays in Honor of Moses Abramovitz*, ed. Paul A. David and Melvin W. Reder, New York, Academic Press, Inc.

6 Andrew J. Oswald, 'Happiness and Economic Performance', *Economic Journal*, 1997, 107, pp. 1815–31; Richard Layard, Andrew Clark and Claudia Senik, 'First World Happiness Report Launched at the United Nations', *The Earth Institute*, 2 April 2012, earth.columbia.edu.

7 Betsey Stevenson and Justin Wolfers, 'Subjective Well-Being and Income: Is There Any Evidence of Satiation?', National Bureau of Economic Research Program, Working Paper No. 18992, April 2013, nber.org.

8 London School of Economics and Political Science, Centre for Economic Performance, Mental Health Policy Group, *The Depression Report: A New Deal for Depression and Anxiety Disorders*, Centre for Economic Performance Special papers, CEPOP15, 2006, pp. 1, 6, eprints.lse.ac.uk.

9 Ibid.

10 See Richard Layard, et al., *Unemployment: Macroeconomic Performance and the Labour Market*, Oxford, Oxford University Press, 1991, which opens with the claim that: 'Unemployment is a major source of human misery', p. xiii. Moreover, the misleading nature of Layard's bland statement that the mentally ill come from every social stratum is at odds with data he presents elsewhere, showing an overwhelming correlation between mental illness and lower educational attainment, in Richard Layard, 'Mental Health: Britain's Biggest Social Problem?', 20 January 2005, Strategy Unit Seminar on Mental Health, p. 26, eprints.lse. ac.uk.

11 Dolan, *Happiness by Design*, p. 77.

12 Michael Marmot, et al., 'Fair Society, Healthy Lives: Strategic Review of Health Inequalities in England Post 2010', *The Marmot Review*, 2010, marmotreview.org.

13 Richard Wilkinson and Kate Pickett, *The Spirit Level: Why Greater Equality Makes Societies Stronger*, London, Bloomsbury, 2010.

14 Randeep Ramesh, 'Top Doctor: Social Inequality in UK

Costing 550 Lives Every Day', *Guardian*, 10 September 2015, theguardian.com.

15 Carole Cadwalladr, 'From Blair to Corbyn: The Changing Face of Islington, Labour's London Heartland', *Guardian*, 9 August 2015, theguardian.com.

16 Kristina Glenn, quoted in ibid.

17 Poppy Danby, 'Islington Has Second Highest Crime Rate of All London Boroughs', *Islington Now*, 25 March 2015, islingtonnow. co.uk.

18 See William Davies, *The Happiness Industry: How Government and Big Business Sold Us Well-Being*, London, Verso, 2015.

19 Paul Baron and Paul Sweezy, *Monopoly Capital*, New York, Monthly Review Press, 1966.

20 Colin Crouch, *The Strange Non-Death of Neoliberalism*, Cambridge, Polity Press, 2011.

21 Mehreen Khan, 'UK Facing "Dreadful" Wage Stagnation: 3 Charts from the IFS, *Financial Times*, 24 November 2016, ft.com. See Tom Crew, 'Strange Death of Municipal England', *London Review of Books*, Vol. 38, No. 24, 15 December 2016, p. 8.

22 See Crew, 'Strange Death of Municipal England'.

23 Laura Bates, 'There Is an Urgent Need to Update Adult Thinking to Catch Up with the Reality of Teenagers' Lives', *Guardian*, 24 August 2015, theguardian.com.

24 Will Davies, Johnna Montgomerie and Sara Wallin, 'Financial Melancholia: Mental Health and Indebtedness', Political Economy Research Centre, 2015, perc.org.uk.

25 Ibid., p. 25

26 Ibid., p. 24.

27 Ibid., pp. 33–4, 1.

28 Rupert Jones, 'Debt Collectors Hit Out at Advice Websites', *Guardian*, 2 December 2009, theguardian.com.

29 Davies, *The Happiness Industry*.

30 Hamilton Nolan, 'At Amazon Even the Part-Timers are Miserable', *Gawker*, 14 May 2014, http://gawker.com.

31 Carl Cederström and André Spicer, *The Wellness Syndrome*, Cambridge, Polity Press, 2015.

32 André Spicer, 'The Cult of Compulsory Happiness Is Ruining Our Workplaces', *Guardian*, 12 December 2016, theguardian.com.

33 Lauren Berlant, *Cruel Optimism*, Durham, NC, Duke University Press, 2011, p. 43.

34 Zadie Smith, 'Find Your Beach', in *The Best American Essays 2015*, ed. Ariel Levy, New York, Houghton Mifflin Harcourt, 2015, p. 194.

35 Sophocles, *Philoctetes*, in *The Greek Classics: Sophocles – Seven Plays*, trans. The Athenian Society, ed. James Ford, El Paso, TX, Norte Press, 2006, p. 205.

36 Aristotle, *The Nicomachean Ethics*, X.9, trans. William David Ross, pp. 262, 263, 269.

37 Martha C. Nussbaum, 'Who Is the Happy Warrior? Philosophy Poses Questions to Psychology', in *Law and Happiness*, ed. Eric A. Posner and Cass R. Sunstein, Chicago, University of Chicago Press, 2010, p. 84.

38 Darrin McMahon, *The Pursuit of Happiness: A History from the Greeks to the Present*, London, Penguin Books, 2007, p. 13.

39 Ibid., p. 181.

40 See David Lyons, *In the Interest of the Governed: A Study of Bentham's Philosophy of Utility and Law*, Oxford, Oxford University Press, 1973.

41 William Blake, *Auguries of Innocence*, London, CreateSpace Independent Publishing Platform, 2014, p. 2.

42 William Blake, 'Eternity', in *Blake Complete Writings*, ed. Geoffrey Keynes, Oxford, Oxford University Press, 1966, p. 179.

43 Baruch Spinoza, *A Spinoza Reader: The Ethics and Other Works*, trans. and ed. Edwin Curley, Princeton, NJ, Princeton University Press, 1994, p. 161.

44 Gilles Deleuze, 'Lecture Courses on Spinoza's Concept of *Affect*', 1978, webdeleuze.com.

45 Georg Wilhelm Friedrich Hegel, *Lectures on the Philosophy of*

World History: Introduction, Reason in History (1830), trans. H. B. Nisbet, Cambridge, Cambridge University Press, 1975, pp. 78–9.

46 Arthur Schopenhauer, *The World as Will and Representation* (1837), trans. E. F. J. Payne, Dover Publications, 1966, p. 573; Arthur Schopenhauer, *Essays and Aphorisms*, ed. and trans. R. J. Hollindale, London, Penguin Books, 1970, pp. 42–3.

47 Immanuel Kant, *Grounding for the Metaphysics of Morals: On a Supposed Right to Lie Because of Philanthropic Concerns* ([1798] 1881), trans. James W. Ellington, Indianapolis, Hackett, 1881, p. 41.

48 'Man Does Not Strive for Pleasure; Only the Englishman Does', Friedrich Wilhelm Nietzsche, in *Twilight of the Idols, or, How to Philosophize with a Hammer* (1889), in *The Portable Nietzsche*, trans. Walter Kaufmann, New York, Viking Press, 1968, CreateSpace Independent Publishing Platform.

49 Sigmund Freud, *Three Essays on Sexuality* (1905), in *On Sexuality*, The Pelican Freud Library (PFL), Vol. 7, Harmondsworth, Penguin, 1977, p. 99.

50 Sigmund Freud, *Civilization and its Discontents*, trans. and ed. James Strachey, New York, W. W. Norton, 1989, pp. 34–5.

51 Sigmund Freud and Joseph Breuer, *Studies in Hysteria* (1895), trans. Nicola Luckhurst, London, Penguin Books, 2004, p. 306.

52 Darian Leader, *The New Black: Mourning, Melancholia and Depression*, London, Penguin, 2009, pp. 1–2.

53 Theodor Adorno, *Minima Moralia: Reflections on a Damaged Life* (1951), trans. E. N. Ephcott, London, Verso, 2005, p. 63.

54 Jack Underwood, *Happiness*, London, Faber & Faber, 2015.

55 Friedrich Schiller, 'An Early Setting of Schiller's "Ode to Joy"' (1785), *Fidelio*, Vol. 2, No. 1, Spring 1993.

56 Adam Potkay, *The Story of Joy: From the Bible to Late Romanticism*, Cambridge, Cambridge University Press, 2007, p. 1.

57 Anaïs Nin, 'Again Towards America: Will I Ever Reach Joy', *Mirages: The Unexpurgated Diary of Anaïs Nin, 1939–1947*, New York, Swallow Press, 2013, p. 2.

58 Anaïs Nin, *The Diary of Anaïs Nin 1944–1947* (1971), New York, Harcourt Publishers, 1980, p. 24.

59 Ann Snitow, 'The Politics of Passion: Ellen Willis, 1941–2006', in Snitow, *The Feminism of Uncertainty*, Durham, NC, and London, Duke University Press, 2015, p. 292.

60 Audre Lorde, 'Uses of the Erotic: The Erotic as Power', *Sister Outsider*, New York, The Crossing Press Feminist Series, 1984, p. 56.

61 Angela Carter, *Wise Children*, London, Chatto & Windus, 1991, p. 256.

62 Ursula Owen, speaking on the popularity of Virago Press, for *Sisterhood and After: The Women's Liberation Oral History Project*, British Museum, recorded 21 November 2011, bl.uk.

63 Lynne Segal, *Making Trouble*, London, Serpent's Tail, 2007.

64 See Michael Klein, 'A Rich Life: Adrienne Rich on Poetry, Politics, and Personal Revelation', *Boston Pheonix*, June 1999, poets.org.

65 Hannah Arendt, 'Revolution and Public Happiness', *Commentary*, November 1960.

66 Hannah Arendt, *On Revolution* (1963), London, Penguin Books, 1990, p. 225.

67 Crouch, *The Strange Non-Death of Neoliberalism*.

68 Wendy Brown, *Undoing the Demos: Neoliberalism's Stealth Revolution*, New York, Zone, 2015, p. 30.

69 Some of the best include David L. Eng and David Kazanjian, eds, *Loss: The Politics of Mourning*, Berkeley, University of California Press, 2002; Heather Love, *Feeling Backward: Loss and the Politics of Queer History*, Cambridge, MA, Harvard University Press, 2007; José Esteban Muñoz, 'Feeling Brown, Feeling Down: Latina Affect, the Performativity of Race, and the Depressive Position', *Signs: Journal of Women in Culture and Society*, Vol. 31, No. 3, 2006, pp. 675–88; David Halperin and Valerie Traub, eds, *Gay Shame*, Pap/DVD, Chicago, University of Chicago Press, 2009; Ann Cvetkovich, *Depression: A Public Feeling*, Durham,

NC, Duke University Press, 2012; Halperin and Traub, *Gay Shame*; Love, *Feeling Backward*; Muñoz, 'Feeling Brown, Feeling Down'.

70 Cornel West, quoted in Gina Dent, 'Black Pleasure, Black Joy: An Introduction' in *Black Popular Culture*, ed. Dent, Dia Center for the Arts, 1992, p. 1.

2. 'Sing No Sad Songs for Me'

1 Ann Cvetkovich, *Depression: A Public Feeling*, Durham, NC, Duke University Press, 2013, p. 154.

2 Barbara Ehrenreich, *Smile or Die: How Positive Thinking Fooled America and the World*, London, Granta, 2009, p. 156.

3 Ibid., pp. 12–13.

4 Ibid., p. 3; Peter Wehrwein, 'Astounding Increase in Antidepressant Use by Americans', Harvard Health Publications, Harvard Medical School, 20 October 2011, health.harvard.edu.

5 Aristotle, *Problemata*, Problema XXX.1, 953a10–14, trans. E. S. Forster (1927), in *The Complete Works of Aristotle*, Vol. II, ed. Jonathan Barnes, Princeton, NJ, Princeton University Press, sixth edn, 1984, as discussed in various sources, for example, Heidi Northwood, 'The Melancholic Mean: The Aristotelian *Problema* XXX.1', *Paideaia*, Summer 1999.

6 William Shakespeare, *The Merchant of Venice*, Act 1, Scene I, pp. 77–79.

7 For one of the fullest discussions of Burton, see Angus Gowland, *The Worlds of Renaissance Melancholy: Robert Burton in Context* (Ideas in Context), Cambridge, Cambridge University Press, 2006.

8 Thomas Dixon, *Weeping Britannia: Portrait of a Nation in Tears*, Oxford, Oxford University Press, 2015, p. 69; George Cheyne, *The English Malady: or A Treatise of Nervous Disorders of All Kinds*, 1733, mentioned in Dixon, p. 42.

9 Clark Lawlor, *From Melancholia to Prozac: A History of Depression*, Oxford, Oxford University Press, 2012, pp. 81–3.

10 Ibid., p. 102.

11 G. E. Berrios, 'Melancholia and Depression During the Nineteenth Century: A Conceptual History', *British Journal of Psychiatry*, No. 153, 1988, pp. 298–304.

12 Émile Durkheim, *Suicide: A Study in Sociology*, trans. John A. Spaulding and George Simpson, Glencoe, IL, The Free Press, p. 248.

13 Sigmund Freud, 'Mourning and Melancholia', *The Standard Edition of the Psychological Works of Sigmund Freud*, Vol. 14, London, The Hogarth Press, 1953–74, p. 246.

14 Julia Kristeva, *Black Sun: Depression and Melancholia*, trans. Leon S. Roudiez, New York, Columbia University Press, 1989, p. 9.

15 Ibid., p. 224.

16 Ibid., pp. 99–100. For criticisms of Kristeva's account of sexual difference, mourning and creativity, which rely upon a rigid reading of the Oedipal dynamic, see Janice Doane and Devon Hodges, *From Klein to Kristeva: Psychoanalytic Feminism and the Search for the 'Good Enough' Mother*, Ann Arbor, University of Michigan Press, 1992, and Elizabeth Grosz, 'The Body of Signification', in *Abjection, Melancholia and Love: The Work of Julia Kristeva*, ed. John Fletcher and Andrew Benjamin, London, Routledge, 1990, pp. 80–103.

17 John Keats, 'Ode to Melancholy', 1819.

18 David Healy, *Let Them Eat Prozac: The Unhealthy Relationship Between the Pharmaceutical Industry and Depression*, New York, New York University Press, 2004, p. 2, italics in original.

19 Edward Shorter, *Before Prozac: The Troubled History of Mood Disorders in Psychiatry*, New York, Oxford University Press, 2009.

20 World Federation for Mental Health, 'Depression: A Global Crisis', World Health Organization, 10 October 2012, who.int.

21 Anna Moore, 'Eternal Sunshine', *Guardian*, 13 May 2007, theguardian.com.

22 Peter Wehrwein, 'Astounding Increase in Antidepressant Use by Americans', Harvard Health Publications blog, 20 October 2011, health.harvard.edu.

23 David Healy, *Mania: A Short History of Bipolar Disorder*, Baltimore, MD, Johns Hopkins University Press, 2008, p. 190.

24 G. I. Spielmans, 'The Promotion of Olanzapine in Primary Care: An Examination of Internal Industry Documents', *Soc.Sci.Med.*, 69, 2009, pp. 14–20.

25 Joanna Moncrieff, 'The Medicalization of "Ups and Downs": The Marketing of the New Bipolar Disorder', *Transcultural Psychiatry*, Vol. 51, No. 4, 2014, p. 593.

26 Gardiner Harris, 'Research Centre Tied to Drug Company', *New York Times*, 25 November 2008, nytimes.com; Moncrieff, 'The Medicalization of "Ups and Downs"'.

27 Irving Kirsch, *The Emperor's New Drugs: Exploding the Antidepressant Myth*, Boston, MA, Basic Books, 2011, pp. 4–5.

28 Marcia Angell, 'The Epidemic of Mental Illness: Why?', *New York Review of Books*, 23 June 2011, nybooks.com; Marcia Angell, 'The Illusions of Psychiatry', *New York Review of Books*, 14 July 2011, nybooks.com.

29 Daniel Carlat, *Unhinged: The Trouble with Psychiatry – A Doctor's Revelations about a Profession in Crisis*, Florence, MA, Free Press, 2010, pp. 25, 134–40; see also Joseph Wegman, *Antidepressant Medication Strategies: We've Come a Long Way, or Have We?*, Eau Claire, WI, Premier Publishing & Media, 2012, p. 25.

30 Angell, 'The Epidemic of Mental Illness: Why?'; Angell, 'The Illusions of Psychiatry'; Daniel Carlet, '"The Illusions of Psychiatry": An Exchange', *New York Review of Books*, 18 August 2011, nybooks.com

31 Oliver Burkeman, *The Antidote: Happiness for People Who Can't Stand Positive Thinking*, London, Canongate, 2013.

32 Nicholas Lezard, 'Darkness Visible', *Guardian*, 29 March 2002, theguardian.com.

33 Andrew Solomon, *The Noonday Demon: An Anatomy of Depression*, London, Vintage, 2002, p. 71.

34 Ibid., p. 25.

35 Ibid. p. 443.

36 William Styron, *Darkness Visible: A Memoir of Madness*, London, Vintage, 1992, p. 62.

37 Kay Redfield Jamison, *An Unquiet Mind*, London, Vintage, 1996, p. 214.

38 Jonathan Dollimore, 'Depression Studies', *London Review of Books*, Vol. 23, No. 16, 2001, p. 32.

39 Ibid., p. 23. Dollimore expands on his life-long struggle with depression in his beautiful memoir: *Desire: A Memoir*, London, Bloomsbury, forthcoming 2017.

40 Dollimore, *Desire: A Memoir*.

41 Cvetkovich, *Depression*, p. 1.

42 Ann Cvetkovich, 'Public Feelings', *South Atlantic Quarterly*, Vol. 106, No. 3, Summer 2007, p. 461.

43 Eve Kosofsky Sedgwick, *Fat Art, Thin Art*, Durham, NC, Duke University Press, 1994, pp. 3, 15.

44 Eve Kosofsky Sedgwick, *Touching Feeling: Affect, Pedagogy, Performativity*, Durham, NC, Duke University Press, 2003, p. 33.

45 Eve Kosofsky Sedgwick, *A Dialogue on Love*, Boston, MA, Beacon, 2000.

46 David Eng, 'Melancholia in the Late Twentieth Century', *Signs*, Vol. 25, No. 4, 2000, p. 1278.

47 David Eng and David Kazanjian, eds, *Loss: The Politics of Mourning*, Berkeley, CA, University of California Press, 2002, p. 4.

48 Cvetkovich, *Depression*, p. 80.

49 Ibid., p. 2.

50 Freud, 'Mourning and Melancholia', p. 246.

51 L. B. Alloy and L. Y. Abramson, 'Judgment of Contingency in Depressed and Nondepressed Students: Sadder But Wiser?',

Journal of Experimental Psychology: General, Vol. 108, No. 4, 1979, pp. 441–85.

52 Munch Museum, *Echoes of the Scream: Arken Museum of Modern Art*, 3 February–5 June 2001, 17 June–30 September 2001.

53 Will Davies, 'The Age of Pain', *New Statesman*, 15 November 2016, newstatesman.com.

54 David Healy, 'Psychopharmacology at the Interface Between the Market and the New Biology', in *The New Brain Sciences: Perils and Prospects*, ed. Dai Rees and Steven Tose, pp. 241–2.

3. *Where Is Joy?*

1 Adam Potkay, *The Story of Joy: From the Bible to Late Romanticism*, Cambridge, Cambridge University Press, 2007, p. 1.

2 Barbara Ehrenreich, *Nickel and Dimed: Undercover in Low-waged USA*, London, Granta, 2002.

3 Barbara Ehrenreich, *Smile or Die: How Positive Thinking Fooled America and the World*, London, Granta, 2009.

4 Barbara Ehrenreich, *Dancing in the Streets: A History of Collective Joy*, London, Granta, 2007, p. 4.

5 Joseph Conrad, *Heart of Darkness* (1902), London, Biblios Books, 2010, p. 56.

6 Ehrenreich, *Dancing in the Streets*, p. 3.

7 Ibid., pp. 8–9.

8 E. P. Thompson, *Customs in Common* (1993), London, Merlin Press, 2009, p. 51.

9 Yosef Stern, *Days of Joy: Sfas Emes – Ideas and Insights of the Sfas Emes on Chanukah and Purim*, New York, Mesorah Publications, 1995.

10 A few scholars, such as Bruce Robbins, have recently looked again at Weber, questioning the extent to which he did believe fully that disenchantment had occurred. See Bruce Robbins, 'Why I Am Not a Postsecularist', *Boundary* 2, Vol. 40, No. 1, 2013, p. 77.

11 Max Weber, *The Protestant Ethic and the Spirit of Capitalism* (1930), trans. Talcott Parsons, London and New York, Routledge Books, 1992, p. 18.

12 Eugen Weber, *Peasants into Frenchmen: The Modernization of Rural France, 1870–1914*, Stanford, CA, Stanford University Press, 1976, p. 3.

13 Ann Laura Stoler, *Race and the Education of Desire: Foucault's History of Sexuality and the Colonial Order of Things*, Durham, NC, Duke University Press, 1995, p. 125.

14 Émile Durkheim, *The Elementary Forms of the Religious Life* (1912), trans. J. R. Swain, New York, Free Press, 1965, pp. 257–8.

15 E. E. Evans-Pritchard, *Theories of Primitive Religion*, Oxford, Oxford University Press, 1965, pp. 14–17.

16 Clifford Geertz, *After the Fact: Two Countries Four Decades One Anthropooglist*, Cambridge, MA, and London, Harvard University Press, p. 17.

17 Max Gluckman, *Rituals of Rebellion in South-East Africa (The Frazer Lecture, 1952)*, Manchester, Manchester University Press, 1954; Victor Turner, *The Ritual Process: Structure and Anti-Structure*, Ithaca, NY, Cornell University Press, 1966.

18 Mikhail Bakhtin, *Rabelais and His World*, trans. H. Iswolsky, Bloomington, Indiana University Press, p. 11.

19 Ibid., p. 341.

20 Ibid., p. 66.

21 Mikhail Bakhtin, *Speech Genres and Other Late Essays*, trans. V. W. McGhee, Austin, University of Texas Press, 1986, pp. 134–5.

22 Stephen Greenblatt, *Learning to Curse: Essays in Early Modern Culture*, London and New York, Routledge, 1990, p. 88.

23 Mary Russo, 'Female Grotesques: Carnival and Theory', in *Feminist Studies/Critical Studies*, ed. Teresa de Lauretis, Bloomington, Indiana University Press, 1986, p. 219.

24 Peter Burke, *Popular Culture in Early Modern Europe*, London, Templesmith, 1978, p. 187.

25 Ken Hirschkop, 'Bakhtin, Discourse and Democracy', *New Left*

Review, No. 160, November–December 1986, pp. 92–3; see also Ken Hirschkop and David Shepherd, eds, *Bakhtin and Cultural Theory*, Manchester, Manchester University Press, 1989.

26 Terry Eagleton, *Walter Benjamin, or, Towards a Revolutionary Criticism*, London, New Left Books, p. 148; Umberto Eco, *The Role of the Reader: Explorations in the Semiotics of Texts*, Bloomington, Indiana University Press,1984, pp. 6–7.

27 Peter Stallybrass and Allon White, *The Politics and Poetics of Transgression*, London, Methuen, 1986, pp. 14, 16, 15.

28 Sigmund Freud, *Civilization and Its Discontents* (1930), Eastford, CT, Martino Fine Books, 2010, pp. 8, 23.

29 Ehrenreich, *Dancing in the Streets*, p. 14.

30 Peter Berger, *Redeeming Laughter: The Comic Dimension of Human Experience*, New York, Walter De Gruyter, 1997, p. 200.

31 Sigmund Freud, *The Future of an Illusion* (1927), in *The Standard Edition of the Complete Psychological Works of Freud*, Vol. 21, trans. and ed. J. Strachey, London, Vintage Press, 2001, p. 43.

32 Julian Barnes, *Nothing to Be Frightened of*, London, Vintage, 2009, p. 1.

33 Charles Taylor, *A Secular Age*, Cambridge, MA, Harvard University Press, 2007, p. 552.

34 See, for example, James O'Donnell, *Augustine: Sinner and Saint – A New Biography*, London, Profile Books, 2005; Bruce Robbins, 'Enchantment? No Thank You!', in *The Joy of Secularism*, ed. George Levine, Princeton, NJ, Princeton University Press, 2011, p. 75.

35 This was the rationale for a conference held by Immanent Frame, 'We Have Never Been Secular: Re-Thinking the Sacred', report on a conference held in New York City on 9 April 2010, http://blogs.ssrc.org/tif/2010/02/01/we-have-never-been-secular-re-thinking-the-sacred/.

36 See, for instance, William E. Connolly, *Why I Am Not a Secularist*, Minneapolis, University of Minnesota Press, 2000.

37 See Karen Armstrong, *The Battle for God: A History of*

Fundamentalism, New York, Ballantine, 2000; Marvin Fox, *Interpreting Maimonides: Studies in Methodology, Metaphysics, and Moral Philosophy*, Chicago, University of Chicago Press, 1990.

38 Taylor, *A Secular Age*, p. 539.

39 John Arnold, *Belief and Unbelief in Medieval Europe*, London, Bloomsbury, 2005; Susan Reynolds, 'Social Mentalities and the Case for a Medieval Skepticism', *Transactions of the Royal Historical Society*, Sixth Series, 1990, Vol. 1, pp. 21–41.

40 See, for example, José Casanova, 'The Secular and Secularisms', *Social Research: An International Quarterly*, Vol. 76, No. 4, Winter 2009, pp. 1049–66.

41 Taylor, *A Secular Age*, pp. 507–10.

42 Callum Brown, *Religion and Society in Twentieth-Century Britain*, Harlow, Pearson Education, 2006.

43 John Robinson, *Honest to God* (1963), Norwich, SCM Press, 2009, p. 22.

44 Bertrand Russell, *Why I Am Not a Christian and Other Essays on Religion and Related Subjects* (1963), second edition, London, Routledge, 2004, p. 41.

45 See, for example, Robert D. Putnam, and Chaeyoon Lim, 'Religion, Social Networks, and Life Satisfaction', *American Sociological Review*, Vol. 75, No. 6, 2010, pp. 914–33; Andrew M. Mckinnon, 'Reading "Opium of the People": Expression, Protest and the Dialectics of Religion', *Critical Sociology*, Vol. 31, No. 1–2, 2005, pp. 15–38.

46 Rowan Williams, 'Archbishop of Canterbury's Christmas Sermon 2009 – Christmas Teaches Us Joy of Dependence', 25 December 2009, archbishopofcanterbury.org.

47 Judith Butler, *Precarious Life: The Powers of Mourning and Violence*, London, Verso, 2006.

48 Rowan Williams, 'Archbishop of Canterbury's 2011 Easter Sermon, Canterbury Cathedral', 24 April 2011, archbishopofcanterbury.org.

49 William Wordsworth, *The Prelude*, New York, CreateSpace Independent Publishing Platform, 2014, p. 246.

50 George Levine, Introduction, *The Joy of Secularism*, Princeton, NJ, Princeton University Press, 2011, pp. 17, 23.

51 Mark Twain, quoted in John Sauer, *Mark Twain Meets Educational Research*, New York, CreateSpace Independent Publishing, 2013, p. 51.

52 Anne Sexton, 'Welcome Morning', in *The Complete Poems of Anne Sexton*, New York, Mariner Books, 1999, p. 446.

53 This quote is widely attributed to Auden, although the exact source remains obscure.

54 Plato, *The Republic*, Book II, trans. R. E. Allen, London, Create Space Independent Publishing Platform, 2014, p. 160; Paul the Apostle quoted in Frank Trentmann, *Empire of Things: How We Became a World of Consumers, from the Fifteenth Century to the Twenty-First*, London and New York, Allen Lane, 2016, p. 405.

55 Trentmann, *Empire of Things*.

56 David Graeber, 'Consumption', *Current Anthropology*, No. 4, August 2011, p. 493.

57 Ibid., p. 499; see also Neil McKendrick, 'The Consumer Revolution of Eighteenth Century England', in *The Birth of Consumer Society: The Commercialization of Eighteenth-Century England*, ed. Neil McKendrick et al., Bloomington and Indianapolis, Indiana University Press, 1985; Stuart Ewen, *Channels of Desire* (1982), Minneapolis, University of Minnesota Press, 2000.

58 David Bennett, *The Currency of Desire*, London, Lawrence and Wishart, 2016, p. 64.

59 William Wordsworth, 'The World Is Too Much with Us' (1802), poetryfoundation.org.

60 Joanna Bourke, *Working Class Cultures in Britain, 1890–1960: Gender, Class and Ethnicity*, London and New York, Routledge, 1994, pp. 53–4.

61 Mica Nava and Alan O'Shea, *Modern Times: Reflections on a Century of English Modernity*, London and New York, Routledge, 1996; Trentmann, *Empire of Things*, pp. 195–7.

62 Vance Packard, *The Hidden Persuaders*, London, Longmans, 1957, p. 7.

63 See Christopher Turner, 'The Hidden Persuaders', *Daily Struggles*, January 2014, daily-struggles.tumblr.com, containing the discussion of Bernays and Freud, and quotes from Dichter; Trentmann, *Empire of Things*, pp. 302–37.

64 Vivienne Sanders, *The American Dream: Reality and Illusion, 1945–1980*, New York, Hodder Education, 2015, pp. 53–8.

65 C. Wright Mills, *The Sociological Imagination* (1959), New York, Oxford University Press, 2000; Herbert Marcuse, *One-Dimensional Man: Studies in Ideology of Advanced Industrial Society*, London, Routledge and Kegan Paul, 1964.

66 John Kenneth Galbraith, *The Affluent Society*, New York, Houghton Mifflin, p. 203.

67 Betty Friedan, *The Feminine Mystique*, New York, W. W. Norton, 1963, p. 24.

68 Karl Marx and Friedrich Engels, *The Communist Manifesto* (1848), York, Empire Books, 2011, p. 8.

69 Theodor Adorno and Max Horkheimer, *Dialectic of Enlightenment*, Stanford, CA, Stanford University Press, 1944, pp. 94–136.

70 See, for instance, Graeme Turner, *British Cultural Studies*, London, Routledge, 2000.

71 Dick Hebdige, *Subculture: The Meaning of* Style, London, Methuen, 1979.

72 Stuart Hall, 'The Emergence of Cultural Studies and the Crisis of the Humanities', *October*, No. 53, 1990, p. 22.

73 Daniel Miller, *The Comfort of Things*, Cambridge, Polity, 2012, p. 1.

74 Pablo Neruda, 'Odes to Things', in *Odes to Common Things*, London and New York, Little, Brown, 1994. Trentmann uses this poem as the epigraph to *Empire of Things*, his own mammoth sweep across the history of things.

75 Elizabeth Wilson, *Adorned in Dreams* (1985), London, I. B. Tauris, revised edition, 2009, pp. 14–5.

76 Alan Bradshaw, Norah Campbell and Stephen Dunne, 'Editorial: The Politics of Consumption', *Ephemera: Theory and Politics in Organization*, Vol. 13, No. 2, May 2013, p. 214.

77 Olga Kravets, 'On Things and Comrades', *Ephemera: Theory and Politics in Organization*, Vol. 13, No. 2, May 2013, p. 421.

78 David Mabb, 'Commodity as Comrade: Liubov Popova – Untitled Textile Design on William Morris Wallpaper for Historical Materialism', *Ephemera: Theory and Politics in Organization*, Vol. 13, No. 2, May 2013, p. 445.

79 Andreas Chatzidakis, 'Commodity Fights in Post-2008 Athens: Zapatistas Coffee, Kropotkinian Drinks and Fascist Rice', *Ephemera: Theory and Politics in Organization*, Vol. 13, No. 2, May 2013, p. 460.

80 Lynne Segal, 'Today, Yesterday and Tomorrow: Between Rebellion and Coalition Building', in Sheila Rowbotham, Lynne Segal and Hilary Wainwright, *Beyond the Fragments: Feminism and the Making of Socialism*, London, Merlin Press, 2013.

81 Zygmunt Bauman, *Does Ethics Have a Chance in a World of Consumers?*, Cambridge, MA, Harvard University Press, 2008, p. 28.

82 Ibid., p. 53.

83 Manuel Castells, *End of Millennium: The Information Age: Economy, Society and Culture*, Vol. III (Information Age Series), Oxford, Blackwell, 1998, pp. 161–5.

84 Juliet B. Schor, 'In Defense of Consumer Critique: Revisiting the Consumption Debates of the Twentieth Century', *The ANNALS of the American Academy of Political and Social Science*, May 2007, p. 25; see also Don Slater, *Consumer Culture and Modernity*, Cambridge, Polity, 1997; Douglas Holt, 'Why Do Brands Matter?: A Dialectical Theory of Consumer Culture and Branding', *Journal of Consumer Research*, Vol. 29, No. 1, 2002, pp. 70–90.

85 See Matthew Hilton, 'Consumers and the State since the Second World War', *The ANNALS of the American Academy of Politics and Social Science*, May 2007, p. 66.

86 See Sam Wollaston, 'Black Mirror Review – This Nightmare Sterile World Is Only Five Minutes Away', *Guardian*, 21 October 2016, theguardian.com; Owen Jones, 'Black Mirror Is an Urgent Reminder of the Fatal Consequences of Empathy Loss', *Guardian*, 28 October 2016, p. 35.

87 Slavoj Žižek, *The Parallax View*, reprint edition, London and Cambridge, MA, MIT Press, 2009, pp. 299, 39.

88 David Graeber, 'A Practical Utopian's Guide to the Coming Collapse', *The Baffler*, No. 22, 2013, thebaffler.com.

4. The Perils of Desire?

1 William Shakespeare, *Romeo and Juliet*, Act 1, Scene 1, Bath and Cheltenham, Nelson Thorness, 2003, p. 27.

2 Lawrence Stone, 'Passionate Attachments in the West in Historical Perspective', in *Passionate Attachments: Thinking About Love*, ed. Willard Gaylin and Ethel Person, New York, Free Press, 1988, p. 19.

3 *Woman's Own*, 6 January 1940, p. 3, as cited in Claire Langhamer, *The English in Love*, Oxford, Oxford University Press, 2013, p. 43.

4 Diane Akerman, *A Natural History of Love*, New York, Random House, 1994; Helen Fisher, *Why We Love: The Nature and Chemistry of Romantic Love*, New York, Henry Holt, 2004.

5 Plato, *Symposium and the Death of Socrates*, trans. Tom Griffith, Hertfordshire, Wordsworth Editions, 1997, p. 9.

6 Ibid., p. 33.

7 Ibid., pp. 45–6.

8 Aristotle, *The Nicomachean Ethics*, X.9, trans. William David Ross, Oxford World Classics, Oxford, Oxford University Press, 1998, pp. 246–7.

9 C. S. Lewis, *The Four Loves*, reissue edition, Houghton Mifflin, 1991.

10 See, for instance, Anne McClintock, *Imperial Leather: Race, Gender, and Sexuality in the Colonial Contest*, London and New York, Routledge, 1995.

11 Anna Clark, *Desire: A History of European Sexuality*, London and New York, Routledge, 2008, p. 1. See also the essays collected in Mark Bradley, ed., *Rome, Pollution and Propriety: Dirt, Disease and Hygiene in the Eternal City from Antiquity to Modernity*, Cambridge, Cambridge University Press, 2012.

12 Heinrich Kramer, *The Hammer of Witches: A Complete Translation of the Malleus Maleficarum* (1486–7), trans. Christopher S. Mackay,

13 Brian P. Levack, *The Witch-Hunt in Early Modern Europe*, New York and London, Longman, 1995; Deborah Willis, *Malevolent Nurture: Witch-Hunting and Maternal Power in Early Modern England*, Ithaca, NY, and London, Cornell University Press, 1995, p. 65; Robin Briggs, *Witches and Neighbours: The Social and Cultural Context of European Witchcraft*, London, Harper Collins, 1998.

14 Simon May, *Love: A History*, London, Routledge, p. 99.

15 See Michael A. Mullett, *Martin Luther*, London, Routledge, 2004, p. 182.

16 Vern A. Bullough, *Sexual Practices and the Medieval Church*, New York, Prometheus Books, 1982; Ruth Mazo Karras, *Sexuality in Medieval Europe: Doing Unto Others*, New York, Routledge, 2005.

17 Author unknown (some suggest William Salmon), *Aristotle's Masterpiece by 'Aristotle the Famous Philosopher'* (1680), published by the Ex-classics Project, 2010, p. 28, exclassics.com.

18 Aphra Behn, *Poems upon Several Occasions, 'A Voyage to the Island of Love' / by Mrs. A. Behn* (1684), EEBO Editions, ProQuest, 2010.

19 Gayatri Spivak, *A Critique of Postcolonial Reason: Towards a History of the Vanishing Present*, Cambridge, MA, Harvard University Press, 1999.

20 John Cleland, *Fanny Hill: Memoirs of a Woman of Pleasure* (1749), London, Mayflower, 1964; see also Roy Porter, 'Material Pleasures in the Consumer Society', in Roy Porter and Mary Mulvie Roberts, *Pleasure in the Eighteenth Century*, Basingstoke, Macmillan, 1996.

21 Sarah Knott and Barbara Taylor, eds, *Women, Gender and Enlightenment: 1650–1850*, London, Palgrave, 2007.

22 Mary Wollstonecraft, *A Vindication of the Rights of Woman* (1792), London, CreateSpace Independent Publishing Platform, 2010, p. 11.

23 See E. A. Wrigley, *Industrial Growth and Population Change*, Cambridge, Cambridge University Press, 1961.

24 Geoffrey Gilbert, Introduction, to Thomas Malthus, *An Essay on the Principle of Population* (1798), Oxford, Oxford University Press, 2008, p. xxii.

25 Judith R. Walkowitz, *Prostitution and Victorian Society: Women, Class, and the State*, Cambridge, Cambridge University Press, 1980.

26 Catherine Gallagher and Thomas Laqueur, eds, *The Making of the Modern Body: Sexuality and Society in the Nineteenth Century*, Cambridge, MA, Harvard, 1997.

27 Author unknown, *Aristotle's Masterpiece*, p. 18.

28 Thomas Laqueur, 'Orgasm, Generation and the Politics of Reproductive Biology', in *The Making of the Modern Body: Sexuality and Society in the Nineteenth Century*, ed. Gallagher and Laqueur, p. 35.

29 Christabel Pankhurst, *The Great Scourge and How to End It*, London, E. Pankhurst, 1913, pp. 13–23, archived at web.archive. org. See also Lesley Hall, 'Sexual Cultures in Britain', in *Sexual Cultures in Europe: National Histories*, ed. Franz X. Eder, Lesley Hall and Gert Hekma, Manchester, Manchester University Press, 1999, p. 45.

30 Richard von Krafft-Ebing, *Psychopathia Sexualis* (1886), New York, Panther Books, 1965, p. 12.

31 Richard von Krafft-Ebing, *Textbook of Insanity*, Philadelphia, F. A. Davis, 1904.

32 From Mass Observation Archive, quoted in Paul Ferris, *Sex and the British: A Twentieth-Century History*, London, Michael Joseph, 1993, p. 1.

33 Michel Foucault, *The History of Sexuality, Vol. 1: An Introduction*, London, Allen Lane, p. 37.

34 Judith Walkowitz, *Prostitution and Victorian Society: Women, Class, and the State*, Cambridge, Cambridge University Press, 1983; Matt Cook, *London and the Culture of Homosexuality, 1885–1914*, Cambridge, Cambridge University Press, 2003.

35 Roy Porter and Lesley Hall, *The Facts of Life: The Creation of Sexual Knowledge in Britain, 1650–1950*, New Haven, CT, and London, Yale University Press, 1995, p. 105.

36 Ferris, *Sex and the British*, p. 29.

37 Matt Cook, *London and the Culture of Homosexuality, 1885–1914* (Cambridge Studies in Nineteenth-Century Literature and Culture), Cambridge, Cambridge University Press, 2003, p. 48.

38 Edward Carpenter, *The Intermediate Sex* (1908), Middlesex, Echo Library, 2007, p. 64.

39 Sheila Rowbotham, *Edward Carpenter: A Life of Liberty and Love*, London, Verso, 2008, p. 330.

40 Ibid., pp. 282, 442.

41 Ibid., p. 1, 204.

42 See also Morris Kaplan, *Sodom on the Thames: Sex, Love and Scandal in Wilde Times*, Ithaca, NY, Cornell University Press, 2005.

43 Adam Phillips, *Unforbidden Pleasures*, London, Hamish Hamilton, 2015.

44 Marie Stopes, quoted and discussed in Porter and Hall, *The Facts of Life*, p. 208. See also Ferris, *Sex and the British*, p. 80.

45 Lesley Hall, *Hidden Anxieties: Male Sexuality, 1900–1950*, Cambridge, Polity Press, 1991.

46 Mitchison, quoted in Porter and Hall, *The Facts of Life*, p. 209.

47 Dora Russell, *The Tamarisk Tree: My Quest for Liberty and Love*, London, Virago, 1977, Ch. XIV.

48 Dora Russell, *Hypatia; or, Woman and Knowledge*, London, Kegan Paul, 1925, p. 39.

49 Stephen Brooke, 'The Body and Socialism: Dora Russell in the 1920s', *Past and Present*, No. 189, 2005, pp. 147–77, 149.

50 Personal communication from Sheila Rowbotham, 27 November 2016.

51 See Seth Koven and Sonya Michel, eds, *Mothers of a New World: Maternalist Politics and the Origins of Welfare States*, London and New York, Routledge, 1993; Sheila Rowbotham, *A Century of Women: The History of Women in Britain and the United States*, London, Penguin, 1997.

52 Peter Mandler and Susan Pederson, 'Introduction: The British Intelligenstia After the Victorians', in *After the Victorians: Private Conscience and Public Duty in Modern Britain*, ed. Susan Pederson and Peter Mandler, 1994, p. 16.

53 Wilhelm Reich, *Sex-Pol: Essays, 1929–1934* (Radical Thinkers), trans. Anna Bostock, Tom DuBose and Lee Baxandall, ed. Lee Baxandall, London and New York, Verso Books, 2012.

54 Alexandra Kollontai, 'Communism and the Family' (1920) in *Selected Writings of Alexandra Kollontai*, trans. and ed. Alix Holt, London, Allison & Busby, 1977; Alexandra Kollontai, *Free Love*, trans. C. J. Hogarth, London, J. M. Dent and Sons, 1932.

55 See Alana Harris and Timothy Willem Jones, eds, *Love and Romance in Britain 1918–1970*, London, Palgrave Macmillan, 2014, p. 2.

56 See, for instance, Gerd-Rainer Horn, *The Spirit of '68: Rebellion in Western Europe and North America, 1956–1976*, Oxford, Oxford University Press, 2007; Arthur Marwick, *The Sixties: Cultural Revolution in Britain, France, Italy, and the United States, 1958–1974*, 1998, Oxford, Oxford University Press.

57 See Lynne Segal, *Straight Sex: The Politics of Pleasure* (1994), London, Verso, 2013, Chapter 1; Clark, *Desire*, Chapter 12; Rowbotham, *A Century of Women*.

58 Aaron Esterson and R. D. Laing, *Sanity, Madness and the Family: Families of Schizophrenics*, Harmondsworth, Pelican, 1964.

59 I wrote about this in my book on masculinity, *Changing Masculinities, Changing Men* (1990), London, Palgrave, 2007, Chapter 1.

60 See Andrew Feenberg and Jim Freedman, *When Poetry Ruled the Streets: The French May Events of 1968*, New York, State University of New York Press, 2001, p. 2.

61 Christine Wallace, *Germaine Greer: Untamed Shrew*, London, Picador, 1997.

62 Erica Jong, *Fear of Flying* (1973), London, Vintage, 1997, p. 12.

63 Sheila Rowbotham, *Woman's Consciousness, Man's World*, Harmondsworth, Pelican Books, p. 30.

64 Rowbotham, *Woman's Consciousness, Man's World*, p. 20.

65 Sheila Rowbotham, 'Women: the Struggle for Freedom', *Black Dwarf*, 10 January 1969, p. 6.

66 Ann Snitow, 'The Politics of Passion: Ellen Willis, 1941–2006', in Snitow, *The Feminism of Uncertainty*, Durham, NC and London, 2015, p. 292.

67 See, for example, Sue O'Sullivan, 'Passionate Beginnings: Ideological Politics – 1969–72', in Sue O'Sullivan, *I Used to Be Nice*, London, Cassell, 1996, p. 22.

68 Audre Lorde, 'Uses of the Erotic: The Erotic as Power', *Sister Outsider*, New York, The Crossing Press Feminist Series, 1984, p. 56.

69 Segal, *Straight Sex*.

70 Alix Kates Shulman, 'Organs and Orgasms', in *Women in Sexist Society*, ed. V. Gornick and B. Moran, New York, Signet, 1971, p. 303; Shere Hite, *The Hite Report: A Nationwide Study of Female Sexuality* (1976), London, Knopf, 1987.

71 Alix Kates Shulman, *Burning Questions* (1978), London, Fontana, 1980, p. 346.

72 Eleanor Stephens, 'The Moon Within Your Reach: A Feminist Approach to Female Orgasm', *Spare Rib*, December 1975, p. 15.

73 I provide many examples, and some critique, of pieces in *Straight Sex*, Chapter 2.

74 See Barbara Ehrenreich et al., *Re-Making Love: The Feminization of Sex*, New York, Doubleday, 1986, pp. 2–3.

75 Lillian Faderman, *Odd Girls and Twilight Lovers: A History of Lesbian Life in Twentieth-Century America*, Harmondsworth, Penguin, 1991, pp. 204–18.

76 Kate Shulman, 'Sex and Power: Sexual Bases of Radical Feminism', *Signs*, Vol. 5, No. 4, Summer 1980, p. 604.

77 Catharine MacKinnon, *Feminism Unmodified: Discourses on Life and Law*, London, Harvard University Press, 1987.

78 Ehrenreich et al., *Re-Making Love*, p. 9.

79 Amber Hollibaugh, in Deirdre English, Amber Hollibaugh and Gayle Rubin, 'Talking Sex: A Conversation on Sexuality and Feminism', *Feminist Review*, No. 11, Summer 1982, p. 44.

80 English in ibid., p. 46.

81 Rubin in ibid., p. 42.

82 See Cindy Patton, 'The Cum Shot: Three Takes on Lesbian and Gay Sexuality', in *Living With Contradictions: Controversies in Feminist Social Ethics*, ed. Allison M. Jagger, Boulder, CO, Westview Press, 1994, pp. 178–80.

83 Angela McRobbie, *The Aftermath of Feminism: Gender, Culture and Social Change*, Sage Publications, 2009, pp. 135, 67.

5. The 'Truth about Love'

1 Andrew Solomon, *The Noonday Demon: An Anatomy of Depression*, London, Vintage, 2002, p. 15.

2 Sigmund Freud, *The Ego and the Id* (1923), *Complete Psychological Works of Sigmund Freud, Vol. 19: The Ego and the Id and Other Works*, London, Penguin, 2001.

3 Sigmund Freud, *Three Essays on Sexuality* (1905), first sentence

added in 1915 edition, in *On Sexuality*, The Pelican Freud Library, Vol. 7, Harmondsworth, Penguin, 1977, p. 145.

4 Sigmund Freud, *An Outline of Psychoanalysis* (1938), The Pelican Freud Library, Vol. 15, p. 423.

5 Ibid., p. 145.

6 Sigmund Freud, 'On Narcissism', in *Standard Edition of Complete Psychological Works*, Vol. 14, trans. J. Stracey, London, Hogarth Press, 1953, p. 85.

7 Julia Kristeva, *Tales of Love*, trans. Leon S. Roudiez, New York, Columbia University Press, 1989, pp. 2, 3.

8 Jacques Lacan, *Seminar VIII: On Transference 1960–1961*, ed. Jacques Alain-Miller, Paris, Seuil, 1991, p. 57.

9 Jacques Lacan, *The Seminar of Jacques Lacan Book I: Freud's Paper on Technique 1953–1954*, trans. Jacques Alain-Miller, Cambridge, Cambridge University Press, 1988, p. 142.

10 Lacan, cited in Darlene Demandante, 'Lacanian Perspectives on Love', *Kritike*, Vol. 8, No. 1, June 2014, pp. 102–18, 110.

11 Jacques-Alain Miller, 'On Love', trans. Adrian Price, *Art and Thoughts*, 3 December 2013, articulosparapensar.wordpress.com.

12 Slavoj Žižek, 'What's Wrong with Fundamentalism Part II', Lacan.Com, 4 May 2004, http://www.lacan.com/zizpassion.htm.

13 Slavoj Žižek, 'Q&A', interview by Rosanna Greenstreet, *Guardian*, 9 August 2008, theguardian.com.

14 Adam Phillips, Preface, in Leo Bersani and Adam Phillips, *Intimacies*, Chicago, Chicago University Press, pp. vii–viii.

15 Adam Phillips, 'Against Self-Criticism', in Adam Phillips, *Unforbidden Pleasures*, London, Hamish Hamilton, 2015, p. 87.

16 Adrienne Rich, 'Women and Honor: Some Notes on Lying', in *On Lies, Secrets, and Silence: Selected Prose*, New York, W. W. Norton, 1979, p. 188.

17 Feona Attwood, 'No Money Shot? Commerce, Pornography and New Sex Taste Cultures', *Sexualities*, Vol. 10, No. 4, 2007,

pp. 441–56; Amalia Ziv, *Explicit Utopias: Re-writing the Sexual in Women's Pornography*, New York, State University of New York Press, 2015.

18 Tristan Taormino, Celine Parreñas Shimizu and Mireille Miller-Young, eds, *The Feminist Porn Book: The Politics of Producing Pleasure*, New York, The Feminist Press at CUNY, 2013; Amalia Ziv, *Explicit Utopias: Rewriting the Sexual in Women's Pornography*, New York, State University of New York Press, reprint edition, 2016.

19 United Nations Statistics Division, 'Violence Against Women', *The World's Women*, Chapter 6, 2015, unstats.un.org; American Psychological Association: Public Interest Directorate, *Intimate Partner Violence: Facts and Resources*, Washington, DC, 2017, apa.org.

20 Katy Steinmetz, 'Why Transgender People Are Being Murdered at a Historic Rate', *Time*, August 2015, http://time.com.

21 Wikipedia, 'List of LGBT Rights Organizations in the United States', en.wikipedia.org, accessed 2 February 2017.

22 Matthew Avery Sutton, *Jerry Falwell and the Rise of the Religious Right: A Brief History with Documents* (Bedford Series in History and Culture), New York, Bedford/St Martin's, 2012.

23 Ruth Murray Brown, *For a Christian America: A History of the Religious Right*, New York, Prometheus Books, 2002; Daniel K. Williams, *God's Own Party: The Making of the Christian Right*, Oxford, Oxford University Press, 2012.

24 See Patrick Buchanan, *The Death of the West: How Dying Populations and Immigrant Invasions Imperil Our Country and Civilization*, Thomas Dunne Books, 2002, pp. 197, 47.

25 James Risen and Judy L. Thomas, *Wrath of Angels: The American Abortion War*, New York, Basic Books, 1998; Jennifer Jefferis, *Armed for Life: The Army of God and Anti-abortion Terror in the United States*, Santa Barbara, ABC-CLIO, 2011.

26 Maurice Godelier, 'The Origins of Male Domination', *New Left Review*, No. 127, 1981, p. 17.

27 The British journalist Laurie Penny writes about the battles she believes we need to wage against the increasing disorders of our times, especially as they impact upon women and our bodies, in her recent book *Unspeakable Things: Sex, Lies and Revolution*, London, Bloomsbury, 2014.

28 Michael J. Rosenfeld, Reuben J. Thomas and Maja Falcon, 'How Couples Meet and Stay Together', Stanford, CA, Stanford University Libraries, 2015, Waves 1, 2, and 3 Version 3.04; Wave 4 Supplement Version 1.02; Wave 5 Supplement Version 1.0, http://data.stanford.edu.

29 S. Roseneil, 'On Not Living with a Partner: Unpicking Coupledom and Cohabitation', *Sociological Research Online*, Vol. 11, No. 3, 2006; S. Duncan and M. Phillips, 'People Who Live Apart Together (LATs) – How Different Are They?', *The Sociological Review*, Vol. 58, No. 1, pp. 112–34.

30 Laura Kipnis, *Against Love: A Polemic*, New York, Vintage, 2004, p. 46.

31 Ulrich Beck and Elisabeth Beck-Gersheim, *The Normal Chaos of Love* (1990), trans. M. Ritter and J. Wiebel, Cambridge, Polity Press, 1995; Anthony Giddens, *The Transformation of Intimacy: Sexuality, Love and Eroticism in Modern Societies*, Cambridge, Polity Press, 1992; Zygmunt Bauman, *Liquid Love: On the Frailty of Human Bonds*, Cambridge, Polity Press, 2003.

32 Beck and Beck-Gersheim, *The Normal Chaos of Love*, pp. 78–9.

33 Giddens, *The Transformation of Intimacy*, p. 62.

34 Carol Smart, *Personal Life: New Directions in Sociological Thinking*, Cambridge, Polity Press, 2007, p. 29.

35 Office for National Statistics, *Families and Households 2014*, January 2015, ons.gov.uk.

36 Mary Evans, 'Love in a Time of Neo-liberalism', *Open Democracy*, 6 November 2013, opendemocracy.net.

37 Sherry Turkle, *Alone Together: Why We Expect More from Technology and Less from Each Other*, New York, Basic Books, 2011, p. 19.

38 Ibid., p. xii.

39 Eva Illouz, *Cold Intimacy: The Making of Emotional Capitalism*, Cambridge, Polity Press, 2007.

40 Eva Illouz, *Why Love Hurts: A Sociological Explanation*, Cambridge, Polity Press, 2012, p. 247.

41 Ibid., pp. 243, 246.

42 Alain Badiou with Nicolas Truong, *In Praise of Love*, trans. Peter Bush, London, Serpent's Tail, 2012, p. 32.

43 Ibid., p. 90.

44 Luc Ferry, *On Love: A Philosophy for the Twenty-First Century*, Cambridge, Polity Press, p. 168.

45 John Lennon and Jan S. Wenner, *Lennon Remembers: The Full Rolling Stone Interviews from 1970*, London and New York, Verso, 2000, pp. 114–15.

46 John Lennon, 'Interview with John Lennon and Yoko Ono by David Sheff, September 1980', *Playboy*, January 1981, john-lennon.com.

47 Jacqueline Rose, *Women in Dark Times*, London, Bloomsbury, 2015.

48 Andrew McMillan, 'The Men Weeping in the Gym', *Physical*, London, Jonathan Cape, 2015, p. 5.

49 Christine Delphy, 'Rethinking Sex and Gender', in *Sex in Question: French Materialist Feminism*, ed. Diana Leonard and Lisa Adkins, Abingdon, Taylor and Francis, 1996, pp. 31–42.

50 Jonathan Dollimore, *Desire: A Memoir*, London, Bloomsbury, forthcoming 2017.

51 Leo Bersani, 'Is the Rectum a Grave?', *October*, No. 43, Winter 1987, pp. 207–9.

52 Cristan Williams, 'Gender Performance: *The TransAdvocate* interviews Judith Butler', *TransAdvocate*, 5 May 2014, transadvocate.com.

53 Arlie Hochschild, *The Outsourced Self: What Happens When We Pay Others to Live Our Lives for Us*, London, Picador, 2013.

54 Angela Carter, *Nights at the Circus*, London, Vintage Classics, 1994, p. 332.

55 Judith Butler, 'On Doubting Love', in *Take My Advice: Letters to the Next Generation*, ed. James Harmon, New York, Simon and Schuster, 2002, p. 65.

56 Eve Sedgwick, *Tendencies*, 1993, Durham, NC, Duke University Press, p. 264.

57 Eve Sedgwick, *A Dialogue on Love*, Boston, MA, Beacon Press, 1999, pp. 24, 25.

58 Ibid., p.168.

59 Gillian Rose, *Love's Work*, New York, New York Review Books Classics, pp. 69, 105.

60 Judith Butler, 'Why Bodies Matter', at Celebrations of *Gender Trouble*'s 25th anniversary, Teatro Maria Matos, Lisbon, 2 June 2015, vimeo.com.

61 Thom Gunn, 'The Hug', *The Man with Night Sweats*, London, Faber and Faber, 2010, p. 1.

62 Seamus Heaney, *The Human Chain*, London, Faber and Faber, 2011, p. 12.

63 Donna Haraway, *The Companion Species Manifesto: Dogs, People, and Significant Otherness*, Chicago, Prickley Paradigm Press, 2003, p. 16.

64 Jackie Kay, 'Darling', *Darling: New and Selected Poems*, London, Bloodaxe, p.79.

65 W. H. Auden, 'O Tell Me the Truth About Love' (1933), poem-hunter.com.

66 Jonathan Dollimore, *Desire: A Memoir*, London, Bloomsbury, in press.

67 Jeffrey Week, *The World We Have Won: The Remaking of Erotic and Intimate Life*, London, Routledge, 2007, pp. 196–7.

68 Simon May, *Love: A History*, New Haven, CT, and London, Yale University Press, 2011, p. 6.

6. Inventing Utopias

1 Terry Eagleton, 'Pretty Much like Ourselves: *Modern British Utopias 1700–1850* by Gregory Claeys', *London Review of Books*, Vol. 19, No. 16, 4 September 1997, p. 6; Fredric Jameson, 'Utopia and Failure', *Politics and Culture*, Issue 2, 2000, https://politicsand culture.org; Fredric Jameson, *Archaeologies of the Future: The Desire Called Utopia and Other Science Fictions*, London, Verso, 2005, p. xv; Immanuel Wallerstein, *Utopistics: Or, Historical Choices of the Twenty-first Century*, New York, The New Press, 1998, pp. 1, 2.

2 Avery F. Gordon, 'Some Thoughts on the Utopian', in Avery F. Gordon, *Keeping Good Time: Reflections on Knowledge, Power and People*, Boulder, CO, Paradigm Press, 2004, pp. 113–32.

3 David Graeber, 'A Practical Utopian's Guide to the Coming Collapse', *The Baffler*, No. 22, 2013, http://thebaffler.com.

4 Plato, *The Republic of Plato*, trans. Allan Bloom, New York, Oxford University Press, 1956, p. 153.

5 Ibid., p. 238.

6 Ibid., p. 55.

7 Aristotle, *Politics* (350 BCE), trans. Benjamin Jowett, http://classics.mit.edu.

8 Martha Nussbaum, *Plato's Republic: The Good Society and the Deformation of Desire*, Washington, DC, Library of Congress, 1998, http://www.harvard.com/book/platos_republic_the_good _society_and_the_deformation_of_desire/.

9 Thomas More, *Utopia* (1516, in Latin), trans. Paul Turner, London, Penguin Books, 2003, pp. 110, 78.

10 Ibid., pp. 84–5.

11 Francis Bacon, *The New Atlantis* (1627), in *The Major Works* (Oxford World's Classics), Oxford, Oxford University Press, 2008, p. 480.

12 Patrick Parrinder, *Utopian Literature and Science: From Scientific Revolution to Brave New World and Beyond*, London, Palgrave, 2015, p. 13.

13 Mary Shelley, *Frankenstein, or, The Modern Prometheus* (1818), London, Penguin, 2003; H. G. Wells, *The Time Machine* (1895), London, Penguin Books, 2012.

14 Simon Schama, *Citizens: A Chronicle of the French Revolution*, New York, Alfred Knopf, 1989.

15 Mary Wollstonecraft, *A Vindication of the Rights of Woman* (1792), Venice, CA, Small World Books, 2010, p. 6.

16 Mary Wollstonecraft, *A Vindication of the Rights of Men* (1790), quoted in Barbara Taylor, *Mary Wollstonecraft and the Feminist Imagination*, Cambridge, Cambridge University Press, 2003, p. 165.

17 Wollstonecraft, *A Vindication of the Rights of Woman*, 1792, p. 46.

18 William Rogers Brubaker, 'The French Revolution and the Invention of Citizenship', *French Politics and Society*, No. 7, Summer 1989; Renée Waldinger, Philip Dawson and Isser Woloch, eds, *The French Revolution and the Meaning of Citizenship*, Westport, CT, Greenwood Press, 1993.

19 Edmund Burke, 'Reflections on the Revolution in France' (1790), constitution.org; Gustave Le Bon, *The Crowd: A Study of the Popular Mind* (1895), Harmondsworth, Penguin, 1977.

20 Charles Fourier, *The Theory of the Four Movements*, ed. Gareth Stedman Jones, Cambridge, Cambridge University Press, 1996, p. 131, italics in original.

21 Robert Owen, *Life of Robert Owen, by Himself* (1857), London, C. Knight, 1971, p. 184.

22 Thompson, quoted in Barbara Taylor, *Eve and the New Jerusalem: Socialism and Feminism in the Nineteenth Century*, London, Virago, 1983, p. 38.

23 Ibid., pp. 220–1.

24 Ibid., p. 105.

25 J. S. Mill, *Principles of Political Economy*, quoted in Taylor, *Eve*, p. xi.

26 Taylor, p. xi.

27 Frederick Engels, *Socialism: Utopian and Scientific*, Chicago, Charles Kerr, 2012, p. 31.

28 Karl Marx and Frederick Engels, *The Communist Manifesto* (1948), Cardiff, Cardiff Books, 2016.

29 Taylor, *Eve*, p. 287.

30 Frederick Engels, *The Condition of the Working Class in England* (1844), London, George Allen and Unwin, 1926, p. 146.

31 See Leonore Davidoff and Catherine Hall, *Family Fortunes: Men and Women of the English Middle Class 1780–1850*, London, Hutchinson Education, 1987.

32 Robert Tombs, 'How Bloody was *La Semaine Sanglante* of 1871? A Revision', *The Historical Journal*, Vol. 55, No. 3, September 2012, pp. 619–704.

33 Kristin Ross, *Communal Luxury: The Political Imaginary of the Paris Commune*, London and New York, Verso, 2015, p. 5.

34 Kropotkin, *The Commune of Paris*, 1881, quoted in Ross, *Communal Luxury*, pp. 123–4.

35 Engels, *Socialism*; see Marx and Engels, *The Communist Manifesto*, p. 17.

36 V. I. Lenin, *What Is to Be Done? Burning Questions of our Movement* (1901), Oxford, Oxford University Press, 1963; E. Levine, 'Levine's Last Speech' (1919), in *Levine: The Life of a Revolutionary*, London, Saxon House, 1973, p. 209.

37 Karl Marx, *The Civil War in France*, in *Marx/Engels Collected Works*, London, Lawrence and Wishart, Vol. 22, p. 335.

38 G. A. Cohen, *If You're an Egalitarian How Come You're So Rich?*, Cambridge, MA, Harvard University Press, 2001, p. 77.

39 David Leopold, 'On Marxian Utopophobia', *Journal of the History of Philosophy*, Vol. 54, No. 1, January 2015, pp. 111–34.

40 Edward Bellamy, *Looking Backwards: 2000–1887 AD* (1880), new edition, ed. Matthew Beaumont, Oxford, Oxford University Press, 2009, p. 92.

41 V. I. Lenin, *The State and Revolution: The Marxist Theory of the State and the Tasks of the Proletariat in the Revolution* (1917), trans. Robert Service, London, Penguin Books, pp. 91–2.

42 William Morris, *News from Nowhere* (1890), Oxford, Oxford

University Press, reissue edition, 2009, p. 80.

43 Ibid., pp. 3, 182.

44 Miguel Abensour quoted in Edward Thompson, *William Morris: Romantic to Revolutionary*, London, Merlin Press, 1976, p. 791.

45 Thompson, *William Morris*, p. 792.

46 Edward Carpenter, *Love's Coming-of-Age: A Series of Papers on the Relations of the Sexes* (1906), London, Forgotten Books, 2008.

47 Edward Carpenter, *My Days and Dreams*, Chapter 11, 'The Story of My Books', The Edward Carpenter Archive, ed. Simon Dawson, edwardcarpenter.net.

48 Sheila Rowbotham, *Edward Carpenter: A Life of Liberty and Love*, London, Verso, 2008, p. 281; George Orwell, *The Road to Wigan Pier* (1936), quoted in Rowbotham, *Edward Carpenter*, p. 442.

49 Ibid., p. 455.

50 Ada Neil Chew, letter to the *Crew Chronicle* (1984), quoted in Sheila Rowbotham, *Dreamers of a New Day: Women Who Invented the Twentieth Century*, London, Verso, 2011, p. 175.

51 Mrs Havelock Ellis (née Edith Lees), 'Olive Schreiner and her Relation to the Woman Movement', quoted in ibid., p. 24.

52 Leon Trotsky, *Problems of Everyday Life* (1924), New York, Pathfinder Press, 1973, p. 65.

53 Jane Hume Clapperton, quoted in Rowbotham, *Dreamers of a New Day*, p. 135.

54 Dora Marsden, quoted in ibid., p. 69. See also Lucy Bland, 'Heterosexuality, Feminism and *The Freewoman* Journal in Early Twentieth-Century England', *Women's History Review*, Vol. 4, No. 1, 1995; Cary Franklin, 'Marketing Edwardian Feminism: Dora Marsden, Votes for Women and *The Freewoman*', *Women's History Review*, Vol. 11, No. 4, 2002.

55 Anna Julia Cooper, quoted in Rowbotham, *Dreamers of a New Day*, p. 176.

56 'Shouting Amazons: Women Emulate Their Brethren and Go on Strike', *Chicago Tribune*, 4 May 1886, p. 1, available at encyclopedia. chicagohistory.org.

57 Rowbotham, *Dreamers of a New Day*, p. 18.
58 Emma Goldman, *Living My Life*, New York, Knopf, 1931.
59 Emma Goldman, *Living My Life*, Vol. 1 (1931), New York, Cosimo Classics, 2011, p. 56.
60 Charlotte Perkins Gilman, *The Yellow Wallpaper*, Old Westbury, NY, The Feminist Press, 1973.
61 *Charlotte Perkins Gilman: Optimist Reformer*, Iowa City, Iowa University of Iowa Press, 2000.
62 Charlotte Perkins Gilman, *Herland [1915] including the The Yellow Wallpaper* (1892), New York, Planet Monk Books, 2015.
63 Rowbotham, *Dreamers of a New Day*, p. 13.
64 Ibid.

7. Living Differently

1 Lyman Tower Sargent, *Utopianism: A Very Short Introduction*, Oxford, Oxford University Press, 2010, p. 26; Ruth Levitas, *Utopia as Method: The Imaginary Reconstitution of Society*, London, Palgrave Macmillan, 2013, p. 85.
2 Yevgeny Zamyatin, *We* (1921), London, Penguin Classics, 1993.
3 Aldous Huxley, *Brave New World* (1932), Harmondsworth, Penguin, 1963; George Orwell, *1984* (1945), London, Penguin Classics, 2004, p. 280.
4 Bertell Ollman, 'The Utopian Vision of the Future (Then and Now): A Marxist Critique', *Monthly Review*, Vol. 57, No. 3, July–August 2005, monthlyreview.org.
5 Karl Popper, 'Utopia and Violence' (1947), in Popper, *Conjectures and Refutations*, Chapter 18, London, Routledge, 1963, p. 357.
6 Howard Zinn, *A People's History of the United States: 1492–Present* (1980), New York, Harper Perennial Modern Classics, 2005.
7 See Gerd-Rainer Horn, *The Spirit of '68: Rebellion in Western Europe and North America, 1956–1976*, Oxford, Oxford University Press, 2007, pp. 77–80.

8 See Arthur Marwick, *The Sixties: Cultural Revolution in Britain, France, Italy, and the United States, 1958–1974*, Oxford, Oxford University, 1998; Lynne Segal, 'She's Leaving Home: Women's Sixties Renaissance', in *1968 in Retrospect: History, Theory, Alterity*, ed. Gurminder Bhambra and Ipek Demir, London, Palgrave Macmillan, 2009, pp. 29–42.

9 Adrienne Rich, 'Towards a Woman-Centered University' (1973), in *Rich: Lies, Secrets and Silences: Selected Prose, 1966–1978*, New York, W. W. Norton, 1979, p. 126.

10 Sue Himmelweit, 'Production Rules OK?', in *What Is to Be Done About the Family?*, ed. Lynne Segal, London, Penguin, 1983, pp. 125–6.

11 Kathy Henderson, Frankie Armstrong and Sandra Kerr, eds, *My Song Is My Own*, London, Pluto, 1979, p. 127; Rita Mae West, *Rubyfruit Jungle* (1973), London, Penguin Books, 1994, p. 141; Ntozake Shange, *for Colored Girls Who Have Considered Suicide when the Rainbow Is Enuf*, New Jersey, Prentice Hall, 1976, p. 43.

12 Lynne Segal, *Making Trouble: Life and Politics*, London and New York, Verso, 2017.

13 Michel Foucault, 'Of Other Spaces' (1967), *Diacritics*, No. 16, Spring 1986, pp. 22–7.

14 Ursula Le Guin, *The Dispossessed* (1974), New York, Gollancz, 1999.

15 Angelika Bammer, *Partial Vision: Feminism and Utopianism in the 1970s*, London, Routledge, 1991, p. 47; Tom Moylan, *Demand the Impossible: Science Fiction and the Utopian Imagination* (Ralahine Utopian Studies), London, Methuen, 1987, p. 10.

16 Diane Elson, 'Economic Crises from the 1980s to the 2010s: A Gender Analysis', in *New Frontiers in Feminist Political Economy*, ed. G. Waylen and S. Rai, Abingdon, Routledge, 2013.

17 Adrienne Rich, *A Human Eye, Essays on Art in Society 1997–2008*, New York, W. W. Norton, 2010, p. 2.

18 Fredric Jameson, *The Seeds of Time*, New York, Columbia University Press, 1994, p. xii.

19 Fredric Jameson, 'Future City', *New Left Review*, No. 21, May–June 2003, newleftreview.org.

20 Wendy Brown, *States of Injury: Power and Freedom in Late Modernity*, Princeton, NJ, Princeton University Press, 1995, p. xiii.

21 Ursula Le Guin, '*On Such a Full Sea* by Chang-rae Lee – Review', *Guardian*, 30 January 2014, theguardian.com.

22 Adam Sternbergh, 'We've Reached Peak Dystopia, But Is It Possible to Imagine Utopia Anymore?', *Vulture*, 22 August 2014, vulture.com.

23 Ibid.

24 Frances Stonor Saunders, 'Where on Earth Are You?', *London Review of Books*, Vol. 38, No. 5, February 2016, p. 7.

25 See Ha-Joon Chang, *Bad Samaritans: The Guilty Secrets of Rich Nations and the Threat to Global Prosperity*, London, Random House, 2007, p. 26; see also Joseph Stiglitz, *Freefall*, New York, W. W. Norton, 2010; Jason Hickel and Khan Arsalan, 'The Culture of Capitalism and the Crisis of Critique', *Anthropological Quarterly*, Vol. 85, No. 1, 2012.

26 M. Grang and N. J. Thrift, *Thinking Space*, London, Routledge, 2000, p. 96.

27 Colin C. Williams, 'A Critical Evaluation of the Commodification Thesis', *Sociological Review*, Vol. 50, No. 4, 2002, p. 525.

28 J. K. Gibson-Graham, *The End of Capitalism (As We Knew It): A Feminist Critique of Political Economy*, Minneapolis, University of Minnesota Press, 2006.

29 Sargent, *Utopianism*, p. 9; Levitas, *Utopia as Method*, p. 19.

30 Fredric Jameson, *Archaeologies of the Future: The Desire Called Utopia and Other Science Fictions*, London, Verso, 2005, pp. 11, 288.

31 Ernst Bloch, *The Principle of Hope*, Vol. 3, London, Basil Blackwell, 1995, p. 1376.

32 Henri Lefebvre, *The Critique of Everyday Life*, Vol. 1 (1961), one-volume edition, London, New York, Verso, 2014, p. 35.

33 See Frances Stacey, *Constructed Situations: A New History of the*

Situationist International (Marxism and Culture), London, Pluto Press, 2014.

34 See David Harvey's account of the rise and fall of urban rebellions, 'The Right to the City', *New Left Review*, No. 53, September–October 2008, http://newleftreview.org.

35 Raymond Williams, *Resources of Hope: Culture, Democracy and Socialism*, London, Verso, 1989, p. 209.

36 Henry A. Giroux, 'Utopian Thinking Under the Sign of Neo-liberalism: Towards a Critical Pedagogy of Educated Hope', *Democracy and Nature*, Vol. 9, No. 1, 2003.

37 Jackie Smith, 'The World Social Forum and the Challenges of Global Democracy', *Global Networks*, 4 October 2004, pp. 413–21.

38 Antonis Vradis, 'Terminating the Spatial Contract: A Commentary on Greece', *Critical Legal Thinking*, 3 July 2012, criticallegalthinking.com; Sebastian Budgen and Stathis Kouvelakis, 'Greece: Phase One', *Jacobin*, 22 January 2015, jacobinmag.com.

39 Paul Mason, *Why It's Kicking Off Everywhere: The New Global Revolutions*, London, Verso Books, 2012.

40 Adam Roberts, 'Civil Resistance and the Fate of the Arab Spring', in *Civil Resistance in the Arab Spring: Triumphs and Disasters*, ed. Adam Roberts, Rory McCarthy and Timothy Garton Ash, Oxford, Oxford University Press, 2016.

41 Ibid.

42 On the unfolding crisis across Europe see Cristos Laskos and Euclid Tsakalotos, *Crucible of Resistance: Greece, the Eurozone and the World Economic Crisis*, London, Pluto Press, 2013; Yanis Varoufakis, *And the Weak Suffer What They Must?: Europe, Austerity and the Threat to Global Stability*, London, Bodley Head, 2016; James Galbraith, *Welcome to the Poisoned Chalice: The Destruction of Greece and the Future of Europe*, London and New Haven, CT, Yale University Press, 2016.

43 Íñigo Errejón and Chantal Mouffe, with Owen Jones (Introduction), *Podemos: In the Name of the People*, London, Lawrence and Wishart, 2016.

44 Rosalyn Fraad Baxandall, 'The Populist Movement Reborn, At Last, in Occupy Wall Street', *On the Issues*, 14 October 2011, ontheissuesmagazine.com.

45 Michael Taussig, 'I'm So Angry, I Made a Sign', *Critical Inquiry*, Vol. 39, No. 1, Autumn 2012, p. 56.

46 Graeber, *The Democracy Project: A History, a Crisis, a Movement*, New York, Spiegel and Gran, 2013, p. xviii.

47 John Holloway, *Change the World Without Taking Power: The Meaning of Revolution Today*, London, Pluto Press, 2005.

48 Terry Eagleton, 'Making a Break: Reviewing *Archaeologies of the Future: The Desire Called Utopia and Other Science Fictions* by Fredric Jameson', *London Review of Books*, Vol. 28, No. 5, March 2006, p. 26.

49 Listen to Alicia Garza, 'Black Lives Matter', speech available on onsizzle.com.

50 Wesley Lowery, *They Can't Kill Us All: The Story of Black Lives Matter*, New York, Penguin Books, 2017.

51 William Fisher and Thomas Ponniah, eds, *Another World Is Possible: Popular Alternatives to Globalization at the World Social Forum*, London, Zed Books, 2003.

52 Rebecca Solnit, *Hope in the Dark: The Never-Surrender Guide to Changing the World*, Edinburgh, New York and Melbourne, Canongate Books, 2004; Naomi Klein, *This Changes Everything: Capitalism vs the Climate*, London, Penguin, 2014.

53 Kate Soper, 'Towards a Sustainable Flourishing: Ethical Consumption and the Politics of Prosperity', in *Ethics and Morality in Consumption Interdisciplinary Perspectives*, ed. Deirdre Shaw, Michal Carrington and Andreas Chatzidakis, London, Routledge, 2016, pp. 11–27; see also Kate Soper, Martin Ryle and Lyn Thomas, eds, *The Politics and Pleasures of Consuming Differently*, London, Palgrave, 2009.

54 Davina Cooper, *Everyday Utopias: The Conceptual Life of Promising Spaces*, London and Durham, NC, Duke University Press, 2014, pp. 2, 149.

55 Andreas Chatzidakis, Pauline Maclaran and Alan Bradshaw, 'Heterotopian Space and the Utopics of Ethical and Green Consumption', *Journal of Marketing Management*, Vol. 28, No. 3–4, 2012, p. 498.

56 Andreas Chatzidakis, 'Syriza and the Rise of a Radical Left in Europe: Solidarity Is the Keyword', *Open Democracy*, 13 February 2015, opendemocracy.net.

57 Russell Jacoby, *Picture Imperfect: Utopian Thought for an Anti-Utopian Age*, New York, Columbia University Press, 2005.

58 David Harvey, *Rebel Cities: From the Right to the City to the Urban Revolution*, London, Verso, 2012, p. 125.

59 Conflicts emerge and sectarian divisions form that can make consensus building almost impossible, especially in building alliances and solidarity between those who may rightly fear for the distinctiveness of their particular oppression, whether along lines of class, race or other vectors of power. Meanwhile, the lack of formal power structures hardly prevents those who, often unwittingly, are more controlling, or perhaps simply more charismatic and enthusiastic, from becoming dominant figures, as the American Jo Freeman complained in an influential early text.

60 Jo Freeman, 'The Tyranny of Structurelessness', *Second Wave*, Vol. 2, No. 1, 1972.

61 Temma Kaplan, *Democracy: A World History*, Oxford, Oxford University Press, 2015, p. 3; see also Temma Kaplan, *Crazy for Democracy: Women in Grassroots Movements*, New York and London, Routledge, 1996.

62 Lynne Segal, 'Today, Yesterday and Tomorrow: Between Rebellion and Coalition Building', in Sheila Rowbotham, Lynne Segal and Hilary Wainwright, *Beyond the Fragments: Feminism and the Making of Socialism*, London, Merlin Press, 2013.

8. *The States We're In*

1 William Beveridge, *The Beveridge Report: Social Insurance and Allied Services*, presented to Parliament, 1942, British Library, www.bl.uk/collection-items/beveridge-report.

2 John Maynard Keynes, 'The End of *Laissez-faire*' (1926), in *Essays in Persuasion*, London and New York, W. W. Norton, 1963.

3 Ibid.

4 David Kynaston, *Austerity Britain, 1945–1951*, London, Bloomsbury, 2007.

5 See, for example, Suzanne Mettler, *Soldiers to Citizens: The GI Bill and the Making of the Greatest Generation*, Oxford, Oxford University Press, 2007.

6 Tony Judt, *Ill Fares the Land: A Treatise on Our Present Discontents*, London, Penguin, 2010, p. 47.

7 David Selbourne, *Against Socialist Illusion: A Radical Argument*, London, Macmillan, 1985, p. 117.

8 Ben Pimlott, 'The Myth of Consensus', in *The Making of Britain: Echoes of Greatness*, ed. L. M. Smith, London, Macmillan, 1988.

9 Stefan Collini, 'Saint or Snake: Review of *Father and Daughter: Patriarchy, Gender and Social Science* by Ann Oakley', *London Review of Books*, Vol. 37, No. 19, 8 October 2015, pp. 29–33, 30.

10 Howard Glennerster, *Richard Titmuss: Forty Years On*, London, London School of Economics, CASEpapers, sticerd.lse.ac.uk.

11 Ann Oakley, *Father and Daughter: Patriarchy, Gender and Social Science*, London, Policy Press, p. 196.

12 Lawrence Black and Hugh Pemberton, *An Affluent Society?: Britain's Post-War 'Golden Age' Revisited* (Modern Economic and Social History), London, Routledge, 2004, p. 1; see also David Dutton, *British Politics Since 1945: The Rise, Fall and Rebirth of Consensus*, Oxford, Blackwell, 1997.

13 Chris Pierson, 'Social Policy', in *The Ideas that Shaped Post-War Britain*, ed. David Marquand and Anthony Seldon, London, Fontana Press, 1996, p. 149.

14 Dennis Kavanagh, *Thatcherism and British Politics: The End of Consensus?*, Oxford, Oxford University Press, 1987.

15 Brian Simon, *Education and the Social Order: 1940–1990*, London, Lawrence and Wishart, 1991; see also Melissa Benn, *School Wars: The Battle for Britain's Education*, London, Verso, 2011.

16 House of Lords, 'Overlooked and Left Behind: Improving the Transition from School to Work for the Majority of Young People', House of Lords Select Committee on Social Mobility Report, 2015–16, thebrokerage.org.uk.

17 Patrick Joyce, *The State of Freedom. A Social History of the British State Since 1800*, Cambridge, Cambridge University Press, 2013, p. 5.

18 Carolyn Steedman, *Landscape for a Good Woman: A Story of Two Lives*, London, Virago, 1986, p. 2.

19 Carolyn Steedman, 'Landscape for a Good Woman' in *Past Tense: Essays in Writing, Autobiography and History*, London, Rivers Oram Press, 1992, p. 36.

20 Gail Lewis, 'From Deepest Kilburn', in *Truth, Dare or Promise: Girls Growing Up in the Sixties*, ed. Liz Heron, London, Virago, 1985, pp. 220, 215.

21 Liz Heron, 'Introduction', *Truth, Dare or Promise: Girls Growing Up in the Sixties*, ed. Heron, p. 6.

22 Alan Sinfield, 'Ideology and Commitment: A Personal Account', new introduction to *Literature, Politics* and *Culture in Postwar Britain* (1997), London, Continuum Press, 2004, p. xii.

23 Valerie Walkerdine, 'Dreams from an Ordinary Childhood', in *Truth, Dare or Promise: Girls Growing Up in the Sixties*, ed. Heron, pp. 74, 76.

24 Oakley, *Father and Daughter*, pp. 218–19.

25 Mary McIntosh, 'The State and the Oppression of Women', in *Feminism and Materialism: Women and Modes of Production*, ed. Annette Kuhn and Ann Marie Wolpe, London, Routledge & Kegan Paul, 1978, p. 256.

26 See, for example, Amina Mama, 'Black Women, the Economic

Crisis and the British State', *Feminist Review*, No. 17, Autumn 1984.

27 Julian Le Grand, *Motivation, Agency, and Public Policy: Of Knights and Knaves, Pawns and Queens*, Oxford, Oxford University Press, 2006, pp. 7–9.

28 London to Edinburgh Weekend Return Group, *In and Against the State*, London, Pluto, 1980.

29 Lynne Segal, *Why Feminism? Gender, Psychology, Politics*, Cambridge, Polity Press, 1999, p. 206.

30 Danny Dorling, *A Better Politics: How Government Can Make Us Happier*, London Publishing Partnership, 2016, p. 26.

31 John Hills, *Good Times, Bad Times: The Welfare Myth of Them and Us*, Bristol, Policy Press, 2014.

32 Danny Dorling, 'Brexit: The Decision of a Divided Country', editorial, *BMJ*, 7 July 2016, bmj.com.

33 Dorling, *A Better Politics*, pp. xvi–1.

34 Richard Titmuss, *The Gift Relationship: From Human Blood to Social Policy*, London, George Allen & Unwin, 1970, p. 225.

35 See Daniel Stedman Jones, *Masters of the Universe: Hayek, Friedman, and the Birth of Neoliberal Politics*, Princeton, NJ, Princeton University Press, 2012.

36 Margaret Thatcher, 'The Renewal of Britain: The Conservatives as a British Party', speech to the Conservative Political Centre Summer School, 6 July 1979, The Margaret Thatcher Foundation, margaretthatcher.org.

37 George Monbiot, *How Did We Get Into This Mess?*, London, Verso, 2016, p. 1.

38 Ken Walpole, *New Jerusalem: The Good City and the Good Society*, London, The Swedenborg Society, 2015, pp. 40, 41–2; see also Lynsey Hanley, *Estates: An Intimate History*, London, Granta Books, 2007.

39 Eric Hobsbawm, *The Age of Extremes*, London, Abacus, p. 304; Chris Rhodes, *Manufacturing: Statistics and Policy*, House of Commons Briefing Paper, Number 01942, 6 August 2015, p. 6.

40 John Lancaster, *How to Speak Money: What the Money People Say – And What It Really Means*, London, Faber and Faber, 2014, p. 115.

41 Jordan Shilton, 'UK: The Wealth of the Super-Rich has Doubled Since the 2008 Economic Crisis', *Global Research*, 21 May 2014, globalresearch.ca.

42 Karl Polanyi, *The Great Transformation: The Political and Economic Origins of Our Time*, second edition, Boston, Beacon Press, 2001, p. 144.

43 Owen Hatherley, *The Ministry of Nostalgia*, London, Verso, 2016, pp. 197–8.

44 See for instance recent polls of doctors and teachers, Dennis Campbell, 'NHS Stress: A Third of GPs Plan to Retire in Next Five Years', *Guardian*, 15 April 2015, theguardian.com; Anna Isaac, 'Unrelenting Pressure and Twelve Hour Days: Headteacher Recruitment Is in Crisis Too', *Guardian*, 28 February 2016, theguardian.com.

45 Thomas Piketty, *Capital in the Twenty-First Century*, Cambridge, MA, Harvard University Press, 2014, p. 21.

46 Ibid., pp. 25–7, 440.

47 Ibid., pp. 422–4, 515.

48 See ibid., pp. 21, 252–5, 515–18.

49 James Meek, *Private Island: Why Britain Belongs to Someone Else*, London, Verso, 2014.

50 Ibid., pp. 114–15.

51 Ibid., p. 15.

52 Ibid., p. 10.

53 Milton Friedman, *Capitalism and Freedom* (1962), Chicago, University of Chicago Press, 2002, p. 3; Mariana Mazzucato, *The Entrepreneurial State: Debunking Public vs. Private Sector Myths*, New York, Public Affairs, 2015, p. 4.

54 Mazzucato, *The Entrepreneurial State*, pp. 79, 32, 48–51.

55 Judith Shapiro, *China's Environmental Challenges*, Cambridge, Polity Press, 2012; Sam Geall, with Isobel Hilton (Introduction),

China and the Environment: The Green Revolution (Asian Arguments), London, Zed Books, 2013.

56 See, for instance, British economic journalist Larry Elliott's reports in recent years, 'George Osborne Told by IMF Chief: Rethink Your Austerity Plan', *Guardian*, 18 April 2013, theguardian.com; Larry Elliott, 'Austerity Policies Do More Harm Than Good, IMF Study Concludes', *Guardian*, 27 May 2016, theguardian.com.

57 John Gray, '*Private Island* by James Meek – Review', *Guardian*, 5 September 2014, theguardian.com.

58 Lancaster, *How to Speak Money*, p. 275.

59 Liz Heron, 'Evolution of the Bond Film', Liz Heron Blog, 26 November 2015, https://lizheron.wordpress.com.

60 Marianna Fotaki, Sally Ruane and Colin Leys, *The Future of the NHS?: Lessons from the Market in Social Care in England*, Centre for Health and the Public Interest (CHPI), 2013, https://chpi.org.uk; Jose-Luis Fernandez, Tom Snell and Gerald Wistow, *Changes in the Patterns of Social Care Provision in England: 2005/6 to 2012/3*, Personal Social Services Research Unit (PSSRU) Discussion Paper 2867, London, LSE, and Canterbury, University of Kent, 2013, pssru.ac.uk; IPC Market Analysis Centre, *Where the Heart Is: A Review of the Older People's Home Care Market in England*, Oxford, Oxford Brookes University, 2012 http://ipc.brookes.ac.uk.

61 Alan White, *Shadow State: Inside the Secret Companies that Run Britain*, London, Oneworld Publications, 2016.

62 Ibid., pp. 2, ix.

63 Mark Leftly, 'Absent UK Boss Adds to Serco's Woes', *Independent*, 26 October 2013, independent.co.uk.

64 Elizabeth Sanderson, 'Paying Myself £8.6m of Tax Payers Money Was the Right Thing to Do', *Daily Mail*, 11 August 2012, dailymail.co.uk; Jason Groves, 'Nine Ex-A4e Staff Charged with Fraud over Offences Relating to Taxpayer-funded Employment Schemes', *Daily Mail*, 27 September 2013, dailymail.co.uk.

65 White, *Shadow State*, pp. 228, 232–3, 250.
66 Mind, 'Mental Health Facts and Statistics', mind.org.ukl; World Health Organization, 'World Health Report: Mental Disorders Affect One in Four People', October 2001, who.int.
67 Mind, 'Mental Health Facts'.
68 Ipsos MORI Global Trends, 'People in Western Countries Pessimistic About Future for Young People', 14 April 2014, ipsos-mori.com.
69 Rebecca Coleman, 'Austerity Futures: Debt, Temporality and (Hopeful) Pessimism as an Austerity Mood', *New Formations*, No. 87, 2016, p. 84.
70 Ipsos MORI, 'Family Matters: Understanding Families in an Age of Austerity', 25 April 2013, ipsos-mori.com; Liverpool Mental Health Consortium, 'The Impact of Austerity on Women's Well-being', August 2014, liverpoolmentalhealth.org.
71 *Boys from the Blackstuff* was a British television five-part drama series, broadcast on BBC2 between 1980 and 1982, written by Alan Bleasdale, and produced by Michael Wearing. *Benefits Street* was a British documentary series broadcast on Channel 4 in five episodes in 2014, directed by Matthew Cracknell for Love Productions.
72 Valerie Walkerdine, 'Communal Beingness and Affect: An Exploration of Trauma in an Ex-industrial Community', *Body and Society*, No. 16, 2010, pp. 91–116; see also Valerie Walkerdine and Luis Jimenez, *Gender, Work and Community After Deindustrialization: A Psychosocial Approach to Affect*, London, Palgrave, 2012.
73 Valerie Walkerdine, 'Coming to Know', *Rhizomes: Cultural Studies in Emerging Knowledge*, No. 27, 2014, rhizomes.net.
74 Kristian Thorup, 'The Dangerous "Zombie Identities" of Those Left Behind by Global Capitalism', *Open Democracy*, 4 December 2016, opendemocracy.net.
75 Gary Younge, 'The View from Middletown: Trump Speaks to Us in a Way Other People Don't', *Guardian*, 27 October 2016, theguardian.com.

76 Tim Strangleman, James Rhodes and Sherry Linkon, 'Work and Community After De-Industrialisation', *International Labor and Working-Class History*, No. 84, Fall 2013, pp. 7–22.

77 Thomas J. Sugrue, *The Origins of the Urban Crisis: Race and Inequality in Postwar Detroit*, Princeton, NJ, Princeton University Press, 1996, p. 149.

78 Jefferson Cowie and Joseph Heathcott, *Beyond the Ruins: The Meanings of Deindustrialization*, Ithaca, NY, Cornell University Press, 2003, p. 5.

79 See Mind, *Life Support*, 7 April 2016, mind.org.uk.

80 John Bingham, 'Britain the Loneliness Capital of Europe', *Daily Telegraph*, 18 June 2014, telegraph.co.uk.

81 Chris Sherwood, Dr Dylan Kneale and Barbara Bloomfield, *The Way We Are Now*, Relate, August 2014, relate.org.uk.

82 John Burn-Murdoch, 'The Demographics That Drove Brexit', *FT Data* blog, 24 June 2016, blogs.ft.com./ftdata/2016/06/24/brexit-demographic-divide-eu-referendum-results/.

83 BBC News, 'EU Referendum: The Result in Maps and Charts', 24 June 2016, bbc.co.uk.

84 Rajnish Singh, 'Brexit Referendum: Voting Analysis', *Parliament Magazine*, 4 July 2016, theparliamentmagazine.eu.

85 See, for example, Tony Travers, 'Why Did People Vote for Brexit?: Deep-seated Grievances Lie Behind This Vote', *LSE BrexitVote* blog, 29 June 2016, http://blogs.lse.ac.uk.

86 David Cameron, quoted in Mathew Weaver, 'David Cameron: Brexit Vote Part of "Movement of Unhappiness"', *Guardian*, 9 December 2016, theguardian.com; Allegra Stratton, 'David Cameron Aims to Make Happiness the New GDP', *Guardian*, 14 November 2010, theguardian.com.

87 Henri Lefebvre, *Right to the City* (1967), in *Henri Lefebvre: Writing on Cities*, trans. and ed. E. Kofman and E. Lebas, Oxford, Blackwell, 1996, pp. 61–184.

88 David Harvey, 'The Right to the City', *New Left Review*, No. 53, 2008, p. 23.

89 See, for instance, Walter J. Nicholls, 'The Urban Question Revisited: The Importance of Cities for Social Movements', *International Journal of Urban and Regional Research*, Vol. 32, No. 4, December 2008.

90 Ati Metwaly, 'Redefining Freedom: Copenhagen's Freetown Christiania', *Ahram Online*, 12 September 2013, http://english. ahram.org.eg.

91 Eugine Losse, *Freetown Christiania: A True Account of Sex, Drugs and Anarchy*, Charleston, CreateSpace Free Publications, 2012.

92 Steve Vickers, 'In Copenhagen's Christiania Neighborhood, the Future Looks More Settled', *Washington Post*, 7 September 2012, washingtonpost.com.

93 Phil Cohen, *Reading Room Only: Memoir of a Radical Bibliophile*, Nottingham, Five Leaves Publication, 2013, p. 121.

94 Ibid.

95 Lynne Segal, 'A Local Experience', in Sheila Rowbotham, Lynne Segal and Hilary Wainwright, *Beyond the Fragments: Feminism and the Making of Socialism*, London, Merlin Press, 1980.

96 Javier A. Reyes and W. Charles Sawyer, *Latin American Economic Development* (Routledge Textbooks in Development Economics), London, Routledge, 2015, p. 48.

97 Justin McGuirk, *Radical Cities: Across Latin America in Search of a New Architecture*, London, Verso, 2015, pp. 80–93, 132–3, 22.

98 Athina Arampatzi, 'The Spatiality of Counter-Austerity Politics in Athens, Greece: Emergent "Urban Solidarity Spaces"', *Urban Studies*, January 2016, p. 2.

99 See Andreas Chatzidakis and others, 'Skoros: Anti-consumption in Crisis', YouTube, July 2015, accessed 19 February 2017.

100 Christy (Chryssanthi) Petropoulou, 'Crisis, Right to the City Movements and the Question of Spontaneity: Athens and Mexico City', *City: Analysis of Urban Trends, Culture, Theory, Policy, Action*, Vol. 18, No. 4–5, 2014, pp. 563–72.

101 Maria Kaika and Luca Ruggiero, 'Class Meets Land: The Social Mobilisation of Land as Catalyst for Urban Change', *Antipode*, Vol. 47, No. 3, 2015, pp. 708–29.

102 Manuela Carmena, quoted in Richard D. Bartlett, 'Commons Technology and the Right to a Democratic City, Madrid, May 2016', *Enspiral Tales*, medium.com.

103 Oscar Reyes and Bertie Russell, 'Eight Lessons from Barcelona en Comú on How to Take Back Control', *Open Democracy*, 8 March 2017, opendemocracy.net.

104 Ibid.

105 Íñigo Errejón and Chantal Mouffe, *Podemos: In the Name of the People*, London, Lawrence and Wishart, 2016.

106 Ronald Butt, 'Mrs Thatcher: The First Two Years', Interview, *Sunday Times*, 3 May 1981, margaretthatcher.org.

107 Hilary Wainwright, 'The Good Old Days: Hilary Wainwright Remembers the Thrills and the Challenges of Working at County Hall in the '80s', *Guardian*, 6 April 2000, theguardian. com; Andy Beckett, *Promised You a Miracle: Why 1980–82 Made Modern Britain*, London, Penguin Books, 2015, pp. 346–71.

108 See Hilary Wainwright, *Reclaim the State: Experiments in Popular Democracy*, London, Verso, 2003; Allan Cochrane, 'Alternative Approaches to Local and Regional Development', in *Handbook of Local and Regional Development*, ed. Andy Pike et al., London, Routledge, 2011; Stewart Lansley, Sue Goss and Christian Wolmar, *Councils in Conflict: The Rise and Fall of the Municipal Left*, London, Palgrave Macmillan, 1989; Andrew Forrester, Stewart Lansley and Robin Pauley, *Beyond Our Ken: A Guide to the Battle for London*, London Weekend Television / Fourth Estate, 1985.

109 Wainwright, *Reclaim the State*, p. 198.

110 Ibid., pp. 56–9; Yves Sintomer, Carsten Herzberg and Anja Röcke, 'Participatory Budgeting in Europe: Potentials and Challenges', *International Journal of Urban and Regional Research*, Vol. 32, No. 1, March 2008, pp. 164–78.

111 Slavoj Žižek, 'Robespierre or the "Divine Violence" of Terror', lacan.com; see also Afterword to Slavoj Žižek, *Living in the End Times*, London, Verso, 2015; Alain Badiou, 'A Speculative Disquisition on the Concept of Democracy', in *Metapolitics*, trans. Jason Barker, London, Verso, 2005, p. 87.

112 Wendy Brown, *Undoing the Demos: Neoliberalism's Stealth Revolution*, New York, Zone Books, 2015; Boaventura de Sousa Santos, ed., *Democratizing Democracy: Beyond the Liberal Democratic Canon*, London, Verso, 2005, p. lxii, italics in the original.

113 Leo Hollis, *Cities Are Good for Us: The Genius of the Metropolis*, London, Bloomsbury, 2013, p. 322.

114 Ibid., p. 326.

115 See, for instance, Janet Newman, 'Austerity, Aspiration and the Politics of Hope', *Compass*, 3 June 2015. See Sarah Lyall and Adrian Bua, 'Responses to Austerity: How Groups Across the UK Are Adapting, Challenging and Imagining Alternatives in the Face of Austerity', New Economics Foundation, 9 February 2015, neweconomics.org.

116 Francesca Polletta, *Freedom Is an Endless Meeting: Democracy in American Social Movements*, Chicago, IL, University of Chicago Press, 2002.

117 Jeremy Gilbert, *Common Ground: Democracy and Collectivity in an Age of Individualism*, London, Pluto Books, 2013, p. 210.

118 Sisters Uncut, '"Suffragette" Protesters Sisters Uncut: Why We Blocked Bridges Around Britain – and You Should Care', *Daily Telegraph*, 21 November 2016, telegraph.co.uk.

Afterword

1 Christine L. Corton, *Fog: The Biography*, Cambridge, MA, Harvard University Press, 2015, p. 243.

2 William Wordsworth, 'Surprised by Joy – Impatient as the Wind',

William Wordsworth: Selected Poems, London, Penguin Classics, 2004, p. 171.

3 Ralph H. Turner and Lewis M. Killian, *Collective Behavior*, second edition, Englewood Cliffs, NJ, Prentice-Hall, 1972; Steve Reicher and John Drury, 'Collective Psychological Empowerment as a Model of Social Change: Researching Crowds and Power', *Journal of Social Issues*, Vol. 65, No. 4, 2009, pp. 707–25.

4 'London 2012: Opening Ceremony – Reviews', *Guardian*, 29 July 2012, theguardian.com.

5 Jenny Diski, 'Collective Joy', *London Review of Books* blog, 30 July 2012, lrb.co.uk.

6 Gordon Rohlehr, *Calypso and Society in Pre-Independence Trinidad*, Port of Spain, Gordon Rohlehr, 1990.

7 Graham St John, 'Altered Together: Dance Festivals and Cultural Life', *American Anthropologist*, Vol. 114, No. 1, pp. 6–18, 9.

8 Janey, Stephenson, 'The Subversive Power of Joy', *Open Democracy*, 26 June 2017, opendemocracy.net.

9 Hannah Arendt, *On Revolution*, London, Penguin Books, 1990, p. 255.

10 Ibid., p. 253.

11 Judith Butler, *Notes Towards a Performative Theory of Assembly*, Cambridge, MA, London, Harvard University Press, 2015, p. 16.

12 Citizenship and Social Justice, 'Comprehensive List of Resources for Resisting Trump', citizenshipandsocialjustice.com, accessed 11 February 2017.

13 Ann Snitow, *The Feminism of Uncertainty*, London and Durham, NC, Duke University Press, 2015, p. 1.

14 Lauren Berlant, *Cruel Optimism*, London and Durham, NC, Duke University Press, 2011, p. 252.

15 Val Plumwood, *Feminism and the Mastery of Nature*, London and New York, Routledge, 1993, p. 196.

16 Bertholt Brecht, 'Motto to the "Svendborg Poems"', trans. John Willett, in *Bertolt Brecht: Poems 1913–1956*, ed. John Willett and Ralph Manheim, New York, Methuen, 1976, p. 320.

Index

Index

Index

'Dreams from an Ordinary Childhood'
(Walkerdine) 225
Duncan, Isadora 185
Durkheim, Emile 36–7, 65
Dworkin, Andrea 126
dystopias 93, 187–8, 197–9
see also utopias

Eagleton, Terry 68, 157, 208
Easterlin Paradox 4
Eco, Umberto 69
economics 3–12, 218–20, 232, 234–5,
242–7
see also capitalism; consumption;
neo-liberalism
education
Owenism 165–6
private 222
sex education 135–6, 178
and the welfare state 218, 224–5,
232–3
for women 105, 159
Edward Carpenter (Rowbotham) 111–12,
179
Egypt 203, 204
Ehrenreich, Barbara 31–3, 60–3, 70
*The Elementary Forms of the Religious
Life* (Durkheim) 65
Eli Lilly and Co. 40–2
Ellis, Edith 181
Ellis, Havelock 110, 178
Empire of Things (Trentmann) 80
Eng, David L. 52–3
Engels, Friedrich 169–70, 171
English, Deidre 127
The English Malady (Cheyne) 35
Enlightenment 35, 75, 80, 103–5
environmentalism 209, 237–8
Ephemera (journal) 88
*An Essay Concerning Human
Understanding* (Locke) 17
An Essay on the Principle of Population
(Malthus) 105–6
'Eternity' (Blake) 18
ethnography 65–6, 86, 264–5
eugenics 36, 105–6, 113, 162
Euripides 61

European Union (EU) 203, 205, 228–9
Evans, Mary 140
Evans-Pritchard, Edward E. 65
Eve and the New Jerusalem (Taylor) 166,
167–8, 169, 170
Everyday Utopias (Cooper) 210
Exarcheia (Athens) 89, 210, 251–2

The Facts of Life (Porter and Hall)
109–10
Faderman, Lillian 125
Falwell, Jerry, Jr. 136
Falwell, Jerry, Sr. 135
Fanny Hill (Cleland) 104
Fat Art, Thin Art (Sedgwick) 51
Fear of Flying (Jong) 121
The Feminine Mystique (Friedan) 84, 186
feminism
American 183–5
and care work 194–5, 200
conflicts 211–12
and education 105
and fashion 87
first wave 107, 180–2
Greenham Common 197
and joy 25–7, 264, 267
and love 137–42
and male violence 126, 134, 213,
259–60
Public Feelings Project 49–50
and sexual difference 144–7
and sexuality 107, 113–15, 120–8,
134, 182
and socialism 164–71
and state provision 224, 226–8, 253–4
and utopianism 163–4, 184–6, 190–5
see also women
Ferry, Luc 143
'Financial Melancholia' (Davies et al.)
11–13
'Find Your Beach' (Smith) 15
*For Colored Girls Who Have Considered
Suicide* (Shange) 192
The Forerunner (magazine) 185
Foucault, Michel 109–10, 192
Fourier, Charles 165
Frankenstein (Shelley) 162

Index

Index

Index

The Protestant Ethic and the Spirit of Capitalism (Weber) 64
psychiatry 36, 39–44, 56–7, 107–9, 118
psychoanalysis 19–22, 37–8, 82–3, 130–3
psychology 2–5, 82–3, 263
  see also mental illness
Psychopathia Sexualis 107–8
Public Feelings Project 49–50
Punch (magazine) 64
The Pursuit of Happiness (McMahon) 17

queer theory 49, 52, 56, 147, 155, 213
Quinta Monroy 251

Rabelais and His World (Bakhtin) 66–8
race
  Black Lives Matter 208–9
  and class 62–3, 64, 222
  and deindustrialization 244
  and imperialism 61–2, 104
  and sex 101, 134–5, 183
  and the welfare state 223–4, 226–7
Race and the Education of Desire (Stoler) 64
Radical Cities (McGuirk) 251
Rathbone, Eleanor 182
Reading Room Only (Cohen) 249–50
Reagan, Ronald 10, 135, 230
Rebel Cities (Harvey) 211
Reclaim the State (Wainwright) 256–7
Red Pepper (magazine) 256
Redeeming Laughter (Berger) 70–1
Reich, Wilhelm 116, 120
religion 35, 37, 62–3, 65, 71–8
  see also Christianity
The Republic (Plato) 80, 159–60
resistance
  alliances 211–14, 256–7, 265–6
  anti-globalization movement 202–5, 256
  Arab Spring 203, 204
  Black Lives Matter 208–9
  and capitalism 89–90, 196–7, 199–200
  and consumerism 94, 209–11
  Greece 203, 205–6, 251–2
  and hope 207–8, 214–15, 259–60
  and love 143, 157

May 1968 190, 201
Occupy movement 204–5, 206–7, 211
Spain 203–4, 206, 253–4
urban spaces 247–53, 258–9
  see also activism; counter-culture (1960s); feminism
revolution
  Arab Spring 203, 204
  and creativity 88
  Marxist 173
  May 1968 201
  Paris Commune (1871) 171–2
  and sex 120, 123–4
  and utopianism 184
  see also Bolshevik Revolution (1917); French Revolution (1789)
Rich, Adrienne 27–8, 133, 190–1, 195
Richardson, Samuel 104
Riesman, David 83, 84
The Right to be Happy (Russell) 114
Rights of Man (Paine) 163
The Road to Wigan Pier (Orwell) 111–12
Robinson, John 74
Rodchenko, Alexander 88
Roger and Me (film) 244
Rohlehr, Gordon 265
Romeo and Juliet (Shakespeare) 97
Rose, Gillian 151
Rose, Jacqueline 144–5
Ross, Kristin 171–2
Rousseau, Jean-Jacques 105
Rowbotham, Sheila 111–12, 114, 121–2, 179–81, 186
Rubin, Gayle S. 127
Rubyfruit Jungle (Brown) 192
Russell, Bertrand 75, 114
Russell, Dora 113–14, 116–17
Russia 66, 88
  see also Bolshevik Revolution (1917)

sadness 18–19, 36, 44, 57, 262
  see also depression; melancholy
Santos, Boaventura de Sousa 258
Sargent, Lyman Tower 187, 200
Saunders, Frances Stonor 198–9
Sawyer, Miranda 264

Index